IBERIAN AND LATIN AMERICAN STUDIES

Néstor Perlongher

IBERIAN AND LATIN AMERICAN STUDIES

Néstor Perlongher

The Poetic Search for an Argentine Marginal Voice

BEN BOLLIG

UNIVERSITY OF WALES PRESS
CARDIFF
2008

British Library Cataloguing-in-Publication Data
A catalogue record for this book is available from the British Library.

ISBN 978-0-7083-2123-2

Typeset by Column Design
Printed in Great Britain by Antony Rowe Ltd,
Chippenham, Wiltshire

Contents

Contents vii

Series Editors' Foreword

Over recent decades, the traditional 'languages and literatures' model in Spanish departments in universities in the United Kingdom has been superceded by a contextual, interdisciplinary and 'area studies' approach to the study of the culture, history, society and politics of the Hispanic and Lusophone worlds – categories which extend far beyond the confines of the Iberian Peninsula, not only to Latin America but also to Spanish-speaking and Lusophone Africa.

In response to these dynamic trends in research priorities and curriculum development, this series is designed to present both disciplinary and interdisciplinary research within the general field of Iberian and Latin American Studies, particularly studies which explore all aspects of **Cultural Production** (*inter alia* literature, film, music, dance, sport) in Spanish, Portuguese, Basque, Catalan, Galician and the indigenous languages of Latin America. The series also aims to publish research on the **History and Politics** of Hispanic and Lusophone worlds, both at the level of region and that of the nation-state, as well as on **Cultural Studies** which explore the shifting terrains of gender, sexual, racial and postcolonial identities in those same regions.

Acknowledgements

An earlier version of this monograph was published as a dissertation for the degree of Doctor of Philosophy at the University of London, King's College. The Arts and Humanities Research Board financed its research and writing. I am also grateful to the University of London Central Research Fund and King's College London's Small Grants for Research in the Humanities for supporting my research in Argentina. Revision of the work took place with the aid of teaching relief at the University of Westminster.

Earlier versions of some of the material included here have been published in the following journals, to whose editors I am grateful for granting permission to republish: *International Journal of the Humanities*, *Arara*, *Tesserae/Journal of Iberian and Latin American Studies*, *Journal of Latin American Cultural Studies*, *Modern Language Review*, *Hispanic Research Journal* and *Hispanic Review*. Full details are given in the relevant chapters.

I am very grateful to the staff at a number of libraries: the British Library, the British Newspaper Library at Collingwood and, in Buenos Aires, la Biblioteca Nacional, la Biblioteca de poesía, la Biblioteca Lincoln, and la Biblioteca del Congreso.

Thanks to all the staff and postgraduates at King's, in particular my tutors Luis Rebaza-Soraluz and Catherine Boyle, who both read versions of this thesis and offered innumerable suggestions; Paul Garner pointed me in the direction of UWP and an anonymous reviewer offered important observations; Alicia Kent offered help with image manipulation and IT; all those who attended CLACS seminars and the University of London School of Advanced Studies Graduate Forums, and the session organizers for invitations to present work in progress; also the board of the *Journal of Latin American Cultural Studies* for their invitation to talk at their 2002 conference; Flavio Rapisardi and Jens Andermann for their advice on research in Buenos Aires; Roberto Echavarren, who was an invaluable interlocutor while I was revising the manuscript in 2006–7 and with whose permission I reproduce Perlongher's work; and, especially, thanks to the Braidas in Argentina. All errors are, of course, no one's fault but my own.

Chapter 1

Towards a Reading of Perlongher[1]

Introduction: Sex, Drugs, Baroque 'n' Roll

As a work in progress this book had the title 'Sex, Drugs, Baroque 'n' Roll: The Poetic Search for an Argentine Marginal Voice in the Work of Néstor Perlongher'. This earlier title was functional for my research because it amalgamates, in a provocative manner, the key areas of activity of the Argentine poet Néstor Perlongher (b. Avellaneda, Argentina 1949, d. São Paulo 1992). These terms are also significant because they pinpoint wider areas of social change in relation to the urban culture of Latin America during the 1960s and 70s, the formative years of the poet, and because these issues later develop into some of the main cultural concerns of the twentieth-century *fin de siècle*.

Under the umbrella term of 'sex', I approach and discuss Perlongher's recurrent interest in the area of sexuality, gender and desire as a means of political provocation and literary experimentation. Throughout Perlongher's work he insisted on the dynamics of desire in the social as predominant in all human behaviour. He co-founded the homosexual activist group Eros in Buenos Aires during the early 1970s and was a vocal member of the Frente de Liberación Homosexual de la Argentina (FLH) from 1971 until the military coup of 1976. This group attempted to draw public attention, particularly that of the left wing, to the existence and specific demands of homosexuals in Argentina. His political activity was informed by a mixture of anarchism and Trotskyism, a dynamic and often contradictory political position also inspired by the Spartacus League's founder and Lenin's intellectual adversary, Rosa Luxemburg. Perlongher insisted that the FLH attend the demonstrations to welcome back General Juan Perón at Ezeize airport in 1973 but also campaigned against Peronist anti-contraceptive laws in the early seventies. He protested against violence committed by the 1976–83 military dictatorship in Argentina, in particular against homosexuals. During the late 1970s and early 80s, he travelled Argentina recording the stories of homosexual people who had been arrested, harassed or beaten by the police. He was repeatedly taken into custody and, on one occasion in Mendoza in 1981, beaten up by local officers. Partly as a reaction to this, Perlongher went into exile in Brazil. In São Paulo he picketed the Cuban embassy in protest at its government's treatment of homosexuals and people living with AIDS and HIV. In his essays from the early 1980s, for example 'Nena, llevate un saquito' (1997b: 25–8; first published 1983, Buenos Aires) or 'Joyas macabras' (1997b: 201–2 [1983, Buenos Aires]), Perlongher dealt with provocative sexual topics such as violence against transvestites and desire in the relationship between Peronism and the working classes. Although Perlongher's membership of the FLH ended in 1976, essays such as 'Matan a una marica' (1985, Buenos Aires), dealing with the murder of transvestites, continued to provoke readers on sexual topics few other writers or essayists ventured near except in sensationalist terms. Meanwhile, in his poetry, beginning with his first collection *Austria-Hungría* (1980, Buenos Aires), Perlongher questioned the idea of a binary division between the sexes through suggestive references to effeminate homosexuals, or *maricas*, transvestites and drag parties. In *Alambres* (1987, Buenos Aires), Perlongher included transvestite characters and problematized the grammatical formulations on which gender is based in language.

With the end of the dictatorship, the democratically elected government of Alfonsín (from 1983) increased the legal and political tolerance displayed towards homosexuality, granting official recognition to groups such as the Comunidad Homosexual Argentina (CHA). Perlongher, however, was largely distanced from the political opening in Argentina, as between 1982 and 1986 he was working in São Paulo on his Masters thesis in anthropology, a pioneering work on male prostitution that drew on the work of sociologists based in the US, such as the Chicago school and Herbert Marcuse, and also the French theorists –

Deleuze and Guattari, Bataille, and Foucault – who had formed the core of his theoretical readings during his membership of the FLH. His work benefited from the more open climate of the Brazilian dictatorship; while in Argentina he had been arrested by the police for breaking city ordinances concerning vagrancy and homosexuality while attempting to carry out research, in Brazil he was awarded a university scholarship for his work. The thesis predated more recent uses of Deleuzean theory, in particular in its attempts to move beyond identitarian readings of homosexuality or Marxist economic interpretations of prostitution, instead stressing the predominance of desire and the social as the most important factors at play.

With the emergence of AIDS and HIV in Brazil, and the sudden wave of publicity that it gave to homosexuality, particularly after the death of international figures such as Rock Hudson, Perlongher at first suggested in essays including 'Disciplinar os poros e as paixões' (1985, São Paulo) that the syndrome and the virus were part of a discourse aimed at controlling desire and social behaviour. However, both the postscript to his essay, 'Avatares de los muchachos de la noche' (1997b: 45–58 [1987, Buenos Aires]), and the subsequent change in the theme of his anthropological work – a move towards popular Brazilian esoteric religions – reveal the effect that AIDS had on Perlongher's views about sexuality, in particular as AIDS and the ensuing public reaction made the *bocas* (gay cruising areas) of central São Paulo increasingly dangerous places to be. Further research into the practices of *michês* (Brazilian male prostitutes who accentuate their masculinity) became impossible and obsolete. The danger of HIV infection or the eruption of violence made the *bocas* no longer the utopia they had once been for Perlongher. In his later poetic collections, Perlongher seemed to question the viability of sex and gender confusion as a basis for alternative politics and, in the essay 'La desaparición de la homosexualidad' (1991, Buenos Aires), Perlongher pronounced sexuality to be no longer of interest. However, many of his later poems still draw on the corporal and sexual elements of his earlier poetry.

Under 'drugs', I address Perlongher's involvement in esoteric drug-related religions, alongside his earlier involvement in drug-taking marginal groups and the ramifications of his prison sentence for possession of drugs in the 1970s, when he spent three months in the Villa Devoto jail. The short story 'Evita vive'

(1975)[2] dealt with drug-taking hippies and *rockeros* (rockers) in the subculture of Buenos Aires in the 1970s. The activist group which Perlongher founded in the early 1970s, Eros, was influenced by and included as members such marginal figures. There is a strong connection between the hippy movement and surrealism, in both their techniques and aims. This connection is also borne out in Perlongher's work but he frequently denied the links between the hippies and his poetry, perhaps owing to his desire to distance his writing from the form of popularized middle-class surrealism found in the lyrics of Argentine singer/songwriters like Andrés Calamaro or Charly García.

The last years of Perlongher's life were characterized by intense engagement with esoteric religions. As AIDS made public displays of 'unsafe' homosexuality increasingly dangerous and subject to censure, Perlongher explored in his research and writing different methods of questioning the individual and seeking ecstasy, methods that offered more formal structure than cruising or casual sex. In the late 1980s he became involved in the Afro-Brazilian religion *candomblé*, before joining the Santo Daime religion in São Paulo. This group believes that the ritual imbibing of Amazonian hallucinogens can offer visions of the divine. Its ceremonies combine the preparation and use of drugs such as *ayahuasca*, also known as *yagé*, with highly ritualized songs, dances, curing, and prayers discovered through divine drug-inspiration. Perlongher travelled to France to carry out postgraduate studies on the cult at the Sorbonne under Michel Maffesoli but abandoned them after Maffesoli failed to show significant interest in the project. During his time in Paris, recounted in scathing tones in his article 'Nueve meses en París' (1999b), Perlongher, after several years of illness, discovered that he was HIV positive. Upon returning to Brazil, Perlongher published a series of articles on the relationship between poetry and ecstasy, the Dionysian and the religion of Santo Daime. In 1991 he also published a collection of poems dedicated to Daime, *Aguas aéreas*, perhaps his most homogenous and formal collection, detailing the ceremonies and visions of the Daime ritual.

As Perlongher's illness worsened, he broke with Daime, largely because of the religion's refusal of orthodox medicine. Perlongher continued to use *ayahuasca* privately, and its effects are apparent in his final, posthumous collection, *El chorreo de las iluminaciones*, published as a collection of four poems in Caracas

(1993) and then as a much longer final section to Roberto Echavarren's edition of Perlongher's *Poemas completos* (1997a, Buenos Aires). The collection demonstrated not only the influence of Brazilian religions but also that of the Christian mystics and popular faith healing as another form of ritual.

With the term 'baroque 'n' roll', I offer a synecdoche for youthful subcultural production in Argentina and Brazil that includes not only music but also poetry and, in particular, the innovative ways in which the lyric interacts with its predecessors. This particularly focuses on poets like Perlongher who were related to the *rockero* subculture of Buenos Aires in the 1960s and 70s and who started publishing in the late 1970s and 80s. The term 'baroque 'n' roll' also attempts to situate these writers politically, as many were vocal opponents of the Argentine military regime of the 1970s. Many were forced into exile. Perlongher lost a number of friends to the dictatorship and is regarded by some critics, for example María Moreno (1996, Buenos Aires), as one of its foremost poetic chroniclers for his poem 'Cadáveres' (1984). Later in the 1980s, many *neobarroco* writers became more interested in purely artistic concerns, particularly those like José Kozer who were involved in the production of the poetry review *Último Reino*. Perlongher though continued his political involvement through writing; throughout the 1980s he published provocative and polemical articles in small-scale magazines such as *El Porteño* of Buenos Aires and in larger organs including Brazil's *Folha de São Paulo*.

As a poet, Perlongher's career began in the limited circles of what he termed the 'secret poetry boom' (1992, London). The military coup and repression from 1976 destroyed almost all networks of opposition within Argentina, culminating in the deaths of around 30,000 people linked, either directly or in the eyes of the military, to the organized left. During this period, the private production of poetry flourished, often by former members of disbanded opposition political groups, and its circulation in writers' workshops and cafés led to a dynamic undercurrent of literary activity. With the limited cultural opening of the early 1980s, after the most significant attacks on the opposition had ceased, there emerged new publications such as the reviews *Último Reino*, *XUL* and *Diario de Poesía*, and publishing houses such as

Tierra Baldía, run by the author Fogwill, which published Perlongher's first collection, *Austria-Hungría,* in 1980. Strong state censorship, and an ingrained tendency towards self-censorship led to the dominance of a refined and mannerist style of writing that circulated in small, hermetic circles.

With the end of the dictatorship, the democratically elected government of Alfonsín saw an increasing market demand for cultural production that had been prohibited under the dictatorship, popularly exhibited by alternative cultural forms and fashions, for example the hard-boiled thriller, the mini-skirt and openly gay discos. These events coincided with Perlongher's shift from marginal, almost cult status, to consecration as a respected, prize-winning poet. In 1987, Perlongher's *Alambres* won the Boris Vian Prize, awarded to works not considered for state or corporate prizes (for example the *Premio Coca-Cola*). The jury included the author Tomás Eloy Martínez and the critic Nicolás Rosa. The collection soon ran to a second edition, in 1989, exceedingly rare for a collection of contemporary poetry in Argentina.

Perlongher's subsequent critical and commercial success as a poet is frequently framed within the so-called *neobarroco* movement. The *neobarroco* is a difficult phenomenon to describe, as it is something of a chimera. The phenomenon I shall examine is the version promoted by Perlongher in anthologies, introductions and reviews, and its legacy, between the years 1980 and 1996. 1980 is the start of Perlongher's poetic career and also the year of the relaxation of the dictatorship's censorship and cultural controls and, with it, the emergence of the review *XUL,* which published many of Perlongher's early works. It is also the year of publication of the two key novels of the dictatorship period, Juan José Saer's *Nadie nada nunca* and Ricardo Piglia's *Respiración artificial.* Perlongher's interest in the *neobarroco* began later, as his essays on the subject date from no earlier than 1985. 1996 represents the change of the *neobarroco* into something else, an increasingly mainstream and retrospective term, as the publication of *Lúmpenes Peregrinaciones,* a collection of criticism on Perlongher's work published by the Beatríz Viterbo publishing house of Rosario, inserted him more firmly into the academic mainstream. The same year *Medusario* was also published, a collection of often explicitly *neobarroco* writing, in some ways stabilizing a *neobarroco* canon.

I regard the *neobarroco* as found in Perlongher's prose and verse work as a form of avant-garde kitsch, where *barroco* techniques such as hyperbaton and chiasmus, or difficult and complex metaphors, are used in a scattergun fashion, not limited by a set form and often as part of poems that include accumulative references to popular culture, consumerism and details from the everyday. There is no sarcasm in my use of the word 'kitsch' – a German term for feigned good taste – for I believe that Perlongher attempts in many of his poems a revaluation of kitsch as an authentic expression of the working and lower-classes. I contend that this international, nomadic, manifesto-less non-group, including figures such as Osvaldo Lamborghini, Wilson Bueno and Reynaldo Arenas, is perhaps most firmly held together by the process of mutual reviewing and anthologizing to which Perlongher was central, in particular through editing, introducing and promoting the bilingual anthology *Caribe Transplatino* (1991, São Paulo), which stands alongside Roberto Echavarren's anthology *Transplatinos* (1990, Mexico) and *Medusario* (1996, Mexico) as one of the key introductions to this heterogeneous poetry, as well as by a reaction against the often didactic and proselytizing political verse of many pre-dictatorship poets in the Southern Cone. Perlongher's own contribution to this not-quite-movement is best exemplified by the collections *Hule* and *Parque Lezama* (1989 and 1990 respectively, both Buenos Aires). Both these collections complicate any attempts to describe Perlongher's poetry as simply *neobarroco*. My use of the term 'baroque 'n' roll' reveals then a desire to problematize the terms 'barroco' and 'neobarroco', which for me have come to obscure the many developments and dynamics within Perlongher's *oeuvre* and the ways in which it differs, often radically, from other supposedly *neobarroco* works.

Perlongher's Poetic Search

I contend that Perlongher's *oeuvre* represents an attempt, in different spheres of activity but specifically focussing on poetry, to identify forms of expression for certain positions distanced from orthodox political, literary and academic concerns, positions which Perlongher identifies as possible alternatives to the contemporary social organization in the Southern Cone.

I focus in this work principally on Perlongher's poems – in prose and verse – as collected in *Poemas completos* but also including Perlongher's unanthologized works. Perlongher wrote his poetry largely in Argentine Spanish and his anthropology initially in Portuguese. He published his poetry in Argentina. Even when resident in Brazil and including elements of the environment of São Paulo in his work, Perlongher was still known as a poet in Argentina and an anthropologist in Brazil. While the situation is changing – bilingual editions and Portuguese translations of Perlongher's poems (1994) and prose texts (2001) have been published in Brazil – during the period that interests me, 1980–96, Perlongher remained an Argentine poet. Throughout Perlongher's academic career he produced poetry, often with a similar thematics to his prose works – *travestis* in his first collection, *michês* while compiling his thesis, esoteric rituals while writing on the Santo Daime religion. Therefore my writing aims to use other material such as essays and theses as support. It is not my intention, however, to divide Perlongher into two writers, as some critics have done. For example, Ariel Schettini (1997, Buenos Aires) separates Perlongher's essays and poems into two competing strands; in doing so he ignores the process of exchange and interaction between his anthropology and his poetry. Indeed in many interviews and articles they overlap completely. Nevertheless, my aim in this work is in the first instance an analysis of his poetry and poetics.

My work also displays a belief in the ability of a poem to affect the reader, not so much as the transmission of a message as in terms of physical effects – voice, but also breath, rhythm and pacing. Thus a poem such as 'Cadáveres' differs from many other poems apparently dealing with military crimes in Latin America in that rather than denouncing these crimes, it attempts linguistic play and mutation, provoking what Perlongher would call in an interview, drawing on Deleuze's terminology, changes on the 'plane of expression' (Ulanovsky, 1990: 11). Many of Perlongher's poems are extremely physical, including stutters, exclamations, lisps and groans. The term 'voice', then, reveals a belief that the poem can be an oral performance, which carries an intellectual and physical charge.

Furthermore, Perlongher's career demonstrated an admirable ability to become involved in movements – homosexual rights, the *neobarroco*, post-structuralist theory, esoteric religion – in their early, dynamic and challenging phases, before abandoning them for other, newer and potentially more provocative themes. These movements were closely linked to political, economic and cultural changes in Argentina and Brazil, for example the dictatorship's end to political opposition, the attempts of the Alfonsín government to draw a line under the events of the dictatorship through the 'punto final' law preventing further prosecutions of military criminals, or the increased acceptance of homosexuality in the marketplace in the 1980s. It is, in my opinion, impossible to divorce the developments and changes in Perlongher's *oeuvre* from their context.

Although he later criticized marginality as a position (1999b), preferring instead the term 'menor' ('minor', as in Deleuze and Guattari's *Kafka. Toward a Minor Literature*) (Ulanovsky, 1990), Perlongher's movement from left-wing politics to sexual activism to the *neobarroco* to esoteric religions represents a dynamic attempt to escape social stratification that other terms obscure. As a student activist in the late 1960s and early 1970s Perlongher represented concerns distanced from those of almost all sectors of the left in Argentina and, then, in his early career as a sociologist – in fact working for a consumer survey firm – Perlongher circulated through lower-class suburbs. His anthropology always placed him on the margins, be they economic, legal, or geographical, interviewing lumpenproletariat prostitutes, or taking part in drug rituals on the edges of the city. Perlongher started writing articles in the 1970s, an era in which the Argentine critic Raquel Ángel claims intellectual activity was often characterized by an attitude of revolutionary praxis in the face of power, and continued through the eighties, which Ángel sees as characterized by a general end to much intellectual political commitment (1992: 9). In his essays Perlongher adopted positions that often turned him into a pariah for both left and right, for example in his condemnation of the Malvinas/Falklands war and the nationalistic fervour unleashed by the conflict, or his portrayal of Eva Perón engaged in sex with male prostitutes and sailors in 'Evita vive'. His later writings on mystical themes distanced him from both the gay rights movement in Latin America and other *neobarroco* poets in another move that kept him on the margins of mainstream culture.

I use the term 'Néstor Perlongher' as shorthand for the material to be studied, the broad body of poems, anthropological

writings, essays, reviews and interviews, with poems being my key
focus, for the reasons outlined above. But 'Néstor Perlongher'
also stands for the conceptual persona, the person, the works by
the person, and the person's construction of the person. The
publication in 1997 of Perlongher's *Poemas completos* and an
anthology of his essays, *Prosa plebeya*, illustrates the market boom
in Perlongher's work in the 1990s. After his death he was even
eulogized by *La Nación* (Schettini, 1997), perhaps the most con-
servative newspaper with a mass circulation in Argentina. The
Colegio Argentino de Filosofía dedicated a major academic sym-
posium to his work in 1991 and a collection of critical and
biographical essays, *Lúmpenes Peregrinaciones*, was published in
1996. His creative writing has begun to increase in renown in
Brazil, where previously he has been known largely as an anthro-
pologist. Key here are the efforts of Jorge Schwartz and the
translator Josely Vianna Baptista, who, alongside the editor
Adrián Cangi, produced the bilingual Brazilian edition of
Perlongher's prose, *'Evita vive' e outras prosas*, in 2001. There are a
great number of websites dedicated either specifically to
Perlongher or with considerable space dedicated to his life and
work, for example *www.literatura.org* and *www.poesia.com*.

In terms of the material to be examined in this study, it is
important to remember that the period in Southern Cone poetry
being dealt with is one in which the public figure of the intellec-
tual and writer has gained increasing importance, perhaps at the
expense of the works themselves. In the twentieth century, Pablo
Neruda's contribution to politics and public life in Chile is
perhaps as well known as his writing; the same may well be said in
Argentina up to the 1980s for Julio Cortázar and his commitment
to revolutionary politics, Jorge Luis Borges and his disagreements
with the Peronists, or, in a more marginal position, Rodolfo Walsh
and his disappearance at the hands of the dictatorship in Argen-
tina. The 1980s and 1990s in Argentina and Brazil witnessed an
increase in the diffusion of cultural production through the mass
media, in particular the growth of literary reviews, such as *XUL* or
Diario de Poesía, and cultural supplements, for example those of
Clarín and *Página 12*, or in Brazil the influential *Folha de São Paulo*
supplement, *Ilustrada*. This format allowed Perlongher space in
Argentina and Brazil to reach a mass audience. As well as articles,
poems and reviews in cultural supplements and specialist maga-
zines – the more traditional staples of the man of letters –

these new organs offered particular coverage for the literary interview, very often coinciding with the release of a book, as described by Kuhnheim (1996) in her work on Olga Orozco. Through this medium, Perlongher and other writers acceded to the status of artist, the intellectual whose difficult art or complex theorizing find a popular and popularized outlet in the mass media. An additional development is that of the internet, which has allowed fans and artists to contribute to the spread of works and the artist as conceptual persona. Fogwill and German García, for example, both have their own websites publishing and promoting their work, and there are several professionally prepared and critically sophisticated literary websites, for example the Uruguayan site *www.henciclopedia.org* [*sic*].

Within this cultural framework then, while owing to my own interests I concentrate on Perlongher's poetry, I also refer to his academic writings, his newspaper articles, and the interviews he gave. As Perlongher became commercially more successful and publicly well known he gave more interviews, and his comments offer a keen insight into his poetics and thinking. I am interested in the creation of a conceptual persona – 'Perlongher' – in poetry, essays, and interviews, as this offers an important insight not only into Perlongher's project, but also into theoretical and social developments in Argentina and Brazil.

I am aware of the great body of critical work that challenges the status of the author and attempts to distance the text from biographical questions. As Michel Foucault observes, the author's proper name has specific links, which are not the same as those of the proper name. The author's name performs a specific classificatory role in narrative discourse (1984: 106–7). For Foucault, the author is a creation that has limited and made safe the dangers posed by fiction (118). Thus, 'the author has played the role of the regulator of the fictive, a role quite characteristic of our era of industrial and bourgeois society, of individualism and private property' (119). Foucault insists on changes in the role of the author, and that it will eventually disappear. Instead of asking the questions associated with authors, Foucault suggests we will ask, 'what are the modes of existence of this discourse? Where has it been used, how can it circulate, and who can appropriate it for himself? [. . .] What difference does it make who is speaking?' (119).

Whereas, for Foucault, the author is a socially limiting strategy, I aim to use Perlongher the author as a starting point for a movement outwards. Thus my examination of articles and poems not examined critically before is an important tool in exploring Perlongher's and critics' constructions of certain truths about his *oeuvre*. Certain articles and poems have been excluded – from anthologies, and from Perlongher's official bibliography – and these pieces offer potentially revealing aporia in the construction of Perlongher as an artist. Fogwill (1993, 1994), in a fashion that perhaps would have found sympathy with Foucault, criticized Perlongher for writing for a specific audience, namely 'la banda gay', as he called homosexual readers of poetry in Argentina, and thereby creating a literary persona as an exercise in marketing his works. Yet this is no reason to dismiss Perlongher's works; it instead allows us to examine the specific processes whereby this may occur in his work and, in particular, the relationship between Perlongher's conceptual persona and his poetry.

Perlongher and Academe: Potential Critical Risks

Perlongher was deeply critical of academic discourse:

> Sucede que el discurso sobre la poesía, campo infestado y saturado por la crítica universitaria, no se parece en lo esencial al modo de fluir de la palabra poética en su gracia lúdica y revelada. En el discurso se habla de otra cosa. El acto de creación poética devela en cambio cierta cualidad estética inmanente de la palabra en el resplandor de su belleza. [. . .] Justamente el aparato de la crítica universitaria funciona como una máquina de sobrecodificación del dispositivo de expresión poética, codificando la radicalidad del misterio oracular en un sentido interpenetrable y sobre todo traducible a la vernacular del ramo. (1997b: 149–59 [1991, Buenos Aires])

Perlongher is suggesting that there exists a problem with academic discourse on poetry. Whereas poetry is radical, unstable and reveals the beauty of the word, academic discourse domesticates and stabilizes language, and so can turn the provocative content of a poem into a set expression. Perlongher seems to be criticizing such practices as rendering verse into prose, or the traditional exercise of *explication du texte* whereby the poem is *explained.* This sceptical attitude towards conservative academic networks is also revealed in scathing writings on his experiences at French institutions (Perlongher, 1999b).

Perlongher was ever keen to distance himself from the university machine. He stated in an interview that, 'hay un destino de los poetas o de los escritores de ser universitarios [. . .]. La mayor parte están ligados [*sic*] a la crítica literaria universitaria' (Friedemberg and Samoilovich, 1992: 32). In these pronouncements, Perlongher is aligning himself with what Vich calls 'una tradición intelectual que no se vinculó a la institución académica' (2000: 25), particularly linked to avant-garde groups. However, Perlongher's work, as a reviewer, poet and anthropologist, was very strongly connected to the university environment. In another interview, he discussed his situation as an academic in Brazil. In answer to the question, '¿el intelectual universitario aquí vive de su trabajo?', he replied, 'sí, y con retribuciones muy aceptables. Además hay un sistema de becas muy desarrollado. Lo malo es que ese mismo sistema universitario es elitista' (Ulanovsky, 1990: 11). The freedom that Perlongher enjoyed to carry out his academic research in Brazil, and the financial rewards that allowed him to write both his thesis and the poems from *Hule* and *Parque Lezama* onwards, were very much part of the university machine that he criticized, as revealed by his caveat with regards to elitism. Thus we have to question whether there is a degree of bluff in Perlongher's criticism of academe.

Furthermore, as a writer who used university literary criticism to promote his own writings and those of others, Perlongher at times smacks of being a victim of his own success. Talking about the intellectual community in Buenos Aires, Perlongher observed:

> Buenos Aires mantiene una virtud de la que todo Brasil carece: la tertulia, la posibilidad de alternar y participar en cafés. La circulación cultural es muy fuerte e intensa, pero pasa mucho por la Universidad. Sus intelectuales se anticipan a los fenómenos, o apenas se insinúan ya hay tres investigadores encima de eso. (11)

Perlongher's comments allow us to shed new light on his stance. He highlights the problem not only of university over-coding but also of university competition: there is always the danger that someone will complete the research before you do. If Perlongher were simply interested in the completion of academic work this would not be a problem. However, there is an implication of purpose in Perlongher's words. Whereas Perlongher seems to present his own academic work as radical, innovative and politically subversive, there is the veiled accusation that the work of others is carried out for personal or purely academic motives. How one would sustain such an argument, however, is not immediately clear. Therefore it becomes increasingly hard to justify Perlongher's attempts to ward off academic discourse from his poems.

The critique of university discourse is one that is full of potential ironies and blind spots, but also one that offers important challenges to the reader of poetry. As William Rowe observes in a discussion of the Chilean poet Gonzalo Rojas, and his 'poems which denounce the deadening activity of the Academy':

> The Academy dreams of a guaranteed reading system, an interpretation machine which will ensure prestige and success for its adherents [. . .]. One way of understanding the interpretation machine is, as I have suggested, to take it as a substitution machine. (2000: 156–7)

Rowe, like Perlongher, presents the university interpretation machine as something that substitutes stable and conservative academic discourse for the content of the poem. This offers a clear challenge to the writer of an academic thesis. If the role of the university critic becomes that of limiting, fencing off and stratifying poetry, turning radical, subversive or experimental poetry into stable and easily summarized discourse, then this role is indeed radically opposed to Perlongher's project with its incessant breaking down of the barriers between literary genres, genders and national territories as presented in contemporary politics, criticism and anthropology. The challenge then that Perlongher's work offers this reader is to attempt a university discourse that does not limit, fence or fix but, instead, allows poems to move, detonate and connect, a reading that respects imagination and creativity – a contact machine rather than a substitution machine. Perlongher's poetry did rely on academic structures, albeit in a difficult and at times conflictive relationship. Many of Perlongher's poems tackle subjects also covered in his or others' academic work – male prostitution, the legal ramifications of prosecuting war criminals, for example – and do so using academic terms and conceptual frames. However, Perlongher's poems are never simply attempts at representing an academic discourse in verse but also include playful and corporeal dimensions that the academic thesis rarely contains. Thus my response to the challenge is to attempt a reading of his poems that exercises academic rigour and coherence without demanding or implying the same rigour and coherence from Perlongher's poems, while exploring the strong relationship between Perlongher's poems and contemporary academic discourses.

Other Critical Approaches to Perlongher

Before I outline my own methodology for approaching Perlongher's work in greater detail, an overview of other critical appraisals is necessary.

Nicolás Rosa was one of the first critics to devote significant attention to Perlongher's work. In his 1987 work *Los fulgores del simulacro* (Rosario de Santa Fe), a study of recent Argentine poetry very much in the French post-structuralist vein, Rosa entitled a chapter, 'Seis tratados y una ausencia sobre los *Alambres* y rituales de Néstor Perlongher'. The work was extended in scope in the 1997 publication, *Tratados sobre Néstor Perlongher* (Buenos Aires). Rosa regards Perlongher's work as an attempt to write the body in language. Whereas psychoanalytic theory following Lacan sees the body as lost in language – the moment we say 'mother', we lose our physical mother in language – for Rosa, Perlongher's use of grunts, stammers, assonance and alliteration, all with a strong effect on the body of the reader, represents a clear inscription of the body's presence in poetry. Perlongher's poetry is thus important because of its physicality, dirtiness and gender subversion, and shows a multiplicity of influences that confuses the notion of the individual author, in keeping with the postmodern technique of pastiche. Similarly, for Rosa, the aesthetic of dressing up in Perlongher's poetry, especially that of the *travesti* – the man whose adoption of supposedly female dress and mannerisms questions the stability of gender and its perception – questions any absolute notions of gender.

Perhaps the central work on Perlongher's life and poetry is the collection of essays, *Lúmpenes Peregrinaciones*, edited by Adrián Cangi and Paula Siganevich (Rosario de Santa Fe, 1996). The volume's contributors include some of the most important modern alternative thinkers in Argentina – María Moreno, Horacio

González and Jorge Panessi, for example – many of whom were friends of Perlongher. The work is too broad in scope to allow me to address each of the contributions individually but several essays do stand out. Jorge Panessi's piece, 'Detritus', views Perlongher's poetry as utilizing that which the classical tradition discards. Tamara Kamenszain examines the links between Perlongher, Góngora and the Christian mystics. Susana Cella offers an astonishingly dense reading of Perlongher's relationship to Jose Lezama Lima's *barroco* and Latin American *modernistas* such as Ruben Darío. Alongside such critical–theoretical work, there are biographical pieces by Osvaldo Baigorria, Christian Ferrer and María Moreno and an authoritative bibliography of Perlongher's work, which has only a few minor, although intriguing, omissions, for example an early essay written in collaboration with Alberto Nigro in 1980.

Elsewhere, Claudio Canaparo's work *El Perlonghear* (Buenos Aires, 2001) is a collection of some previously published works and chapters from his as yet unpublished magnum opus, *El navegador. Retórica del ensayo y escritura del conocimiento*. As an application of Deleuze and Guattari's *What is Philosophy?* and as a way in to certain theoretical aspects of Perlongher's work, *El perlonghear* is unique. Similarly, the work in undoing certain academic attempts at limiting or 'reterritorializing' Perlongher's work is vital. Chapter Two is provocative and revealing in its analysis of the relationship between writing, theories of writing, and the risks of the ≪puro acontecer≫ [*sic*], Canaparo's concept of the prelinguistic, unformed matter with which Perlongher's writing engages. Important also is Canaparo's refusal to separate the different areas of Perlongher's work into academically convenient blocks.

The poet, academic and critic Roberto Echavarren edited Perlongher's complete works (1997a, Buenos Aires); he has also written the introduction to the same volume (Echavarren, 1997) and an introduction to the collection *Medusario* (Mexico, 1996), which represents something of an overview of the *neobarroco* self-image. The former details Perlongher's poetics and political commitments, and their dynamic development. Echavarren focuses on the movement across borders in Perlongher's poetry and touches on his mystical phase in *Aguas aéreas* as a complication of the female figures in his earlier poetry. He then examines the notions of victims and priests in Perlongher's later work, before addressing Perlongher's final collection as an attempt to incorporate disjunctions and paradoxes into poetry, in a manner similar to but much more extreme than Góngora. Echavarren's introduction to *Transplatinos*, meanwhile, gives the origin of the *neobarroco* as the post-*modernista* vanguards in Latin America. Writers such as Vicente Huidobro, Oliverio Girondo and Octavio Paz broke with the signifier as an integral unit and instead focused on the explosion of phonemes. He distinguishes this poetry, which concentrates on what Roman Jakobsen called the poetic function, from socially committed poetry. The *neobarroco* also has roots in the Golden Age via José Lezama Lima, according to Echavarren, celebrating the impure and the pleasurable; it shares certain characteristics with the vanguard but differs in other respects. The vanguard is experimental, didactic and cultivates images and metaphors. The *neobarroco* experiments, is not didactic, and functions around connections formed through complex syntax. Echavarren also distinguishes between the *neobarroco* and colloquial poetry. Both are direct and anecdotal but colloquial poetry is communicative, public and based on speech, whereas *neobarroco* poetry is not, and cultivates a style. Echavarren, as is common in writings on the *neobarroco*, subsequently slips into observations on the *barroco*. For Echavarren, the *barroco* is a form of poetry that challenges the natural and the signifier, and cultivates self-referentiality and plurality. Echavarren concludes by suggesting that the *barroco* and the *neobarroco* coincide in 'una necesidad de ir más allá de las adecuaciones preconcebidas entre el lenguaje del poema y las expectativas supuestas del lector, el despliegue de las experiencias más allá de cualquier límite' (1996: 17). I would question, however, whether his insistence on the *neobarroco* as a form of *art pour l'art* does not overlook the political and contextual circumstances of the emergence of the poets involved in the *neobarroco* and the emergence of the term itself.

José Amícola's collection of essays *Camp y posvanguardia* (2000) contains a chapter entitled 'Campeones camp: Copi y Perlongher'. It opens by suggesting that Perlongher's poem 'Por qué seremos tan hermosas' (from *Austria-Hungría*) offers a paradigm of camp provocation, whereby literary parody (of the *modernistas* and the Golden Age, in particular) attacks genre boundaries and the notion of the poem as occupying a separate territory of its own, and redeems the gay world through a favourable view of difference. Similarly, Jill Kuhnheim's piece 'La promiscuidad del

significado' (1999) suggests that Perlongher's work demonstrates
a shift from a homosexual subtext to a homosexual text, in
particular in the evolving use of the figure of Evita. Her conclu-
sion, suggesting the need for a political reflection on the *barroco*,
is suggestive but perhaps revealing of an omission in the piece.
While her observations of the changing position of homosexuality
in Perlongher's work are sound, the question of *why* this position
changes is never asked. Responding to her own imprecations for a
political reading of the *barroco* would, I believe, allow us to
contextualize Perlongher's work and provide more profound
observations of his poetics.

   A work on which I have drawn heavily in this study, particularly
for biographical data on Perlongher, is *Fiestas, baños y exilios* (2001),
a study of gay culture during the most recent Argentine dictator-
ship carried out by Flavio Rapisardi and Alejandro Modarelli. This
work, while not dealing specifically with Perlongher's poetry, does
address his political commitments, starting in the 1970s with the
Eros group and moving on to his much-discussed religious activities
in the 1990s. The authors interview a number of friends and
colleagues of Perlongher and thus provide a detailed portrait of the
poet and his environment that offers useful insights for readers of
his poetry.

Perlongher and Politics: 'Evita vive'

Having examined other critical approaches and before detailing
my own methodology, I aim in this section to exhibit the ques-
tions that Perlongher's own writing throws up for the potential
reader of his work. My focus here will be on Perlongher's most
infamous text, the short story 'Evita vive'. There are several
reasons why I feel that 'Evita vive' offers an introduction to my
methodology. The short story was the first text by Perlongher that
I examined in my studies of his work and many of the problems
and potential methods for reading Perlongher's work arose first
in my work on this text. Secondly, the piece is arguably
Perlongher's best-known text in Argentina, both popularly owing
to the scandal that it caused upon republication in Buenos Aires
in 1989, in *El Porteño*, and academically because of its presence on
university literature and sociology courses. Moreover, the text,
written in 1975, was the first mature artistic piece completed by

Perlongher and I believe it offers an overture to Perlongher's writing on desire and the social. Finally, Perlongher's text is closely related to the political circumstances of its writing – the breakdown of Argentine democracy under the government of Evita's real-life ghost, Perón's third wife Isabelita – and its publication – the break-down of Argentine democracy in the last stages of Alfonsín's government – and so asks provocative questions about the relationship between literature and its political context.

'Evita vive' is a work in three sections, each with a different narrator. The first section is narrated by a *travesti*, the second by a young homosexual hippy, and the third by a *chongo*, in Argentina a lumpenproletariat male prostitute. The three sections deal with the fictional yet all-too-believable return of a visceral and sexually vibrant Evita Perón to the low-rent districts of 1970s Buenos Aires, where she mixes and has sex with male prostitutes, transvestites and drug dealers. It is these characters who then recount their experiences with Evita and the scandalized and often violent responses that these elicit. As the emotionally drained editorial committee of *El Porteño* noted in their piece 'Un mes movido' (May 1989), the reaction to their 1989 publication of Perlongher's text in Buenos Aires was spectacular. *El Porteño*'s staff found themselves facing political censure, the wrath of national dailies and anonymous death threats.

A glance through the newspapers of 1975, the year Perlongher completed the piece, and 1989, reveals keen similarities. *The Buenos Aires Herald* records both years as times of political apprehension, the Isabelita Perón and Alfonsín governments both months away from dramatic conclusions. Shops suffered shortages while robberies and civil violence both appear frequently in the paper. Argentina's currency slumped and inflation ridiculed the average pay cheque. There is a general sense that organized politics is floundering, and the possibility of violent collapse is clear on the horizon. Page six of *The Herald*, 13 February 1974, reports that the Buenos Aires Insurers Convention had met to discuss raising premiums on kidnapping, while on 22 March 1989, page six records that the supposed growth of so-called 'microterrorism' had led police to patrol supermarkets. National ghosts haunt various pages, in particular the Peróns and Juan Manuel de Rosas, emblems of past struggles as yet unresolved within the country.

Perhaps the most noticeable element of 'el caso Evita', as the
1989 scandal came to be known, was the breadth of the condem-
nation towards the story and *El Porteño*. Peronists and radical
politicians alike condemned the offence to Evita's memory. Of
the national newspapers only *The Herald* defended the piece,
reminding readers that the era of censorship was legally over (*El
Porteño*, May 1989: 3). A brief view of the changing role of the
intellectual in Argentina may offer some explanation for the
offence caused. As stated previously, Ángel (1992: 9) suggests that
in Argentina the 1960s were marked by a contestatory intellectual
spirit – Terán (1993) talks of the emergence of a 'new intellectual
left' in Argentina in the period 1956 to 1966 – the 1970s by
revolutionary praxis, but the 1980s by an end to much political
commitment.[3] Masiello (1987: 23) remarks that after 1976 there
was little room in Argentina for an articulation of intellectual
resistance. Similarly Piglia (1990: 178–80) offers a broad outline
of intellectual activity after the coup. While modernist culture, be
it Joyce, Picasso or Stravinsky, celebrates transgression and socio-
sexual freedom – their Argentine equivalents would probably be
Oliverio Girondo or Enrique Molina – the late 1970s and early 80s
saw many Argentine intellectuals realize the uncomfortable
strength of the gun over the pen. Piglia sees postmodernism,
particularly inside Argentina, as characterized by a lack of confi-
dence in the transformative powers of art and a general intellec-
tual conformism, which avoids socially committed or combative
stances. The military's truth-creation of, for example, the idea of
the nation as a sick body needing to be cleansed, as described by
Torre and Riz (1993: 329–30) among others, was followed by the
Alfonsín government's dissemination of the notion of generalized
guilt, the idea that violence was a result of a general weakness in
the Argentine character (Piglia, 1990: 181), or the 'two demons'
theory of shared responsibility by the extreme right and left. The
piece by Perlongher emerges from an era – before the 1976
military coup – of intellectual provocation and confrontation,
characteristics that by 1989 had in many cases been overtaken by
discourses of falsely harmonious amnesia. The socio-political
instability, however, had not gone away. Thus Perlongher's text
struck raw nerves that in the late 1980s many Argentine intellec-
tuals tended to ignore.

Bronfen talks of the ghost as a harbinger of death (1992: 301).
Sadly, the case of 'Evita vive' illustrates this all too well. Argentina

collapsed into bloody military rule the year after the text was completed, and three years after its public scandal, Néstor Perlongher died. There is frightening perspicacity to the text, a piece that in a time of political uncertainty identified and attacked key binary systems within society and illustrated the violence required to maintain such a system. The text can thus be seen as 'anti-fascist', in Foucault's terms (2000: xiii), working against unitary or totalizing systems, aiming for positive, associative and nomadic description, attacking notions such as 'truth' or the 'individual' and connecting 'desire to reality' with 'revolutionary force' (xiii). While the text uses Evita's body, it is not as an idealized figure of Woman or as a vilified castrating 'phallic woman', as Diana Taylor (1997: 83) suggests many versions of Evita do, but rather as a visceral, sexual, problematic (non) being, a (dead) woman shuttling between the real and the stereotyped within marginal communities that struggle for survival inside yet outside respectable society. As Lucy indicates (1997: 247), thinking a ghost offers an affirmation of struggle for – and as – democracy. 'Evita vive' is a complex, oppositional piece that demands awareness of political context and demonstrates the provocative potential of reading. I realize the paradox of demanding plurality while appearing to insist on political readings. However, I wish only to suggest that a practical openness to critical plurality must include the *possibility* of political analysis. Completely removing the political aspects and connotations of 'Evita vive' appears simultaneously to remove a key aspect of any response to the question 'why read?' and to close off many avenues of reading seemingly called for by the language *on the paper*, including references to Alice Cooper, popular drugs and certain police practices. Furthermore, one must remember, pragmatically, that texts receive political reactions, in this case attempted censorship and death-threats. In answering the question 'why read?' the text demands one follow Kaufman (1997: 33) in asserting the need for culture as a means of forcing memory. Sarlo (1987: 122) also insists upon the power of literature against 'los perros del olvido', creating a shuttle between the past and the present. 'Evita vive' suggests a role for the critic, reader, specialist or student as a mediator in a complex process of cultural encounter, focused firmly on the language of the text, but keenly tracing form and content through the context of writing and reading.

Methodology

As this study has progressed, it has become increasingly clear that readings of Perlongher's work require an engagement with the theorists Perlongher himself read and studied: Deleuze and Guattari, Bataille, and Foucault, for example. Simultaneously, a reading of Perlongher's writings on gender and sexuality, and his poetry, with its clear challenge to rigid gender structures, pushes the reader towards more recent theorists in this field, such as Judith Butler and Leo Bersani. However, as this list may suggest, any reading of Perlongher demands that I adapt the methodological tools offered by these theorists to the literary and contextual specificities of Perlongher's writing and also to my own purposes of allowing Perlongher's poems freedom to perform without overencoding through the application of rigid theoretical frameworks on my part.

What then is the methodology that I will use in this study? One of the most influential writers in Britain on Latin American poetry and poetics in recent years is William Rowe. Rowe holds a key position as an academic within Latin American Cultural Studies working specifically on poetry and poetics, seeing the poem as a performative event in language, rather than a vessel of meaning. The title of his 1996 collection of essays is revealing of the project he undertakes: *Hacia una poética radical. Ensayos de hermenéutica cultural* (Rosario de Santa Fe/Lima). Thus there are two processes at work: radical poetics, or the study of poetry in terms of both the poetic operations carried out and the radical political implications this possesses; and cultural hermeneutics, or the study of meanings in a text within its cultural context, in the broadest sense of 'culture' as the relationships between the elements of a society. Rowe's reading, continued in the collection of essays *Poets of Contemporary Latin America. History and the Inner Life* (2000, Oxford), allows the full detonation of the poem in its context. Vital here, however, are both the close attention to poem and context and also the frequent subversion of the search for unified or unambiguous meaning by a poem. Very often poems mean nothing, or many things. The reader must not abandon the poem in the face of nonsense or ambiguity. Instead we must consider the political consequences of poetic withdrawal or refusal.

Important here is the influence on my work of Tzvetan Todorov's seminal essay, 'A Complication of the Text: *Les illuminations*' (Paris, 1982). Todorov's piece outlines and critiques four methods of reading Arthur Rimbaud's notoriously difficult prose poem. *Euhemerist* readings use the text to find out about the world in which it was written; *aetiological* readings examine possible inspirations for the text (drugs the author took or paintings he saw, for example); *esoteric* readings examine the text by looking for special codes that may unlock its symbolism; and, finally, *paradigmatic* readings – structuralism, in other words – examine the structural equivalences at play in the work. These options effectively dismissed, Todorov moves on to his own reading, which sees Rimbaud's piece in terms of the cultivation of a poem that is about nothing and which revels in this status.

While Todorov's reading is provocative and his taxonomy suggestive for critical self-reflection, his reading suffers the possibility of radically flattening out the differences between poems. Rimbaud's poem can be situated within the stage of *l'art por l'art* within France and there are social and economic factors, such as the triumphant rise of the bourgeoisie, that contextualize the emergence of a poetry that celebrates its divorce from language as a social medium and, for the first time, becomes aware of its status as socially independent but also socially ineffectual. However, Todorov's division of types of reading and final suggestion of a reading that focuses specifically on the text itself, do allow me to conceive a reading that is sensitive to all five of Todorov's divisions – a reading that Todorov was himself to suggest in his later work, *Literature and Its Theorists* (Paris, 1988). Many of Perlongher's poems contain direct references to real people, to other literary works, are resonant of events in the poet's life, or cultivate remarkable formal patterns and structures. Moreover, there are poems where pure sounds and sonic connections predominate over any linguistic sense. My reading therefore has to be sensitive to all of these possibilities.

What then of critical voices that would suggest that my attempts to read poetry for its textual, intertextual, historical, personal and political interactions suffer from the same problems of 'interpretation' suggested almost forty years ago by Susan Sontag (1967)? Sontag argues in the essay 'Against Interpretation' that interpreting texts follows a Platonic model by limiting the text as a shadow of the real world, expresses dissatisfaction with the text, and attempts to turn it into something else. I am not fully convinced by Sontag's esoteric and at times rather elitist arguments in favour of an 'erotics' of art; for example, her insistence on transparency and transcendence in great art in the companion piece, 'On style' (1967: 15–36), seems to remove from consideration those works that engage directly with their circumstances, such as the protest song, the political poem or the testimonial. Nevertheless, her suggestion that interpretive criticism falls into the Platonic trap of seeing the universe as organized along hierarchical principals – ideal forms, reality, art as mimesis, in that order of precedence – and in effect dismissing poetry, is useful for my work. A political reading can easily become a reading that ignores the poem itself, thus performing the Platonic relegation of art from the critical Republic. Instead of Sontag's 'erotic', 'incantatory' and 'magical' approach to art (1967: 3), and the problems that such an approach presents, what allows us to escape the Platonic refusal of art as first and foremost art?

The anti-Platonic, anti-rational tradition that has found followers in the likes of William Empson and Paul de Man has its most obvious modern roots in the work of Friedrich Nietzsche. In *Beyond Good and Evil*, not only does Nietzsche anticipate deconstruction – 'it could even be possible that whatever gives value to those good and honorable things has an incriminating link, bond, or tie to the very things that look like their evil opposites; perhaps they are essentially the same' (2002: 6) – but also, in his insistence on 'perspectivism' and the contextual and relative nature of truth claims, forces the 'new philosopher', as Nietzsche calls him/her, towards a detailed analysis of the socio-historical context of truth claims and, by implication, all forms of cultural production.

Following this suggestion, perhaps the most notable theorists who have in recent years addressed the problems and insufficiencies within the Platonic system are Gilles Deleuze and Félix Guattari, whose two volume *Capitalism and Schizophrenia – Anti-Oedipus* (Paris, 1972) and *A Thousand Plateaus* (Paris, 1980) – bore a considerable influence on Perlongher's theoretical and anthropological work. They conceived rhizomatics – a philosophical approach based on non-hierarchical, flat connecting networks like those of grass – in opposition to the 'tree-logic' they detected at the heart of Platonism. Their thinking is keenly focused on multiplicities and paradoxes; 'a disjunctive that remains a disjunctive, that affirms them throughout their entire existence, *without restricting one by the other or excluding the other from the one*, is perhaps the greatest paradox. "Either . . . or . . . or", instead of "either/or"' (2000a: 76). In their readings of literature – Kafka, Beckett and Artaud in particular – they insist on 'the unimportance of "What does it mean?" [. . .] How it works is the only question' (180). In *A Thousand Plateaus* they suggest:

> Contrary to a deeply rooted belief, the book is not an image of the world. It forms a rhizome with the world, there is an aparallel [*sic*] evolution of the book and the world; but the world effects a reterritorialization of the book, which in turn deterritorializes itself in the world [. . .]. Mimicry is a very bad concept, since it relies on binary logic to describe phenomena of an entirely different nature. (1999: 7)

The rhizome, they contend, 'has no beginning or end; it is always in the middle, between things, interbeing, *intermezzo*' (25). Their reading insists on movement, connection and contradiction, as Guattari suggested in *Molecular Revolution*, calling for a 'politics of experimentation that takes hold of the existing intensities of desires and forms itself into a desiring mechanism in touch with historical social reality' (1984: 87). He opposes this to the sign 'machine':

> The totality of intensive reality is then 'processed' by the formulizing duo, signifier/signified; the totality of fluxes is held in the 'snapshot' of signification which places an object facing a subject; the movement of desire is sterilized by a relationship of representation; the image becomes the memory of a reality made impotent, and its immobilization establishes the world of dominant significations and received ideas. (87–8)

My reading of Perlongher then focuses on movement, dynamism, contradiction and ambiguity in his work, breaking down the barriers between text, author and world.

In relation to the work of the French theorists and their insistence on the function and dynamics of writing, there are three terms that feature prominently in the analysis to follow: 'thematics', 'aesthetics' and 'poetics'. I use these in a fashion close to their Greek derivations. 'Thematic', from the Greek *tithenai*, to lay down, is my way of describing what is 'laid down' in Perlongher's poetry, in vulgar terms, what his poetry does or contains, or as Deleuze and Guattari might suggest, how the work connects with the world. This term does not deny the possibility

that many of Perlongher's poems are deliberately 'about' nothing
and attack the very notion of 'aboutness'. However, it forces close
attention to the words on the page, to what they might mean. This
attention is vital in reading poetry that is as allusive and suggestive
as Perlongher's. 'Aesthetic', from the Greek *aisthanesthai,* deals
with feeling and perception, and therefore the shapes, move-
ments and patterns in Perlongher's works. In relation to this
term, in particular in chapter 2, I also employ the word 'dynamic'
to describe specifically the movements and lines of flight traced by
Perlongher's poems. Finally, 'poetics', from the Greek *poiein,* to
make, encompasses the techniques Perlongher uses in his poems,
and deals with the small-scale, perhaps traditional, analysis of the
poem. As an example, in chapter 4, my discussion of the *travesti*
details the thematics of cross-dressing, the aesthetics of crossing,
and the poetics, or technique of chiasmus.

In fact, Perlongher himself offers pointers for techniques of
reading, in an interview with Ekhard and Bernini:

> De algún modo, para ese tema [male prostitution] que yo estudié y
> la manera en que lo enfoqué, o sea, enfocar la prostitución a partir
> de la propia territorialidad – trabajando en campo –, a mí me
> parece que es difícil trabajar con otras herramientas que no sean
> ésas. (1991: 83, Buenos Aires)

The field suggests the tools, and so Perlongher's reading of other
theorists allows the reader to follow this process out of the text,
into the world, and back into the text. Perlongher, a linguistic and
territorial nomad, created a succession of dynamic movements in
his *oeuvre.* As Rosi Braidotti suggests,

> La gran teoría es una máquina caníbal destinada a asimilar todos
> los cuerpos nuevos y hasta los extraños. Afortunadamente, los
> nómades pueden correr más velozmente y soportar viajes más
> largos que la mayoría de las personas: por lo tanto no pueden ser
> asimilados fácilmente. (2000: 74, Buenos Aires, first published in
> New York)

Perlongher, a nomad in Braidotti's terms, shifted between genres
and theoretical approaches. Thus, my reading has to slide within
Todorov's taxonomy in its adoption of Deleuze and Guattari's
rhizome. My readings aim to connect Perlongher's works to other
texts, be they literary, historical, poetic or political, to
Perlongher's own life and comments on his life and works.

Perlongher's poems offer critical comment on contemporary political and intellectual developments and vice versa. The critical assessment of difficult texts like Perlongher's poetry thus offers an opportunity for expanding the traditional role of both critic and author and the political and artistic potential of the text.

A brief word on my chapter headings will suffice to conclude this introduction. They have been chosen for what I feel is the facility with which they frame an examination of Perlongher's interaction with the world, its thinkers and poetic tradition. These headings have a threefold function. Firstly they are a product of my own reading of Perlongher's work, as what I see to be the key strands that run through his work, and which allow me to compare and contrast Perlongher's poems over the period studied. They are also tools allowing me to group and separate Perlongher's writings and to avoid repetitions in my argument. Finally, they display the development of my own ideas and the areas where I feel that my own analytical tools have the greatest potential for innovative developments in reading Perlongher's works.

In terms of the works included in these chapters, the reader will notice that several poems and essays, which I consider key in Perlongher's *oeuvre*, appear in more than one chapter. This is because of the multiple functions and effects that his works, in particular his poems, undertake. Furthermore, it is my suspicion that Perlongher, in many of his collections, repeated tropes and themes in several poems. Rather than generalizing about collections or trends I have preferred to select those poems that I feel to be illustrative of Perlongher's efforts and then perform my own detailed and specific analysis. From this the reader may surmise that my chapters are intended to be both independent and complementary. Each chapter is intended to stand on its own but reading the chapters together presents a more complete assessment of Perlongher's varied, difficult and challenging work.

NOTES

[1] Some of the material used in this chapter, in particular the section on 'Evita vive', was also dealt with in a different form in the paper '"Evitá hablar de la política": Multiple critical readings of Perlongher's "Evita vive"', published in *Tesserae: Journal of Iberian and Latin American*

Studies, vol. 9 no. 1, available at *www.tandf.co.uk/journals*, and in 'Prolegomenon to the Political reading of Poetry: The Argentine Neobarroco as Test Case', *International Journal of the Humanities*, 2003.

2　'Evita vive' was written in 1975, and first published in 1983 in San Francisco as 'Evita Lives.' Further publications followed: 1985, *Salto Mortal* 8/9 (Jarfalla, Sweden); 1987, *Cerdos y Peces* 11 (Buenos Aires); 1989, *El Porteño* 88 (Buenos Aires); 1997, *Prosa plebeya*; 2001, *'Evita vive' e outras prosas* (São Paulo).

3　See Riz (2000) for an incisive overview and examination of the political scene in Argentina in the period 1966 to '76.

Chapter 2

Perlongher and Territory[1]

Introduction

I wish to examine in this chapter Perlongher's treatment of the concept of territory. Collins (1999: 1538) defines territory as '1: any tract of land; district. 2: the geographical domain under the jurisdiction of a political unit'. The word is drawn from the Latin *territorium*, the land surrounding a city, from *terra*, land. It is in relation to the second of these definitions, the relationship of land to politics, that I feel Perlongher's work to be particularly interesting, as his writing consistently defines and presents territories that are based on desire in relation to the social and are opposed to the conservative views of territory that dominated contemporary Argentine thought.

Perlongher's first collection of poems, *Austria-Hungría* (1980, Buenos Aires), details an aesthetic of border-crossing and 'in-betweenness' that questions the solidity of the nation. The collection *Alambres* (1987, Buenos Aires) proposes an aesthetic of drift that is more complex than the border-crossing and shuttle effects found in *Austria-Hungría* and contains reflections on the experience of exile and political defeat. Both *O negócio do michê* (1987, São Paulo) – Perlongher's Masters thesis in anthropology – and the collection *Parque Lezama* (1990, Buenos Aires) present a cartography of desire in the urban environment, where desiring subjects often function as nomads, or wanderers around the city. The collection *Aguas aéreas* (1991, Buenos Aires), which draws on Brazilian esoteric religion, is dominated by an aesthetic of the rhizome, connections in a horizontal and non-hierarchical fashion that continue and complicate the nomadic aesthetic of the earlier collections. Perlongher's final, posthumous collection, *El chorreo de las iluminaciones* (1997, Buenos Aires), demonstrates a contradictory attempt to reconcile the Christian teleological aesthetic of the mystics with his earlier nomadic and anti-essential writings.

Border-crossing in *Austria-Hungría*

The opening poem of *Austria-Hungría* details various movements in territory:

> Es una murga, marcha en la noche de Varsovia, hace milagros
> con las máscaras, confunde
> a un público polaco
> Los estudiantes de Cracovia miran desconcertados:
> nunca han visto
> nada igual en sus libros
> No es carnaval, no es sábado
> no es una murga, no se marcha, nadie ve
> no hay niebla, es una murga
> no hay serpentinas, es papel picado, el éter frío
> como la nieve de una calle de una ciudad de una Polonia
> > > que no es
> > > que no es
> lo que no es decir que no haya sido, o aún
> que ya no sea, o incluso no esté siendo en este instante
> Varsovia con sus murgas, sus disfraces
> sus arlequines y osos carolina
> con su célebre paz – hablamos de la misma
> la que reina
> recostada en el Vístula
> el proceloso río donde cae
> la murga con sus pitos, sus colores, sus chachachás carnosos
> produciendo en las aguas erizadas un ruido a salpicón
> que nadie atiende
> puesto que no hay tal murga, y aunque hubiérala
> no estaría en Varsovia, y eso todos
> los polacos lo saben
> (Perlongher, 1997a: 23 [1980, Buenos Aires])

Perlongher creates two horizons: Warsaw and Buenos Aires, the home of the *murga*, in Argentina a rowdy musical procession and the style of singing and chanting that accompany it. The game is then to throw the reader between the two, talking of one as the other, distracting the reader's attention with one while talking about the other, and thus creating two spaces and crossing between them. This effect of shuttle, where the reader is thrown forwards and backwards in the text, is achieved particularly through the use of proparoxytone words ('hubiérala', 'máscaras', 'Vístula') and alliteration ('murga [...] marcha [...] papel picado'), or by the juxtaposition of two disparate elements ('murga', 'Varsovia'). Other techniques that create this effect of shuttle are phonic and visual, for example the repetition of the 'es' / 'no es' formula, as in lines one and seven ('Es una murga [...] / [...] No es carnaval'), or the poem's nearly symmetrical shape, which creates a mirroring effect around lines twelve and thirteen – another movement back and forth. This is aided by the form and rhythm, for example the absence of full stops and the use of capital letters without any accompanying punctuation.

Perlongher's poem immediately demands an unconventional logical agility from its reader. Contradictions placed closely together ('no es una murga [...]/ [...] es una murga'), deny conventional logic in favour of connections and contradiction, as in orations such as 'en la noche de Varsovia / [...] no esté siendo en este instante [...] / [...] Varsovia. Once either Poland or Buenos Aires is established as a coordinate, the negation takes us to another space, the other space being by a process of elimination Buenos Aires or Poland.

These logic-defying negations and the complex web of connections allow two different discourses and spaces to overlap. Although a number of logical propositions and rhetorical formulas are used, for example 'no es', 'hablamos', 'puesto que' or 'aunque', the prevalence given to enumerative descriptions such as 'con sus' with four nouns ('murgas', 'disfraces', 'arlequines', 'osos carolina') and then again with three ('pitos', 'colores', 'chachachás') suggests a poem that is sensuous rather than rational. This is further emphasized by the self-contradictory grammar and syntax of the poem. The repetition of 'que no es' in lines twelve and thirteen could be a double negative, or a refrain. The reader is again left in an undecided shuttle. Buenos Aires and Warsaw are separated in space; Perlongher's poem, however, leaves the reader in a position of not being able to distinguish between the two owing to the rapid movement traced in the poem. Thus in answer to the question 'are we in Buenos Aires or Warsaw?', a question that demands the limitation of two exclusive spaces, Perlongher's reader must affirm that he or she is in a space that is at the same time *either* Buenos Aires *or* Warsaw. This interstitial statement could be taken as an expansion of the border into an overlapping and duplicitous margin.

We can illustrate the importance of this point by examining the position of the border in the formation of the Argentine nation state. If one considers Argentina's often difficult and violent relationship with its neighbours, as in the War of the Triple Alliance against Paraguay, or the Siege of Montevideo, one can see that the history of Argentina has been marked by attempts to fix monads, or individual and self-contained units. These monads have included units such as 'Argentina' and 'Uruguay' or, on a smaller but no less critical scale, such binary distinctions as 'loyal' and 'disloyal'. The latter was visually achieved under the dictator-ship of Juan Manuel de Rosas (from 1835 to 1852) through enforcing the wearing of a red armband or, in the Peronist era, through observing mourning for the general's wife Evita Perón after her death in 1952.

Perlongher's poem significantly complicates such a portrayal of the world; the opening poem of *Austria-Hungría* details a strong aesthetic of the between. Like the collection's title, the poem hints at the political reality of the contemporary era: the impor-tance of geographical boundaries in Argentine politics.[2] In 1977 the Videla government had officially entered into dispute with the Pinochet administration of Chile over several islands and water-ways in the Beagle Channel area. In 1979 the matter was placed in the judgement of the Vatican, who would later find in Chile's favour. The Chilean government under Pinochet had published school geography textbooks showing much of Patagonia as Chil-ean, while Argentine atlases have for years read 'Islas Malvinas (Arg.)'. It is the latter dispute with the United Kingdom, deals struck between the army and the navy, and growing public discontent about military rule that would culminate in Galtieri's decision to invade the Malvinas/Falklands on 2 April 1982. The dictatorship's fixing of the nation is an attempt to define Argen-tina as a pre-given territory inhabited by people with a shared relationship to and affiliation for that territory – patriotism, or the love of the *patria*, the land belonging to the father. Perlongher's poem on the other hand reveals the difficulties masked by attempts to fix the nation to a given space, and attempts to create an alternative form of nation, where national borders do not disguise their penetrability.

It is worth outlining at this stage Perlongher's early political commitment. The Argentine sociologists Rapisardi and Modarelli (2001) draw attention to Perlongher's early activism with the Trotskyite Partido Obrero, and to the Trotskyite tactics that characterized Perlongher's early activism. Perlongher was a member of the Trotskyite group Política Obrera between 1968 and 1971 and was an *ultraizquierdista*, or ultra-leftist, member of the Frente de Liberación Homosexual (FLH) in the 1970s (Ferrer and Baigorria, 1997: 255). He dedicated a poem, 'Lago Nahuel', from *Hule*, to Nahuel Moreno, the most prominent Argentine Trotskyite. This commitment is revealed for example in the participation of the FLH, following Perlongher's demands, in the demonstrations to welcome General Juan Domingo Perón back to Argentina in 1973, although the group had no official links to the Peronist movement (Rapisardi and Modarelli, 2001: 156–7).

This participation draws attention to two key elements in Trotskyism, firstly, its need to cultivate alliances with other groups and, secondly, the international character of the Permanent Revolution promoted by Leon Trotsky, as opposed to the more limited national aims proposed by Lenin. As Trotsky stated, 'the permanent revolution [is] a revolution whose every stage is rooted in the preceding one and which can end only in the complete liquidation of class society [. . .]. Therein lies the permanent character of the socialist revolution as such' (1962: 6, 9). This revolution also had to cross national boundaries: 'The international character of the socialist revolution [. . .] is no abstract principle but a theoretical and political reflection of the world economy [. . .], a national revolution is not a self-contained whole; it is only a link in the international chain' (9).

Many of Perlongher's early writings for the feminist review *Persona* in the 1970s were signed with the name Rosa L. de Grossman, the hispanicized married name of the Spartacus League's founder, Rosa Luxemburg, and this anti-Leninist internationalism is also highlighted in the writings of Luxemburg, Perlongher's mentor, for example in her critique (1976) of Lenin's insistence on the self-determination of nations. Luxemburg instead focuses on federations and the self-determination and autonomy of the working class, brought about by the international socialist revolution. While it is important not to attempt to subsume Perlongher's poetry within an orthodox Trotskyite or even Spartacist position drawn from turn of the twentieth-century thought, it is clear that in his proposition of alternative national spaces, Perlongher is drawing on his early political commitments.

Alongside the political implications of Perlongher's *murga*, there are other connotations relating to the smaller configuration of a territory for sexually marginalized or persecuted groups. The *murga* represents an uprising, a Dionysian force. In terms of content it is a combination of various forms of art: music ('pitos'), dance ('chachachás') and costume ('colores'). This 'marcha' recalls the drag parties recounted by Juan José Sebreli (1997) and Rapisardi and Modarelli (2001), particularly with the fleeting reference to 'reina' – in Buenos Aires, slang for an effeminate homosexual man – in Perlongher's poem, which is also, perhaps, an ironic and sideways reference to the alternative possibilities of desiring sovereignty, where the *reina* ('queer/n') *reina* ('reigns'). For much of the poem the *murga* exists in a subjunctive space, as a possibility ('que no haya sido', 'que ya no sea', 'no esté siendo') that is ignored or denied ('que nadie atiende', 'no estaría en Varsovia'). Thus the artistic, cross-dressed, Dionysian uprising lasts only an instant, before its denial and disappearance in the river. This scene alludes to a political reality, suggested by the 'célebre paz' of Warsaw, the agreement that from 1955 gave the Soviet government the right to station troops in satellite countries and provided justification for the invasion of Czechoslovakia in 1968.

The word 'proceloso' also offers a telling allusion to the contemporary political situation. In an interview with Guillermo Saavedra, Perlongher spoke of the secretive codes used by left-wing militants in the seventies as key to the orality of *Austria-Hungría*. He gives the example of calling calle Alberdi, 'alba mierda', in a form of *faux-lunfardo* (Saavedra, 1991: 2). The word 'proceloso', in similar fashion, contains the word 'proceso', short for the *proceso de reorganización nacional*, or 'dirty war' against the Argentine left in the late 1970s. Thus the river, site of the dumping of many victims of the Argentine dictatorship, is linked to the *proceso* through a telling political allusion. The disappearance of the *murga* in Warsaw, by a river, therefore traces connections between two statist, centralizing governments (Moscow and

Buenos Aires) and shows the risks for that which attempts to disturb the rigid organization of society, namely disappearance, both physically and from official history. The relationships that characterize Perlongher's *murga* are relationships that disappear, that cease to exist, not only in the poem but also in history, as occurred with the repression or disappearance of opposition groups in the late 1970s and with the concomitantly necessary process of self-censorship and survival. Hence Perlongher's crossing of national boundaries alludes sharply to the repression of the late 1970s.

Perlongher's attempts to cross national borders are borne out in his other writings from this period, first between Argentina and Brazil and the rest of Latin America, and later between Argentina and its historically problematic neighbour Uruguay. If Argentine national identity has historically been based on its isolation from the rest of Latin America – and conversely, its historical importation of European ideas such as opera and psychoanalysis – Perlongher seems to propose in his writings from his early period an Argentina more open to Latin America.[3]

The poem 'Los orientales' allows us to examine further these early dynamics in Perlongher's poetry. 'Orientales' are, for *Bonaerenses*, Uruguayans, as they come from the east bank of the River Plate, also known as the Banda Oriental:

Sordo
era el silencio de la 18 de Julio cuando empezaron a apagarse
las últimas luces y Nelson y tú perdieron a los botijas
nada más
estaba la pareja de argentinos dando giros en el oscuro
las Fuerzas de Seguridad y el sol de Carrasco a las 19 yéndose
Cómo te vestías de justo porque los señores
de Sally ya habían emigrado, y no la amabas. . .
Faltaban cigarrillos; Walter, Franklin
conocían porteños y fumaban
en Colonia, a la llegada del vapor, en tanto
el país se vaciaba y fuera de las colas
apenas se veían lustrabotas, y nadie
compra tu amor que se desvaluaba como el peso   Los turistas
te miraban fascinados y enamorándose de ti
querían llevarte a Río, a San Isidro
pero siempre desaparecían del hotel una hora antes

y qué sentido tenía vagar por el embarcadero y despedirlos:
hacían bay bay con una mano y se reían
y te preguntaban por los topos, en el Carnaval de Ciudad Vieja
entre los negros descoloridos, con fastidio
Sólo pensaban en el sexo sexo sexo   Líber, Derby
desde los hoteles de Retiro escribían a las familias y buscaban
en medio de la noche otros muchachos que los llevaban a vivir
por una hora o dos y los abandonaban
después de darles de drogar
y caminaban por calles interminables donde se olía
el ácido del río
(Perlongher, 1997a: 24–5 [1980, Buenos Aires])

In simple terms, the poem traces movements of crossing the River Plate. This is given a particular resonance by the use of character names. The character names – 'Walter', 'Franklin', 'Nelson' and 'Sally' – are not only all non-Castilian imports, they are also the type of names adopted as homosexual pseudonyms, the *nombres de guerra* detailed by Rapisardi and Modarelli (2001: 25) in their assessment of the second baptism in homosexual circles, either for effeminate male homosexuals to accentuate their female side and international pretensions – 'Sally', for example – or as adopted by male prostitutes for a certain anonymous exoticism – the other names listed. Perlongher recorded these practices in his early sociological work, as illustrated by his contribution to Acevedo's work on homosexuality in Argentina (Buenos Aires, 1985). Overtly then, this is a poem describing the aimless wanderings of underemployed Uruguayan prostitutes, menaced by the security forces – from 1973 Uruguay also had a dictatorship, with similar repressive practices to its Argentine counterpart – and lacking clients as a result of economic hardships in the country. To this end Perlongher uses a number of geographical markers: 'Carrasco' is a beach resort near Montevideo, '18 de Julio' (with capitals) is a central street in Montevideo, while 'Ciudad Vieja' is a part of Montevideo. Overtly then, also, Perlongher is writing about Uruguay and the hardships observed there, a common tactic during the dictatorship when non-exiled writers would talk of political outrages in other countries, for example supposed Uruguayan political victims being washed up on the Argentine side of the Río de la Plata, as a covert way of criticizing their own country's government.[4]

However, the situation is rather more dynamic than that. Perlongher complicates the territory dealt with here through various references and techniques. The poem proposes a geographical movement across the River Plate – the 'vapor', or steamship – but also the creation of a permissive space, by expanding the border into a between-territory, what Hakim Bey (2002) calls the Temporary Autonomous Zone,[5] as seen in 'La murga'.[6] Colonia is the shortest crossing point to Argentina, having been an Argentine, Brazilian and Uruguayan territory in the past. 'La Ciudad Vieja' is also a rather generic name for the old part of a town. The tourists write from hotels in Retiro in Buenos Aires, want to go to 'Río' (de Janeiro) or 'San Isidro' (in Argentina), and say 'bay bay', a phonetic inscription of English. The poem's insistence on naming as a form of nationality for those who the contemporary dictatorships would prefer to expel or arrest – the 'Argentinos' are cruising for boys; the 'Orientales' are homosexual prostitutes – questions the rigid construction of a national identity for the countries involved, while proposing a more fluid and interchanging approach to the nation. Whereas 'La murga' problematized the separation in space between two countries by creating a Dionysian shuttle effect between the two – the *murga* itself – 'Los orientales' questions the solidity and autonomy of the nation by displaying the problematic or foreign elements within it that the nation state would prefer to avoid.

What is also interesting about this poem is its relationship to Perlongher's early sociological studies of prostitution and homo-sexuality, for example the co-authored study *La familia abandónica y sus consecuencias* (1981, Buenos Aires), or the essay 'Prostitución homosexual: el negocio del deseo' (1981, Buenos Aires). In these works, Perlongher translated the personal contact he had had with *chongos* (male prostitutes who accentuate their masculinity and look for effeminate clients, or *maricas*) into an attempt to theorize the position of the male prostitute in a way that did not stress either disguised homosexuality or economic factors, both of which would lead to essentialist conclusions. Instead, in Perlongher's assessment of the movements of these boys, very often starting with expulsion or voluntary exit from the family home, Perlongher focused on the unpredictable movements of desire within the social. These studies detail complex and intriguing movements and sexual contacts very similar to those traced in 'Los orientales'. This poem's defiance of geopolitical borders and its intersection of historical horizons is inscribed within the secretive circuits of clandestine homosexual activity outlawed by the military dictatorship through the imposition of pseudo-legal police edicts that criminalized vagrancy or suspected previous convictions (*antecedentes*), or by the curfews and limitations on movement described by Diana Taylor (1997: 95). This defiance represents, like much of *Austria-Hungría*, a challenge to the dictatorship's obsession with territorial fixing that is typical of Perlongher's first collection.

The Malvinas Conflict in Perlongher's Work

The dictatorship's obsession with fixing territory reached its apogee with the invasion of the Falklands/Malvinas Islands. Although *Austria-Hungría* was written before the conflict, Perlongher's confrontational approach to territory is in keeping with his attitudes to the Islands, as borne out in three essays: 'Todo el poder a Lady Di: Militarismo y anticolonialismo en la cuestión de las Malvinas' (1982, Buenos Aires); 'La ilusión de unas islas' (1983, Buenos Aires); and 'El deseo de unas islas' (1985, Buenos Aires). The first of these represents a direct criticism of militarism and the Malvinas campaign. Perlongher suggests that:

> Antes que defender la ocupación de las Malvinas, habría que postular la desocupación de la Argentina por parte del auto-denominado *Ejército Argentino*. El sólo hecho de que guapos adolescentes, en la flor de edad, sean sacrificados [. . .] en nombre de unos insalubres islotes, es una razón de sobra para denunciar este triste sainete. (Perlongher, 1997b: 179).

Perlongher stands out for several reasons: firstly, he is not swayed by patriotic, anti-imperialist rhetoric; and, secondly, he questions who decides on issues of nationhood. By placing the 'Ejército Argentino' in italics and calling it 'autodenominado', Perlongher insists that it is not just the country's unelected military rulers who have the power to define the nation. For Perlongher, Argentina under military rule is as much an illegally occupied country as the Malvinas under British rule. The young soldiers sent to fight in the conflict are potentially being murdered, as the military is not the legitimate decision maker in matters of national sovereignty. Furthermore, through his insistence on the *sexual* waste of having boys killed in the Malvinas, he inserts desire, rather than notions of love or honour, into the political situation. For Perlongher the greatest tragedy, it seems, is the loss of potential sexual partners.[7] This antipatriotic stance was supported by his reading of the work of the founder of the Spartacus league, Rosa Luxemburg, on the invasion of Poland. She had refused to support patriotism, which, according to Perlongher, she saw as a reactionary bourgeois deception (178). Rosa Luxemburg's criticism of nationalism can be found in, for example, *The National Question* (1976 edition), a collection of earlier pamphlets and essays, where she argued that the quest for self-determination was an obstacle to socialism, criticizing defenders of an independent Poland, which she felt would consolidate the bourgeoisie's hold on power. For Luxemburg, the enemy was not international oppression but oppression per se, which could only be combated through class struggle, as workers and peasants from different countries have more in common with each other than they do with the middle and ruling classes of their own countries. Perlongher's insertion of desire into national politics complicates Luxemburg's work and represents a radical challenge to the contemporary left in Argentina.

In the second of the essays mentioned above Perlongher engaged in a polemic with those writers and theorists who had criticized his 'traición' (Perlongher, 1997b: 182) – not supporting the campaign – in a 1983 article in *Sitio*, a group that Perlongher states included [Ramón] 'Alcalde', [Eduardo] 'Grüner', [Luis] 'Gusmán', and [Jorge] 'Jinkis' (1997b: 181),[8] some of the most prominent contemporary intellectuals of the Argentine left. Perlongher's approach to the Malvinas contrasts to the vast majority of Argentine writers, whose attitude to Galtieri's venture was one of qualified support. In poetry, the deluge of patriotic pieces supporting the campaign was collected, alongside earlier pieces and Borges's 'Juan López y John Ward' in *Nuestros poetas y las Malvinas* (Müller, 1983). Most are in the neoclassical style and are almost self-parodic in their machismo and indignation, for example the following medically confused line by Jose María Castieñeira de Dios: '¡que estas islas nos duelen como si nos castraron!' (58), or Alberto Blasi Brambilla's 'Canto de amor a las Malvinas', which celebrates 'amor normal' for the Islands – femininized in their 'ternura' – in terms of 'sangre, corazón' and

'El Señor' (32). The only prominent critic was Jorge Luis Borges, who suggested that the islands be given to Bolivia so it could have a seaport (Perlongher, 1997b: 179) and whose poem 'Juan López y John Ward' (1982) follows Wilfred Owen in presenting the irrational and inexplicable bloodshed of war. Even the prominent left-wing critic Atilio Borón, writing a retrospective condemnation of the campaign in 1992, still insists on Argentine sovereignty for the islands and the correctness of non-military attempts to regain them. Borón's use in the article of terms such as 'ganado' to describe diplomatic advances in reclaiming the islands is closer to the military's discourse than he might like to imagine; again a figure on the political left uses military vocabulary to discuss political negotiations regarding the islands. This reinforces the radical nature of Perlongher's stance on the composition of the national territory, in contrast to the massive cross-party displays of support in the Plaza de Mayo (Escudero Chauvel, 1996: 23–4) and the support for the campaign by unions (Egurbide, 1982: 32; Ortiz, 1982: 8) and even the exiled revolutionary leader Mario Firmenich.

Perlongher can be seen therefore in the early 1980s proposing an alternative approach to territory – soldiers as lovers, mobile communities based on desire, porous borders – not only to the *proceso* dictatorship but also to the left-wing opposition to the dictatorship. The key difference, again, is that Perlongher's writing focuses on desire and the social. In his poems and essays, Perlongher uses the concept of nationality to discuss communities united by specific interests, in this case desire, and the social organizations that challenge or oppose them. Furthermore, he uses the concept of territory to present and discuss the places or sites where such a community, perhaps only briefly or as a possibility, may find its very marginalized space. These sites, once acknowledged or recognized in Perlongher's poems, can question the rules for the construction of the nation state that combat the development of new forms of political communities. This process in Perlongher's writing can be seen as closely related to the radical ways in which the destruction of traditional left-wing opposition groups – parties, unions or guerrilla groups – changed the possibilities for political organization in Argentina in the late 1970s and 1980s.

Alambres and Exile

In 1981, after the publication of *Austria-Hungría* and another arrest, this time accompanied by a beating from the Mendoza police, Perlongher went into exile in São Paulo.[9] Perlongher's Brazilian exile is reflected in two areas of his work. Firstly, the fieldwork among street prostitutes, which so often ran the risk of pseudo-legal police reprisals, in Brazil gained him a university scholarship (Perlongher, 1999a: 12 [São Paulo, 1987]). Secondly, the delirious sexuality of the poems in the 'Frenesí' series, especially '*carnaval – río 1984*', clearly exhibits the new freedom Perlongher found under the less repressive regime in Brazil:

[. . .]   Terciopelo, correhuelas de ter-
ciopelo, sogas de nylon, alambrecitos de hambres y sobrosos, sabro-
sos hombres broncos hombreando hombrudos en el refocilar, de la
pipeta el peristilo [. . .]

                                                                        el
alcahuete paga el servicio de la consumición, ahoga en cerveza lo
furtivo del lupanar, tupido, apantallado por maltrechas écuyères en
caballitos de espinafre, la pimienta
haciendo arder el sebo carnoso del ánade.
(Perlongher, 1997a: 105 [1987, Buenos Aires])

The accumulation, misspelling and physicality of this poem all point to Perlongher's identification of a Dionysian exuberance not found in Argentina. It is worth stressing the basic cultural difference between Argentina and Brazil embodied by the absence of a major carnival, specifically the absence of a permitted space for the Dionysian in Argentina, in contrast to the appeal Brazil held for Perlongher, as highlighted by Rapisardi and Modarelli: 'Brasil, ya a fines de los setenta, parece disfrutar de una cierta libertad de pensamiento' (2001: 183). Sex and sexuality – particularly images of the beach and carnival – played an important role in exporting the notion of Brazil as a permissive society in both the political propaganda of its dictatorship and in its attempts to increase foreign trade, especially tourism. Many adverts can be found in the pages of the conservative Argentine daily *La Nación* from the 1970s promoting travel to Brazil – often sponsored by the Brazilian tourist board or VARIG, the national airline – that use images either of scantily clad carnival sambistas, or beachgoers sporting the famous *tanga*. In contrast, Perlongher regarded Argentina as a particularly un-Dionysian country: 'la Argentina [es] una sociedad en la que la orgía no existe. Una sociedad muy ordenadita. No hay orgías, no hay carnaval. Y sin embargo, una sociedad tan ordenada y limpita produce los horrores de la dictadura' (Ekhard and Bernini, 1991: 86).

The position of the bewildered and exultant foreign observer is highlighted as the poem creates an effect of wonderment through taking the carnival performance at face value – these are riders ('écuyères'), this is a (sea) horse ('caballitos') – and not ordering the spectacle but, instead, attempting to transpose the confusing and sensual experience directly onto the poem. This is achieved through the unordered juxtaposition of sensuous elements, for example 'terciopelo', a texture to be felt, 'sabrosos' or 'pimienta', taste, and 'hombres' or 'correhuelas', sight and potentially touch. Moreover, in the manner of Oliverio Girondo and his collection *Veinte poemas para ser leídos en el tranvía* (1922), the poem concentrates on public displays of sexuality – the hypermanliness of the 'hombres', the pimp and the brothel, the suggestive burning of the 'ánade', a proparoxytone close in sound to 'ano'. However, unlike the situations described in Girondo's poetry, here there are no bourgeois values to control this sexuality and no social mores to force a hypocritical denial of desire. Instead, Perlongher's poem suggests the carnival environment as a pure explosion of Dionysian sensuality and kitsch art. What is intriguing is that this uprising is wholly inscribed within the territory of Brazil, not only by the endnote almost boastfully setting the poem in *'carnaval – río 1984'*, but also through the inclusion of very specifically Brazilian carnival details, such as the 'lanzaperfumes', the ether jets used as a drug in early carnival celebrations. It is this sort of Dionysian uprising, here found in the Brazilian carnival, that Perlongher had proposed in 'La murga'. Thus *carnaval* offers a Brazilian *murga*, a Brazilian TAZ, a concrete and state-supported example of the glimpsed possibility in the earlier poem. If the poems of *Austria-Hungría* attempt to find a nation for the desiring, Perlongher's poem dealing with Brazil instead detects, exultantly, a desiring nation state. Whereas his earlier poems attempted to find a possible space for desire, here Brazil at carnival time is identified as a concrete example of that possibility. Within this, the status of the exile is an intriguing one, in many ways an extension in time and degree of the uprootedness of the 'turistas' in the earlier poem 'Los orientales'. If poems like the latter and

'La murga' attempted to create an in-between space of freedom and desire, the in-betweenness of the exile – more than a tourist, but not a resident – is a more concrete example of the freedom sought out by the earlier poems.

Alongside this Luso-tropicalist exuberance, however, Perlongher's poems from this era also contain telling allusions to the notion of exile as defeat, a reality for many political militants whose exile distanced them from oppositional activities, as in the poem 'India muerta':

> noticiándose del malhadado suceso del 27
> volví a sufrir otro revés que nos obligó a pasar el Yaguarón
> un poco apurados
> yo perdí parte de la montura pero salvé bien desde aquel día
> estamos bajo la protección de las autoridades imperiales
> que nos protegen y nos respetan en todo aquello que puede ser
> para mantener la esperanza de salvar la república
> mirar con indiferencia las desgracias del país
> un enemigo fuerte y poderoso que tenemos al frente
> no me horroriza ni me infunde terror
> árbitro de la fortuna de este honrado
> pueblo compuesto de patriotas cuyo patriotismo los ha hecho callar
> un atrevimiento sin límites
> En la frontera de Santa Teresa nada hay nuevo: los enemigos
>   continúan ocupándola
> mi idolatrada Bernardina
> en brazos de un poder americano
> (Perlongher, 1997a: 67 [1987, Buenos Aires])

The first person of the historical letter is strongly maintained throughout the poem ('volví', 'sufrí', 'perdí'); were it not for the division into verse, the text would be almost indistinguishable from one of the nineteenth-century Uruguayan patriot José Fructuoso Rivera's letters describing his struggles with Rosas and General Oribe for an independent East Bank, as found in the appendices to Adolfo Saldías's *Historia de la confederación argentina* (1881–1907). However, the effect of versification, causing the break-up of sentences and the intrusion of physical sensations, in particular breathing, into the orderly telling of history – the surface of the poem, one might say – to give the impression of a complex pleating, whereby other realities beyond Rivera's defeat are alluded to. Furthermore, the historical and geographical references ('autoridades', 'la república', 'las desgracias del país',

'terror'), and the geographical references, for example 'las autori-
dades imperiales' (Brazil, in the context of Rivera's letter), allow
the process of exile to echo Perlongher's own exile, also in Brazil
escaping a violent dictatorship. Perlongher therefore examines
through a reframing of history the negative connotations of exile
as political defeat and loss. Perlongher's own life offers intriguing
parallels with that of Rivera. The general, whose nicknames were
'pardejón', *gaucho* slang for a homosexual, or 'Don Frutos', a pun
on his second name Fructuoso, was frequently attacked by his
political opponents not just for his nationalist ambitions but also
for his supposed perversion. More interesting still is that Rivera,
against the efforts of the dictators Rosas and Oribe, proposed an
alternative and marginal nation, Uruguay, an expansion of the
border between Argentina and Brazil. Historical distance may
strip this project of some of the scandalous audacity that
Perlongher's efforts still preserve but, nevertheless, the inscrip-
tion of this attempt to create an independent Uruguay and the
political and personal hardships that this entailed, allows
Perlongher to draw parallels to his own failed efforts with the FLH
at creating a similarly marginal desiring community in Argentina.

Exile is one of the key movements in *Alambres* but is also
accompanied by drift, or 'deriva', a relational aesthetic of flows
and passing contact that to a great degree takes over from the
two-dimensional aesthetic of crossing that dominated in *Austria-
Hungría*, as in the poem 'Mme. S.':

> pude acaso pararme como un macho ebrio de goznes, de tequilas
>   mustio,
> informe, almibararme, penetrar tus blonduras de madre que se ofrece,
> como un altar, al hijo – menor y amanerado? adoptar tus alambres de
> abanico, tus joyas que al descuido dejabas tintinear sobre la mesa,
> entre los vasos de ginebra, indecorosamente pringados de ese rouge
> arcaico de tus labias?
>   cual lobezno lascivo, pude alzarme,
> tras tus enaguas [. . .]
> (Perlongher, 1997b: 88_9 [1981, Buenos Aires])

The poem investigates the perversion and violence that exists at
the heart of the bourgeois family, an organization that delimits a
territory – 'the home' – and individual roles within that territory.
The poem alludes to these relationships, talking of mothers and
sons ('madre', 'hijo'). However, it complicates these roles. Firstly,

the roles are qualified; the mother, who should be reserved for the father, offers herself ('se ofrece'), and the son is both young and 'amanerado', affected, effeminate even. Furthermore, the technique of simile, centred on 'como' and 'cual' shows how the roles, a form of performance themselves, perform themselves into something else, the 'macho' lover or a predatory wolf cub ('lobezno'). Moreover, the home develops a sickly atmosphere through references to alcohol ('tequila', 'ginebra') and glasses ('vasos'), common trappings of bourgeois entertainments, but now faded ('mustio') or dirtied ('indecorosamente pringado'). This recalls Tennessee Williams's play *A Streetcar Named Desire* (1947), with its unwholesome domestic air of casual alcoholism, brittle sanity and incestuous violence.

Within this atmosphere Perlongher creates a connecting net-work of space through a reference to the collection's title, 'alam-bres' (wires). Perlongher uses wires as a form of separation (through the partitioning of lands, as in barbed wire), as a means of connection (in telegraph or electricity wires), and also as a way of depicting the complex network of connections involved in human sexuality: here the wires of the mother's fan ('abanico'), but also those of a dress's bustle. The crisis in Perlongher's text, which leads to the apparent murder of the mother, revolves around attempts to escape stratification within the preordained roles of a family, to be son *and* lover, to be mother *and* fiancée. The poem, which was published as 'Mme. Schocklender' in *XUL* in 1981, was a response to the polemical 'Schocklender' case in Argentina, where a well-to-do Buenos Aires couple were found dead in their house with their children missing. After a dramatic police search, the sons were found. The investigation blamed the eldest son for the murders, and suggested that he had been engaging in sexual relations with his mother. In Perlongher's poem, as the bourgeois order collapses, its divisions no longer have meaning and paranoid violence erupts. We see in 'Mme. S.' how attempts to escape the sedentary and striated socio-territorial organization of the bourgeois family result in violent retribution.

In the poem 'El palacio del cine', such complex relationships between desire and space are investigated further:

Hay algo nupcial en ese olor
o racimo de bolas calcinadas
por una luz que se drapea

entre las dunas de las mejillas
el lechoso cairel de las ojeras
que festonean los volados
rumbo al olor del baño, al paraíso
del olor, que pringa
las pantallas donde las cintas
indiferentes rielan
guerras marinas y nupciales

Los escozores de la franela
sobre el zapato de pájaro pinto
dan paso al anelar o pegan toques
de luna creciente o de frialdad
en el torcido respaldar
que disimula el brinco
tras un arco de fumo
y baban carreteles de goma
que dejan resbaloso el rayo
del mirador entretenido en otra cosa.

Aleve como la campanilla del lucero
el iluminador los despabila
y reparte polveras de esmirna
en el salitre de las botamangas
y en el rouge de las gasas
que destrenzan las bocas
esparciendo un cloqueo diminuto
de pez espada atrapado en la pecera
o de manatí vuelto sirena
para reconocerlos.
[. . .]
(Perlongher, 1997a: 100–1 [1987, Buenos Aires])

The poem creates a set of drifting connections. This is achieved
through the great density of conjunctions and prepositions in the
stanza-long sentences, connecting through 'por', 'que', 'entre'
and 'de' (all within the first four lines), in a pattern that is
repeated throughout. Each connection thus leads to another
clause or phrase, so that while grammatically each clause or
phrase gives the impression of completing the last, in fact it
complicates it, to be then followed by a further complication.
Furthermore, while this might suggest an orderly construction of
syntax, gerundives, 'para's and 'que's complicate the syntactical
connections in such a way as to leave phrases, for example 'para

reconocerlos' or 'esparciendo un cloqueo diminuto', grammatically adrift. In an interview with Daniel Molina, Perlongher highlighted this syntactical aspect of his poetry: 'Comparándolo [Spanish] con el protugués [*sic*], te das cuenta de que el español – inclusive en las escrituras más convencionales, menos poéticas –, permite, casi exige, el encastre de las frases subordinadas, unas dentro de otras' (Molina, 1988: 17). This insertion allows Perlongher to cultivate a complicated drifting movement between elements in this poem.

The second process at work is the creation of 'snippets'. In the first stanza, lines four and five appear to lack punctuation: 'entre la dunas de las mejillas / el lechoso cairel de las orejas', sandwiched as they are between 'que's in lines three and six. These tropes have two effects: firstly, the poem is in constant movement, a complication of the movement above; secondly, the hyperbaton becomes an unresolved and folded syntax; unlike the Golden Age hyperbaton, the poem cannot be restored to a grammatically correct syntax. Rather than a self-contained construction, Perlongher's poem instead opens out like a fan. The reader then is left grammatically adrift, a syntactic nomad between the various sensuous phrases that constitute the poem.

This grammatical construction, whereby the reader is left unable to reconstruct the poem's syntax, allows the poem's lexicon to come to the fore. This can be categorized into several semantic fields: the body ('mejillas', 'bolas', 'baba', 'ojeras'); clothing ('zapato', 'botamangas'); cinema or theatre technology ('luz', 'pantallas', 'respaldar', 'iluminador'); and toilets ('olor' repeated three times, 'baño'). This lexicon, also including *lunfardo* vocabulary, like 'franela', sexual excitement by touch, recreates the various sensations of visiting a porno cinema. The presentation of a cinema as a space for sex has a number of sociological implications. Perlongher's poem uses the cinema as an example, and a positively valorized one at that, of drift in the urban environment. Specifically, this movement in the *salas populares* of central Buenos Aires cinemas, which the Argentina sociologist Juan José Sebreli calls 'hacer el ajedrez' (1997: 344 [Buenos Aires]), involves moving from seat to seat or from seat to toilets to seat in search of sexual partners. Rapisardi and Modarelli, in their work on gay rituals in the last Argentine dictatorship, relate the importance of the porno cinema to changes in the Buenos Aires ghetto that have accompanied the insertion of homosexuality into the market place in the post-dictatorship era. One of their interviewees, 'La Richard', a former devotee of homosexual cruising areas in Buenos Aires, details the changes that this entailed:

> *Cada vez se hace más chico el ghetto, a pesar de que se abren locales nuevos todos los días [. . .]. Para mí, antes toda la ciudad era un escenario para armar sexo, a pesar de la policía, de los militares [. . .]. Hoy, en cambio, todo queda reducido a los cines pornos, los saunas, los boliches y los taxi-boys.* (Rapisardi and Modarelli, 2001: 24, italics in the original)

Despite the repression of the military era, secretive homosexual activity still carried on in clandestine spaces – like the earlier *murga.* For La Richard, 'coming out' has meant greater freedom in the reduced frequency of physical violence but reduced freedom in that the new freedom is inscribed within the market place as a channelling agent to circumscribe all types of sexual activity within relationships of capital. Freedom now costs money. Perlongher's poem however celebrates the cinema; it is worth remembering that Perlongher did not witness the changes in the Buenos Aires *ghetto* first-hand, owing to his exile, and his writings on the change in sexual practices, particularly the postscript to his work on male prostitution (1997b: 56–7 [1987, Buenos Aires]) focused on AIDS as the root cause of a new sedentarization, or settling down, of sexual exchanges. AIDS was perhaps central in Brazil, but less so in Argentina, where insertion into the market-place had a more important effect. For Perlongher the cinema is still a space of excitement, freedom, and sexual exchange. The cinema itself seems to inhabit a space between Argentina and Brazil, where it has the pre-exile Argentine secrecy required for sex, and the post-exile Brazilian exuberance found on the streets of São Paulo. Thus in contrast to the poems of *Austria-Hungría*, this poem cultivates a combination of drift and an *intermezzo* between Argentina and Brazil.

This attitude to territory suggests the beginning of Perlongher's interest, one might say obsession, with the nomad. Perlongher defined the nomad, a term that he drew from the writings of Gilles Deleuze and Félix Guattari, in an interview with Ekhard and Bernini (1991: 83):

> Los chicos [male prostitutes in São Paulo] son nómades. [. . .] El nomadismo está en la circulación, no solamente de los muchachos

– los taxi boys –, de los homosexuales también. El eje básico de la circulación es esa área, en el centro de la ciudad, el área – yo te diría – de baja prostitución. Sería el equivalente de Lavalle aquí [in Buenos Aires], Lavalle hasta Santa Fe inclusive. La modalidad de circulación erótica es la errancia, la deriva. La gente sale a derivar y a ver qué pasa. El problema es que el nomadismo no se puede pensar a la manera dialéctica, como una oposición a la sedentariedad, como polos, o una cosa o la otra. El nomadismo siempre está en lo intersticial.

The nomad, for Perlongher, is the person who is in-between. The roots of the word can be found in the Greek *noumos*, the parceling of land, and the Latin, *nomas*, a wandering sheepherder. I would suggest that the popular image of the nomad is most clearly illustrated by wandering African tribes such as the Tuareg, who travel with their animals between different points where pasture, water, shelter and so on can be found. Perlongher's suggestion, perhaps at odds with the common conception, is that the points are less important than the movement. Therefore unlike the movement of a commuter or a migrant, where the points of departure and arrival are determinant, what determines the nomad's movement is the need for movement itself. That is why, then, the nomad does not settle down in the places where pasture and water can be found. 'Nomad' is the term that Perlongher begins to adopt for his in-between states, after his move to Brazil, and with his increasing interest in Deleuze-inspired urban anthropology.

Three poems in *Alambres*, '(*grades*)', '(lobos)', and '(Mamparas)', the most nonsensical in the collection, highlight a linguistic form of nomadism, a new sensitivity to in-betweenness in language. '(lobos)' serves as a perfect example:

> lebos lobos ajax rodrigo guesevenda
> gruesa venda venérea madreselva del ánade
> cohonestas ebúrneos mercados
> tasa la marca del pito
> rito colomí cárpido lesma
> leve losa lontano lamé
> (Perlongher, 1997a: 94 [1987, Buenos Aires])

The poem defies grammatical rules (the need for verbs, especially), unites unrelated elements ('lobos ajax'), and ignores metrics and rhyme. Its lexicon imports foreign words ('ajax') and

uses non-words ('lebos'), and uses words with suggestively similar
sounds to others ('ánade' again suggests 'ano'). As in Vicente
Huidobro's *Altazor* (1931) or Oliverio Girondo's *En la masmédula*
(1956) and perhaps to a greater extreme, Perlongher creates a
poem in an almost-language, between sense and non-sense. The
poem thus exhibits the key characteristic of Perlongher's nomad,
being in-between. The Italo-Australian French-based theorist Rosi
Braidotti discusses this opening up of the space between in her
book *Sujetos nómades*. As Braidotti suggests, 'el políglota es un
nómade lingüístico' (2000: 37). Through Perlongher's move to
Brazil and his difficult relationship with having to learn Portu-
guese (Perlongher, 1999a: 12; Rapisardi and Modarelli, 2001:
198), he had become a linguistic nomad, mixing Spanish and
Portuguese in his everyday speech and his poetry, writing prose in
Spanish for Buenos Aires publications and Portuguese for his
academic work and articles in Brazil. For Braidotti this type of
polyglot has an innate tendency towards sound games of the type
exhibited in '(lobos)':

> Una especie de perversidad polimorfa acompaña la capacidad que
> tiene un políglota de deslizarse entre los idiomas, robar huellas
> acústicas aquí, sonidos de diptongos allá, en un constante juego
> infantil de broma. Los desplazamientos son intraducibles, pero no
> por ello menos eficaces' (Braidotti, 2000: 44).

She adds: 'la escritura políglota, nómade, desprecia la comuni-
cación dominante [. . .]. La escritura nómade [. . .] anhela el
desierto, las zonas de silencio que se extiende entre las cacofonías
oficiales, en un flirteo con una pertenencia y una condición de
extranjería radical' (48). Thus these three poems in *Alambres*
demonstrate a development in Perlongher's poetry that compli-
cates his earlier crossings and moves further towards nomadism.

Hule: State Power and Territory

In *Alambres*, then, we can detect a complication of the aesthetic of
border-crossing through the experience, both positive and nega-
tive, of exile, whereby drifting becomes the dominant movement.
Furthermore, we may observe the first signs of the nomad ethos,
drawn from Deleuze and Guattari, which later characterized
Perlongher's anthropology. It is the latter, perhaps, which most

tellingly reveals the political changes between *Austria-Hungría* and *Alambres*. In *Hule*, the collection Perlongher wrote in the second half of the 1980s, Perlongher examines the new power that the state has over movements of people, and how the types of movement that Perlongher celebrated in his earlier work – crossing borders, exodus, for example – can be exploited by the state. Such is the case with the poem 'Viedma':

> ¡Envoltura! ¡Envoltorio! En el yuxtaponer inmiscuir un grano, una briznita, entre la costra del pan flauta y el papel de almacén, rojo de vino, vino la Orden: horda de pámpanos, estallo de astillero en el rebote de la voz, tomada, embargada la fuga, en el Dictatum. El dístico, el adiós [. . .]
> (Perlongher, 1997a: 155 [1989, Buenos Aires])

The poem alludes to the discovery of an order to leave Buenos Aires, found on a newspaper wrapping one's shopping. The poem is prefaced by two epigrams, one from the *modernista* poet Rubén Darío, '*¡Exodos! ¡Exodos! Rebaños*', and another from Perlongher's contemporary Emeterio Cerro, '*Perla alfonsinita caracolas*'. Together with the opening order ('¡Envoltura!'), the poem draws attention to the proposal by the Alfonsín government (1983–9) to move the capital of Argentina to the town of Viedma, in an attempt to stimulate development in the south, similar to the development of Brasilia as capital city of Brazil. Although the move never took place, some *bonaerenses* anticipated the move and still live in the town today. While Perlongher's poem is mock epic in tone, hence the frequent exclamation and the juxtaposition of legal proclamations with French bread, nevertheless there is a serious point at stake, vital for the development of Perlongher's attitude to territory. In the dictatorship era, crossing borders and rethinking the national territory offered a provocative gesture against the military's political and legal mechanisms; in the post-dictatorship, neo-liberal era, characterized by the increasing insertion of Latin American countries into networks of global capital, in Argentina's case specifically through the privatization of national companies, or through trade agreements that opened up borders and created easily traversable 'border trade zones', for example the Ciudad del Este–Foz de Iguaçú–Puerto Iguazú triangle on the border with Paraguay and Brazil, or opened the country to European or US imports while imposing tariffs on national exports, this aesthetic is no longer so challenging, as it has been assimilated into the capitalist project itself.[10] Instead it is the nomad that comes to dominate Perlongher's poetics.

Perlongher's Nomadology

The 'nomad' appears very clearly in the collection *Parque Lezama*, written while Perlongher was researching his anthropological thesis, in the mid 1980s. The collection clearly shows the influence of the contact with *michês* – male prostitutes who, like *chongos*, accentuate their masculine attributes, such as strength, activity, and erectility – and their clients in São Paulo. Three terms are key in Perlongher's thesis, and will be used frequently in my analysis of his poetics in this period: territorialization, deterritorialization, and reterritorialization. All three are drawn to some degree from the work of Deleuze and Guattari. The first refers to the organization of human beings that sees them fixed or 'striated' within a given and limited space. The family or the village would be a territorialization. Deterritorialization is the movement out of this situation, a line of flight or escape, such as leaving home. Reterritorialization is the subsequent process whereby the deterritorialized settles down again. The successful economic migrant is the reterritorialized par excellence, while the nomad is the deterritorialized. The language of the poem '(lobos)' examined above, could be seen as deterritorialized from Spanish.

The poem 'Nostro mundo' from *Parque Lezama* deals with the processes of de- and reterritorialization within the circuits of homosexual exchange in the urban environment:

> Luces negras avinagradas
> en ese mar de bolas recubiertas
> por fragancias espúreas
> de violeteras que se vuelven lobos
> cuando el acohol de los volcanes
> da paso al laminado tiburón
> que raspa con su aleta las burbujas
> y haciéndolas estallar desparrama el sinsentido
> por un plano de brujas en vacaciones.
> (Perlongher, 1997a: 212 [1990, Buenos Aires])

The title alludes to the first gay rights organization in Argentina, 'el grupo Nuestro Mundo' (1969–71). The delimitation of such a space as 'our world', which many of Perlongher's early poems appeared to seek, would represent territorialization, a physical space for a certain group of people. There are two key processes at work in this poem that allow Perlongher to describe this type of space in 'Nostro mundo'. Firstly, Perlongher continues the use of conjunctions and prepositions to connect phrases in the drifting manner exhibited in earlier poems; thus on a grammatical level processes of deterritorialization dominate. Secondly, and in a more complex fashion, Perlongher examines the linguistic processes of a territorialized community. Again, Perlongher uses half-words ('acohol') and focuses on the sensual, both linguistic deterritorializations but there is also a strong set of references to magic ('brujas') and processes of change. In line four, a street flowerseller becomes a wolf; this anthropomorphic change is then followed by the appearance of a shark. Thus a process of becoming is traced:

```
violeteras————————lobos
x———————————————tiburón
```

The 'violetera' is a mercantile profession based on the street and thus has keen similarities to the *michês* that Perlongher studied in his thesis. Furthermore, the Buenos Aires street meaning of 'tiburón' is a *Don Juan* or sexual predator. Just as the 'violeteras' become wolves, the 'tiburón', a second term of a metaphor whose first term is erased, has all the attributes one would expect of a real shark such as an 'aleta' (fin), and giving off bubbles ('burbujas'). The poem flirts between being a flight of fantasy, presenting a zoological cornucopia of ill-matched animals, and being a homosexual ghetto reworking of the type of animalistic metaphors used by Luis de Góngora (1561–1627) in his *Soledades*, whereby men who cruise are metaphorically sharks and *michês* are like flowersellers selling their stalks. Thus the poem is open to overencoding, or fixing, as a depiction in street slang of homosexual practices. At the level of meaning reterritorialization dominates. Thus 'Nostro mundo' deals with the politics of the ghetto, the deceptively privileged space of the marginal group. The question it asks is whether limited freedom within a limited space, a reterritorialization of a deterritorialized group, as found in so-called gay 'ghettos' such as that in San Francisco in the 1970s and 80s, is really freedom at all.

These movements of de- and reterritorialization are also dealt with in the poem 'Pavón':

[. . .] si él por no cruzar su puntapié los
flecos de la bota o la media inmedia estambres no hubiese vuelto
suavemente la mirada pupila en un interno huida de la pecera en
un interno externo de un interno anterior del interior venido deve-
nido exterior demás cercano a mí en ese aliento a fresas aplastadas
mascadas carcomidas uñas de laca en la ribera aviesa que un carro
de nereidas atravesaba el rizo que sobre su frente el telón del talón
amarillear tornar el dorado doblón húmedas ascuas porras rocia-
das caracolas en la baba del bucle el reflejo de su entrepierna aleve
flotando en el aire cercano invadido el hollín por el espeso spray de
su sudor humor olor tan breve tan ligero que en su escaso parénte-
sis alzase la amenaza de un dejarse ir de un irse de un afuera de
agüero después que nos sería jamás seguro [. . .]
(Perlongher, 1997a: 229 [1990, Buenos Aires])

Again, Perlongher's poem examines territory in homosexual exchange, particularly through a poetics of deterritorialization. Grammatically, the poem's massive sentence (it stretches in the same vein over twenty-five lines), with four seemingly unlinked 'si. . .' clauses, and familiar density of connectives between sub-clauses seems to stretch hyperbaton to an almost ridiculous extent, and this alongside the repetition of near homonyms ('anterior', 'interior', 'exterior') makes the poem physically diffi-cult to read: one often finds oneself reading the same line twice by mistake. Again Perlongher incorporates elements from Argen-tine street slang; the 'pecera' is a goldfish bowl and, by extension anywhere people go to be seen, such as a street-corner bar, or merely a street corner. 'La pecera' was also the name of an infamous dictatorship detention centre. These poetic elements all suggest processes of deterritorialization, both in grammar – to nonsense – and in the content being dealt with, specifically cruising for sex. Within this, Perlongher seems to suggest that fixedness, or striation, can be abandoned for a fluid, unsure state, in the suggestion of an 'irse', a 'dejarse ir' and of being 'jamás seguro', all found within two lines. However, the 'dejarse ir' is presented as an 'amenaza', a threat. Thus the poem suggests that while some may seek deterritorialization – those who are cruising, in the poem the first person position – for others it represents a concern – the other party in the poem, by implication a prosti-tute. Perlongher's poem thus presents a relationship between the prospect of deterritorialization and the perception of deterritorialization as a threat, a perception that may lead to potentially violent reterritorialization. This is also – and more clearly – dealt with in his Masters thesis:

> *Ese problema de dejarse o no es un punto de explosión de la violencia. Hay situaciones en que el michê ya va de antemano con la intención de robar. Pero otras veces está dispuesto a transar, o prostituirse realmente, y una vez llegado a la cama le da un brote sexual de culpa, se enloquece, empieza a romper todo, puede llegar a matar al cliente.* (Perlongher, 1999a: 196–7 [1987, São Paulo] italics in the original)

In the environment of São Paulo, with its clash between the old, hierarchic and popular model of homosexuality (active–masculine–positively valorized/passive–feminine–negatively valorized) and the modern, egalitarian and petit bourgeois model (gay–gay) (190), there are several movements: deterritorialization of the prostitute from the home or district, reterritorialization in the circuits of the sex market, which leads to deterritorialization in opening up to homosexuality, followed by reterritorialization in the proscription of the prostitute's anus as a site of pleasure (194). The same movement is also traced in Perlongher's poems: the opening up of the poem to uncertainty in the floating and folded syntax and the reterritorialization in ghetto codes and marginal clichés.

Perlongher's poems from this era also present processes of de- and reterritorialization in the techniques of anthropology, as in the poem 'Kayak':

> Kayak despavorido en el horror de aguas empalagosas, salpicón en enaguas del enjuague, jabona, hala el desliz por la correa que se lima, deslizase hacia el plano inferior; hade aplanado pero que en las puntas hería, en los bordes del plan, en las pistolas planas del evoque [. . .]
> (Perlongher, 1997a: 234 [1988, Buenos Aires])

The poem stages a play between force ('aguas') and form ('kayak'), and the notion of drift is immediately present in the poem – a kayak in the water. The poem's grammar also creates appropriate physical sensations in the reader. The poem has only one full stop, at the end, and an ungrammatical approach to the distribution of commas and semicolons. Added to this, the use of

Latinate words with oxytone stress ('habrá', 'mirará', 'invocación') forces the reader into unnatural breathing patterns and indeed breathlessness: a physical sensation similar to that of being dragged forward and down, as if by a river. This is highlighted by a lengthy ellipsis; we read '............................ caída en el caer de / un cuerpo muerto en el torrente: en la navegación accidentada [. . .]' (234). Not only does the pause suggest a loss of breath, but also after the pause the effects of the dangerous journey are revealed: a dead body washed ashore. Thus the kayak adrift in the waters is an experience of danger and possible death. Intriguingly, the design of a kayak is such that, unlike a raft, it can gyrate easily in the water. This allows full immersion for the kayaker, but also the possibility of escape.

Throughout the poem the kayak is linked to sordid social details. There is an interplay here between language in various fields: the body and clothes (underwear, for example, as in 'enaguas' and 'correa'), various types of tactile sensation ('jabona', 'hería') and language drawn from Deleuze and Guattari (1994: 36–8), for example the 'plano inferior', the abyss underlying our existence. Much of the language also has sensual, if not sexual implications; the 'correa', or thong (as in Brazilian-style swimming costumes), slips down; thus the 'plano inferior' is not just philosophical, but also suggests illicit, below the waist pleasures. This includes the object of study in *O negócio do michê* with his suggestively masculine pavement posturing: 'si sobándose el bulto en / la baranda' (234). Thus we see how the anthropological tracing of desire – 'nomadology', in Deleuze and Guattari's terms – always risks the possibility of death, and the kayak can thus be seen as the *form* with which the anthropologist or poet attempts to navigate that movement of desire. The desire to be charted drifts and flows, but is potentially lethal, and so thus requires a form – poetry, anthropological rigour – to prevent death. Therefore in Perlongher's anthropological poems, although drift is an important factor, reterritorialization also takes place.

The approach to territory and movement within that territory in *Parque Lezama* is at times very complicated, as in 'Anochecer de un fauno', where we see the Faun of Stéphane Mallarmé's 'L'Après-Midi d'un Faune' (1876) in a drifting, labyrinthine chase.

En el lacar lunado del espejuelo lácteo
estatua de neón posa el corto circuito
de los patines en el hielo, arbóreas
fintas y voiles susurran
la nitidez flambada del contorno.

En lo alunado, transparece
en el élitro de libélula afilándose
en el filtro del lago:
                    en el foco capcioso
de esa luz
china, pajarerías
de chicuela en el lazo,
moños chirles
fuman contorsiones del mirante.

Vitrina de opio, cristalina
parapetando en la mucosa
destartalados flecos: mosquiteros
de tul por cuyos poros
húyese la piragua de una náyade. . .
¡Ah cachas! ¡Ah espirales!
Cada caza es un laberinto (Perlongher, 1997a: 237 [1990, Buenos Aires])

The poem, with its intertextual relationship to Mallarmé's symbol-
ist masterwork and rather esoteric theme, full of spirits ('náyade')
and archaic creatures ('libélula', 'fauno'), is seemingly unrelated
to issues of territory in the circuits of homosexual sex-exchange.
Nevertheless, Perlongher's poem contains references to kitsch
('tul', 'espejuelo'), feminine adornment ('moños', 'flecos') and
the city ('neón'), which allow it to occupy a space between the
fantasy world of Mallarmé's poem and the city of Perlongher's
anthropology. Like Mallarmé's poem, Perlongher's piece presents
an observer spying on two figures, who he then attempts to
pursue for sexual purposes. Within this framework, however,
Perlongher complicates not only Mallarmé's failed chase/rape
but also his own conception of territory and movement. For
example, 'cachas' are horns (of the faun), and buttocks or thighs
(of the naiad); thus the ambiguity allows a shuttle between hunter
and hunted, as well as a shift between perceptions of what the
faun sees as he chases and what the naiad sees upon turning to
observe her attacker. The 'espirales' suggest both the spiralling

horns on the faun's head – like those of the mountain goat – and the movement of the chase, round in circles. Furthermore, Perlongher's poem states that the 'caza', chase, is also a 'laberinto', a maze. Two types of movement are involved here: the chase and the maze. The chase, never completed in Mallarmé's poem, represents (sexual) teleology. The chase posits a movement by A to B, relying on A moving faster than B and reaching B. The attraction of the chase is the desire A feels for B, the inspiration for the chase itself. On the other hand the maze is a movement from place A to place A – in and out again – relying on being able to negotiate the local geographical rules. The attraction of the maze is its flirtation with the possibility of getting lost, potentially overcome by success. However, as we know from the work of Jorge Luis Borges, the maze can easily be fatal. Thus Perlongher complicates Mallarmé's chase using Borgesian territory, as in the two mazes of 'La muerte y la brújula' (1956) or the maze Theseus penetrates to kill the Minotaur in 'La casa de Asterión' (1956).[11] The reader is therefore left with two contradictory approaches to movement. The chase is teleological, proposing a purpose and an end point, whereas the maze's appeal is largely based on the possibility of not reaching an end-point. This is further complicated by 'espirales', which provide a historical–baroque edge, folding in the unending manifold surfaces of the fractal. Perlongher's poem, itself between canonical literature and street prostitution, exemplifies the complex relationship between sexual purpose and nomadic wandering in the circuits of male prostitution. Thus the poem illustrates complex movements of desire in the social.

The question that one must therefore ask, is what sort of nomads is Perlongher describing in his poems? For Perlongher, as displayed above, the *michê* was a nomad and therefore was characterized by the predominance of drift ('deriva') and in-betweenness ('intersticial'). However, another factor is also introduced, in the poem 'Caza', from *Parque Lezama*:

> Veredas, veredas trabajadas
> por la inconsecuencia de un pez palo, escueto, casi rígido en la es-
> padez que explande, que despide, para encantar, ojos babosos, li-
> mos de azufre jabonoso en la argentina transparencia.
> (1997a: 228 [1990, Buenos Aires])

The poem creates a play between desiring ('babosos') drift in the city – the repetition of 'veredas' – and mercantile calculation – the notion of pavements 'trabajadas', and the 'para', suggesting purpose, which provides the central axis to the actions. The nature of the relationship between the two factors, drift and calculation, means that they are often inseparable. The poem creates a relationship between display and observation, or, perhaps, advertising and consumption, between the 'espadez', 'swordness', the rigidity of the *miché* so sought by the homosexual client, and the desiring and synaesthetically drooling eyes. Thus the prostitute is wandering, but also working, with purpose. The nature of this wandering as work, however, is called into question by the *potlatch*, the wastage in the piece, through the 'inconsecuencia', the pointlessness and lack of direction of this movement. Perlongher's poem therefore strikes an uneasy balance between presenting the *miché* as a nomad – the theory of his thesis on anthropology (Perlongher, 1999a/1987b), and on which he insisted in articles and interviews such as the one above – whereby wandering would be the important factor, and presenting the *miché* as a sex worker, whereby the points to which he goes and the purpose with which he displays himself are key. The latter point of view is closer to that held by more identitarian theorists such as Sebreli (1997: 338–57).

In Perlongher's thesis he spoke of the processes of de- and reterritorialization that take place in the circuits of male prostitution. He also dealt with the predominance of certain stereotypes within the *miché* community – a form of reterritorialization of identity. The poem 'Al deshollinador' deals with some of these stereotypes:

> el suplente es un moreno aceitunado
> que tiene tiznados los resortes
> por la bruma de un madero que se reaviva
> y clava sus estocadas gelatinosas
> en la brillantina de las sombras, [. . .]
> (1997a: 196 [1990, Buenos Aires])

The poem creates a relationship between a client and a chimney sweep. The relationship is couched in terms from his anthropological work: class (higher to lower), skin colour (lighter to darker), wealth (richer to poorer) and gender (feminine to masculine) (Perlongher, 1999a, chapter 3 [1987, São Paulo]).

This is reinforced by the repeated references to 'hollín', a word used throughout *Parque Lezama*, for example in 'Pavón' (1997a: 229), associated with excrement and thus the anus. The sweep, a replacement, is just another of the dark, lower-class masses, capable of adopting the required pose and hardness. Practically then, the *michê* is both labelled and carries out a process of self-labelling. Such a set of clichés, or stereotypes, applies to the sexual partners observed in almost all the poems in *Parque Lezama*. Dirtiness, hardness, strength, erectility, and violent energy are all constants in these poems. This would suggest that reterritorialization dominates in the circuits of male prostitution, not just in the adoption of certain territories but also in settling down to certain roles, at least in terms of the technique for picking up work. Perlongher insisted that the *michês* offered the possibility of a break with the social order through beginning a process of becoming woman (1997b: 50 [1987, São Paulo]). However, the space of the *boca* (a term Perlongher preferred to *gueto* or *ghetto*) is also one of reterritorialization and striation, as pointed out by an interviewee in Perlongher's thesis: '*En mi cabeza, imaginaba que* [prostitution] *sería un puro placer. Pero no: las locas son tontísimas, crean sus patrones, rotulan, uno tiene que ser algo dentro de esa clasificación*' (51). This is the process of reterritorialization that Perlongher refers to: the codes and regulations of the ghetto. In *El negocio del deseo*, Perlongher describes this process of labelling:

> Esta reinscripción del sujeto deseante en otro código no es meramente simbólica sino literal: producción de marcas en el cuerpo, tipificación de la indumentaria, modelización de tics y movimientos, seriación de moldes gestuales y sexuales, selección y valorización del compañero sexual, etcétera. (1999a: 166 [1987, São Paulo])

Nevertheless, Perlongher seems to give primacy to the quality of desire whereby it always transgresses and can never be fully reterritorialized: 'Aunque considerablemente eficaces, todos los mecanismos de reterritorialización internos al circuito parecen no ser suficientes para apagar esos pálidos fuegos' (1997b: 56 [1987, São Paulo]). In Perlongher's anthropology, no complete reterritorialization occurs, despite the many codes and rules that limit the nomadism of the prostitutes. But, in his introduction to Perlongher's work, Echavarren highlights the need expressed by certain clients for younger prostitutes: 'Por eso los clientes se afincan en *michês* más jóvenes [. . .] que en algunos casos llegan hasta los 11 años, cuando la criatura no sabe aún qué se espera de ella' (Echavarren, 1999: x). The youngest prostitutes have not yet been fixed within the ghetto and are thus more mutative and prone to suggestion. This need on the part of the client seems to suggest the high degree of sedentarization that may occur in the *bocas.*

Thus there is an important distinction to be found between Perlongher's anthropological studies and his poetry. In his anthropology Perlongher adapted Deleuze and Guattari's nomadology, as found in the section 'Treatise on Nomadology' (1999: 351–423) and insisted on the *michês* and clients as nomads (1999a: 219–31), often despite his own evidence to the contrary. In his poetry, on the other hand, he leaves the reader in a more problematic position regarding the movements within the circuits of male prostitution.

This is further illustrated by the poems that exhibit the effects of AIDS in the later collections *Hule* and *El chorreo de las iluminaciones.* These clearly display a new and problematic stasis in Perlongher's work, for example 'Dolly' (1997a: 146 [1989, Buenos Aires]), from *Hule*:

> La telaraña de jeringas
> diestros cintazos pernoctaba
> el *pernod* junto al jarabe
> que en el vaho de alcohol
> cierne la pierna,
> > renga de un
> hijo, en el jolgorio de las venas
> de celuloide que penetran
> bajo la piel al centro, lían
> hacia lo que bombea [. . .]

In 'Dolly', Perlongher creates two fields of meaning. One is related to addiction or medication. The second is that of being trapped or physically immobile, completely striated or sedentary in the terms Perlongher would have borrowed from Deleuze. Furthermore, the poem takes elements that would have been celebrated in earlier poems, such as 'jolgorio' or 'penetran', and juxtaposes them to ideas of pain and fixedness. Thus the former nomad is shown sick and dying. Similarly, in 'El mal de sí', from *El chorreo de las iluminaciones,* a poem whose title puns on SIDA (AIDS) we read:

> Mientras estamos dentro de nosotros duele el alma,
> duele ese estarse sin palabras suspendido en la higuera
> como un noctámbulo extraviado.
> (1997a: 355 [Buenos Aires])

Again, Perlongher focuses on being stuck. This is achieved though the repetition of parts of 'estar', instead of the verbs of movement that dominated earlier poems, and through the creation of internal spaces ('dentro'). The 'noctámbulo, a sleepwalker, but also a nightwalker, the cruiser of his earlier poems, is now lost. If part of the attraction of the prostitution chase–maze was the possibility of losing oneself, this poem reveals the fatality that this entails. The poem's backdrop is the dual immobility imposed by the mass spread of AIDS in Brazil, both through killing people and through making urban nomadism no longer as appealing as before. While this stillness has its valorized counterpart in the movement and cruising in the *bocas* that Perlongher studied in his anthropology and portrayed in complex and provocative style in his poetry, the poem presents the negative effects that cruising had. Perlongher, in a postscript to his essay 'Avatares de los muchachos de la noche', adds that the irruption of AIDS has created a new model of control that can carry out a more effective reterritorialization of the nomadic elements:

> A partir de la irrupción del Sida, un dispositivo mucho más potente está montándose en el contexto de la creciente medicalización higienista de la existencia. Sólo de pensar la diferencia entre el valor intensivo concedido a la vida en esos circuitos ardientes, con todas sus violencias interiores y sus complejas paradojas, y la imposición de un control clínico sobre el deseo, que mide la vida a partir de un patrón extensivo y normativo, puede intuirse, a despecho del horror, toda la potencia radical del goce que en esas turbias, sino torpes, fugas [. . .].
> (1997b: 56 [1987, São Paulo])[12]

The new medical discourse allows us retrospectively to see the potential that the ghetto had – you don't know what you have until you've lost it, in other words. Perlongher's tone is one of nostalgia for the *bocas* that formed the subject of his thesis, now heavily controlled by state medical discourse after the emergence of mass death from AIDS. What the internal codification and reterritorialization of the circuit could not in Perlongher's anthropological eyes control fully, the flow of desire that the *michês* exhibited in their nomadic wanderings, is now controlled by terror and the clinic.

Thus there is an intriguing difference between Perlongher's poetics from this period, and his anthropological readings of the *michês* and their clients. In fact, Perlongher's anthropological characterization of the *michês* and clients as nomadic owes a lot to a perhaps simplistic comparison that he makes to heterosexual relationships:

> Es que esas prácticas no se agotan en la monótona extenuación de los recursos anatómicos, sino que sirven de cimiento a verdaderas redes de sociabilidad 'alternativas' respecto de la cultura oficial, 'desviantes' o marginales respecto de la norma social dominante, nómades en relación con los módulos de heterosexualidad sedentaria. (1999a: 168 [1987, São Paulo])

Perlongher fails to identify these 'módulos de heterosexualidad sedentaria', and does not take into account the possibility of *heterosexual* perversion or cruising. He insists on the practical ways in which the prostitutes and clients exhibit nomadic qualities, in particular in the reaction they draw from the state apparatus. He underlines:

> Las solidaridades prácticas que se establecen entre los diversos marginales del área tras las rejas de las celdas donde todos acaban, una vez u otra, recluidos, en un máximo de sedentarización compulsiva con que la maquinaria policial pune sus excesos nómades. (47)

Perlongher identifies the prison as the maximum stage of state sedentarization, or the maximum *striation*, to continue using Deleuze's terms. As the state forces sedentary life for the nomad, then by implication, those who are in prison must have been nomads. This argument suffers from two weaknesses. Firstly, the prison does not represent the absolute stage of the sedentary; unstriated or 'smooth' space can exist anywhere, even in prison, as the novels of Jean Genet testify, and the nomad likewise. Secondly, Perlongher's concrete solidarity seems too heavily dependent on certain concepts strong in the 1970s and drawn

from Herbert Marcuse's *One Dimensional Man* (1957) about the
possibility of solidarity between the intellectual and lumpenprole-
tariat classes.

Furthermore, while Perlongher highlighted the randomness in
the *michê*'s wanderings and the amount of time spent between
points, his focus on movement overlooks a key part of Deleuze
and Guattari's description of the nomad, specifically their insist-
ence that the nomad clings to smooth space and is not therefore
characterized by movement, but by stillness: '[t]he nomad distrib-
utes himself in a smooth space; he occupies, inhabits, holds that
space; that is his territorial principle. It is therefore false to define
the nomad by movement [. . .] The nomad knows how to wait, he
has infinite patience' (1999: 381). Problematically for our reading
of Perlongher, then, there is a clear contradiction between his
words and those of Deleuze and Guattari. Furthermore, there is
another with regard to the matter of reterritorialization:

> If the nomad can be called the Deterritorialized par excellence, it
> is precisely because there is no reterritorialization *afterward* as with
> the migrant, or upon *something else* as with the sedentary (the
> sedentary's relation with the earth is mediatized by something else,
> a property regime, a State apparatus). (381)

It is worth remembering a point upon which Perlongher does
not insist in his anthropology but which is often implicit in his
poems. Many of the prostitutes are economic migrants, attempt-
ing reterritorialization in the urban environment, a project that
often includes prostitution, or whose failure results in prostitu-
tion. While the *michê* does wait, and does exhibit patience in the
rigid poses adopted on street corners, movement and striation are
still key. The poems analysed above, furthermore illustrate the
centrality of reterritorialization in Perlongher's conception of the
bocas. Perlongher's poetry reveals some of the blind spots and
simplifications in his anthropology. It becomes clear that
Perlongher is not only *adapting* Deleuze and Guattari's nomadol-
ogy to a different time and place, but also *adopting* it, through an
insistence on the application of key terms and concepts.

In the conclusion of Deleuze and Guattari's chapter on the war
machine, we find a clue, perhaps, to the importance of defining
the *michê* as a nomad for Perlongher. Deleuze and Guattari
(writing in 1980) discuss the growing strength of the war machine

as related to states in their 'counterguerrilla' fights against the 'Unspecified Enemy' (422):

> World war machines [. . .] reconstitute [. . .] a smooth space to surround and enclose the earth. But the earth asserts its own powers of deterritorialization, its lines of flight, its smooth spaces that confront one another in the two kinds of war machine, according to the two poles. War machines take shape against the apparatuses that appropriate the machine and make war their affair and their object: they bring connections to bear against the great conjunction of the apparatuses of capture and domination. (423)

In Brazil in the 1980s, dictatorship death squads were hunting out transvestites and homosexuals on the streets of São Paulo, as Perlongher (1997b: 35–40 [1988, Buenos Aires]) recounted; in Buenos Aires, *razzias* – raids on bars, homes and public toilets where those suspected of homosexuality were arrested – had been common throughout the dictatorship years (Rapisardi and Modarelli, 2001). Faced with this statist war machine, sedentarizing and striating, the importance of the circuits of the *michês* and clients is as an alternative war machine, one which undermines the work carried out by the state to pin them down. Perlongher's nomadology is an attempt to attack state striation on a smaller scale than his earlier *murguista* political projects. Thus Deleuze and Guattari provide tools for a micropolitical yet still desiring project.

In an interview from 1991 with Marcelo Ekhard and Emilio Bernini, Perlongher rejects the model of identity, and insists on the primacy of desire in his study of prostitution. This represents a way out of Marxist theories of prostitution that see the prostitute as a product of social deprivation (Ekhard and Bernini, 1991: 85). Perlongher's observations in the ghetto had led him to believe that not all the *michês* were working because they had been thrown out of their homes or were desperate for money. Both of these theories can lead to an essentialist conception of sexuality: the prostitutes are born gay and an uncaring, homophobic society marginalizes them; or the prostitutes are heterosexuals forced to act as homosexuals for financial reasons; or they are essentially homosexuals forced by society to mask the fact. Perlongher, however, aims to steer away from identity, the reason being that a liberal interpretation of identity for Perlongher would potentially lead to ghettoisation in the gay–gay couple, while a conservative interpretation might lead to attempts to 'cure' homosexuals. Perlongher therefore uses Deleuze and Guattari because of their constant privileging of 'deseo en lo social', something that is, according to Perlongher, lacking in Marxism (Eckhard and Bernini, 1991: 85) and vital for his continual validation of desire.

Mystical Territory

Later in his career, Perlongher became increasingly involved in the Brazilian esoteric drug religion, Santo Daime. Perlongher attended their rituals, took the hallucinogenic drug *yagé* and dedicated the collection *Aguas aéreas* (1991) to one of the Daime churches in São Paulo (Perlongher, 1997a: 293 [1991, Buenos Aires]). The first half of this collection (poems I to XIX in the collection) is similar in many ways to his earlier anthropological poems, detailing his participative immersion in the rituals of the group. The movement of the urban anthropologist, by now familiar to the reader of Perlongher, takes him down into the city, into a lower-middle class, slightly kitsch environment of chequered table clothes and astral projection (Poem I, in particular), in an escape from the self through drugs that replaces the sex that dominated the earlier collections.

However, from poem XX onwards, a different movement is traced. Many of the latter poems in *Aguas aéreas* have distinctly sylvan and maritime elements, in radical contrast to his very urban earlier poems. As part of his research into and participation in Santo Daime, Perlongher undertook a journey to the religion's forest sanctuary in the Amazon.[13] Poem XXI demonstrates the complications that occurred in Perlongher's mystical approaches to territory as he undertakes a dangerous and exotic journey on the Amazon River. Poem XXII opens with a quotation from the Conde de Villamediana, Góngora's great friend and poetic disciple.[14]

> *Este en selva inconstante pino alado*
> **Conde de Villamediana**

ASCESIS FORESTAL:
          el agua sólo como excusa o cauce para el entroncamiento del tronco en el ramaje, sutileza fluvial, el fluir de la

canoa por el divertimiento de las ramas, haciéndole de concha al si-
bilante estuche, chispas de borravino nacían del encuentro amoro-
so del codo de la piragua con el nudo del árbol adamado, inclinado
a enguantar o feminar sus redes, al otro lado del arroyo, envuelto,
vegetales que entraban en el agua, un devenir ácueo del palo,
navegan en el bosque.
(Perlongher, 1997a: 276 [1991, Buenos Aires])

The epigram is the Count's metaphor for a boat, 'a winged pine',
steering a course in the sea-as-forest during one of his many
journeys in exile. Like many of Perlongher's poems, drift and
exile are dominant themes; the notion of the count as a wanderer
in exile – like Perlongher's earlier exiles – provides material for
the presentation of the boat adrift on the forest waters. The
metaphor of a boat as a winged pine provides a dyad of water and
forest for Perlongher's exploration of the space between the two,
an abstract between-space similar in conception to the *murga*-
space of earlier.

Various movements, however, complicate Perlongher's earlier
dynamics. The poem opens with 'ascesis', abstaining from worldly
pleasures for religious purposes. This suggests a movement up,
towards God, and teleology – the search for ends – appropriate to
Judaeo–Christian religion. There is a proliferation of tree and
wood-related vocabulary ('entroncamiento', 'tronco', 'ramaje',
'ramas', 'árbol', 'palo'). This allows an ironic play on the origin of
the *silva* style frequently used by Góngora and his contemporar-
ies, in the word *selva*, meaning forest.[15] Also, Perlongher is calling
to the idea of 'tree-logic', a characteristic of western philosophy
after Plato, which functions in terms of origins, roots and hierar-
chy. However, in the becoming-boat of the tree and the becoming-
water of the oar ('devenir-ácueo del palo'), tree-logic is put into
flux as the Count's boat-as-tree metaphor is taken quite literally,
thus opening up a space between tree and river. This is reasserted
by the watery vocabulary interspersed among the once-
hierarchical trees: 'agua', 'cauce', 'fluvial', 'fluir', 'arroyo' and
'ácueo'. This leads us into another field of language, namely
drifting: 'canoa', 'piragua', 'concha', in the forest and on the
water. Perlongher thus creates a shuttle between two planes, the
horizontal of the river's branches and the vertical of the trees. If
we imagine a map of the Amazon, its branches resemble the
branches of a tree. Perlongher flattens out the branches of the

tree, showing its connections with the river and thus dehierarchizing the tree-logic of Judaeo–Christianity into a rhizome, a connecting network like grass.

Importantly here, desire is an all-important factor, as we have an 'encuentro amoroso' between the canoe and the tree (line seven), and 'feminar', crossing the preconceived boundaries between the sexes, in line seven. Key in Perlongher's poem is the idea of 'sutileza' (line three), subtlety, and sensitivity to grey areas and fuzzy sets. This is described as 'fluvial', for the flowing of the water gives mixed, between states, like the between state of a feminized man.

The difference from Perlongher's earlier poems is the willingness to engage with elements from religion. The journey is part of a dangerous pilgrimage on the river. Hence the importance of 'navega[r]' (line nine); its Latin roots, 'navis' (ship) and 'agere' (to drive), give both drift and a guiding hand. Perlongher outlined this force–form diptych in the essay 'Poesía y éxtasis' (1997b: 153 [1991, Buenos Aires]): the force of the ecstatic experience, with the risk of annihilation, and the form of the religious ceremony allowing the line of flight to avoid destruction in the abyss. As Perlongher stated, 'lo puro dionisíaco es un veneno, imposible de ser vivido, pues acarrea al aniquilamiento de la vida. Para mantener la lucidez en medio del torbellino, hace falta una forma. Sabemos que esa forma es poética' (153). The pure Dionysian had been found in the pre-AIDS orgies and cruising Perlongher had studied. As he knew, these led to destruction, particularly through violence and HIV/AIDS; instead, then, the religious ceremony and poetic form provide a method of escape from striation that does not lead to death. Perlongher's approach to territory in this collection combines the Deleuzean aesthetics that we observed in earlier collections, particularly the rhizome and drifting, with new religious aesthetics that imply movements upwards, towards a divine end, with a greater degree of control than before.

These spatial dynamics are further complicated and developed in Perlongher's final, posthumous collection, *El chorreo de las iluminaciones*. 'Alabanza y exaltación del Padre Mario', from this collection, takes the form of a long prayer with refrains and imprecations of the priestly and quasi-divine figure of the title:

Oh Padre

Cúrenos

la salud y las escoriaciones del alma y los pozos del trauma y las he-
ridas que hilan en el fondo de sí de cada cual las babas de la sierpe
y nos enriedan la cabeza enrulada hasta hacernos perder toda ra-
zón y arrastrarnos enloquecidamente con el absurdo sueño de salir
por abajo bajando descendiendo sin ver que la iluminación viene de
arriba como un sol que fijo sobre los ventanales de voile atravesán-
dolos de luz divina luz de la que irraban sus ojos claros ojos abrien-
do una vereda de fulgor en la tiniebla floreciéndola

(1997a: 332 [1991, Buenos Aires])

According to Perlongher's friend Sara Torres, the poem was
composed in honour of a popular *curandero,* or faith healer, from
the Buenos Aires suburb of González Catán, in whom Perlongher
became interested after discovering he was suffering from AIDS,
and breaking with the Santo Daime religion (Rapisardi and
Modarelli, 2001: 198). Much of the poem stands in radical
contrast to Perlongher's earlier poetics. Perlongher's treatment of
the up–down binary demonstrates a significant change in
approach. Whereas in earlier work Perlongher has moved down
(to the anus, the penis, the petticoats, the sewer, or the streets), as
in the opening story of 'Evita vive', or in the discovery of bodies in
'Cadáveres', here a change occurs. Perlongher's poem suggests
that up is good and down is bad. This is achieved by the
association of the below ('pozos', 'abajo') to the mad or the
painful ('trauma', 'absurdo'). Secondly, the poem proposes a
centre to the universe, a source of all light and goodness ('luz
divina'), that is above us, traditionally in Christian thought the
position of heaven – hence the shape of gothic cathedrals.

Another, perhaps even more remarkable change to Perlongher's
aesthetics occurs in the next stanza:

Y Oh Padre

Párenos

en nuestra prisa loca no nos deje caer tan fácilmente llévenos don-
de está y se refugia cuando sale de sí cuando se nota su alma desli-
zándose en vez de caminar sobre un mantón de hojas acuáticas
mbucuruyás victorias regias camalotes en el igarapé atascado de
flores que permite que flote el vivo escorzo de su presencia astral

(332)

Stasis seems to be preferred to movement; although the notion of 'salir de sí' is maintained, it is a leaving with a purpose, at odds with earlier drifting 'salidas' around the city. These earlier 'salidas' are characterized by madness, 'prisa loca'. If the previous verse presented 'razón' as a positive attribute, here this is contrasted to the unwanted 'prisa loca': reason over madness for the first time in Perlongher's poetry and, furthermore, a clearly negative allusion to queening ('loca'). The 'locas escandalosas' were seen in 'La desaparición de la homosexualidad' as the last vestige of homosexual provocation in the face of increasing liberal acceptance of certain types of homosexual practice (Perlongher 1997b: 87 [1991, Buenos Aires]); here now even they are condemned.

Instead, Perlongher's poem praises stillness and stasis, not drifting, but instead the static floating islands of 'camalotes', and, perhaps vitally, the blocked Amazonian network, the 'igarapé atascado'. The 'igarapé' is the network of connecting rivers around the Amazon. In poem XXII of *Aguas aéreas* we saw Perlongher turn the tree on its side to form a rhizomatic network of connections in a river basin; here however Perlongher presents this network only to block it up as a stable platform for his divinity, a paradise of rivers that are as still as earth. Instead of creating a space between the tree and the river, a contradictory fluid solidity, here Perlongher creates a stable solid fluidity, whereby the flow and drift that had earlier characterized his mystical river are now stopped still. Thus 'Párenos' gives a new positive value to stopping, also linked to the notion of changing one's ways. However, there is an innate contradiction to Perlongher's logic; if earlier we saw an up–good/down–bad binary, now the 'igarapé' and 'camelotes' suggest a levelling out, the rhizome mentioned above. Thus Perlongher in his divine teleology still finds terminology and models in the distinctly antiteleological philosophy of Deleuze and Guattari; this I feel reflects an underlying unease about religious vocabulary and models that even in his most mystical stage Perlongher cannot shake off. This unease is borne out in the clash between two types of vocabulary. The first is that demanding closeness to the divine ('escorzo' in stanza eight); the second is that drawn from critical theory, ('reichiana' stanza eight), in particular Deleuze and Guattari ('el cuerpo sin órganos' stanza nine).

The tenth stanza reveals a tension between seeking and not finding:

Oh Padre
Háganos
llegar a sí a llegar a usted llegar adónde quiera que lleguemos mas
con la sensación de no llegar cual si estuviéramos siempre de vuel-
ta dando círculos en la ruleta de las voces circuyendo de nieve aca-
ramelada bolas de frenesí fervor dándonos vuelta siempre de vuel-
ta a sí volver a usted (333)

The poem thus formulates two requests. Firstly, it expresses a desire to arrive ('Háganos / llegar a sí'), reiterated by the repetition of parts of 'llegar' (also 'lleguemos'). Secondly, it expresses a desire to feel as if one has not arrived ('la sensación de no llegar'). Not arriving is similar to the nomadic wandering we encountered earlier, where each point simply leads to another movement; this is reflected in the unfinished grammar and paradoxical statements, all of which defy teleology. There is a clear tension though between this nomadic 'salir de sí', which is centrifugal in form and a return to (divine) origins, which is centripetal. This constitutes an irreconcilable tension between sceptical atheism and credent mysticism. This tension leads to a new movement of gyration or rotation, perhaps similar to that facilitated by the kayak (above), of turning around, backwards and forwards, highlighted by the vocabulary related to turning ('vuelta' three times, 'volver'). In this particular search for God, God is always behind you. The constant turning around – after each turn, God is still behind you – reminds us of the difficult spirals of 'Anochecer de un fauno', when the teleology of the chase was complicated by the maze. Here now the insertion of mystical and religious thematics allows us to see the difficult relationship between popular mysticism that relies on direct contact with God and a sceptical atheism – closer to Perlongher's earlier writings – that refuses to believe in God.

As the poem continues, the journey towards the divine becomes increasingly complex, particularly with the introduction of the concept of velocity in the eighteenth stanza:

Oh Padre
Espérenos
no vaya tan rápido que no podamos alcanzarle no nos deslumbre
con una velocidad vertiginosa que no podamos comprender qué lo

> lleva lejos no nos asuste con la amenaza de que un día no vuelva no
> nos deje con el remordimiento de su ida no nos deje de lado en su
> ascensión no nos olvide en el sobrevuelo de su ala volaz sobre los
> cándidos cipreses del bañado
> (335)

This complicates the earlier journey towards a divinity; the move-
ment is in the favourable up direction and the movement of the
divinity is at high speed. Therefore the idea of Padre returning
could well be a trick of relativity. Rather than

man —————→ X —————→ Padre

we have

man —→ X —————————→ Padre

Thus if the Padre slows down, a backwards, returning movement
would be perceived by man:

man —————————→   ←——— Padre

Here we cross with Zeno's paradoxes, where objects in motion can
never reach their end. Zeno of Elea, a fifth-century BC disciple of
Parmenides, a fellow Eleatic, designed to show that any assertion
opposite to the monistic teaching of Parmenides leads to contra-
diction and absurdity. Parmenides had argued from reason alone
that the assertion that only Being is leads to the conclusions that
Being (or all that there is) is (1) one and (2) motionless. The
opposite assertions, then, would be that instead of only the One
Being, many real entities in fact are, and that they are in motion
(or could be). Zeno thus wished to reduce to absurdity the two
claims, (1) that the many are and (2) that motion is (*Encyclopaedia
Britannica* 2001). Thus, even if Padre Mario slows down, he can
still never be reached, like Achilles' tortoise. In this notion of
chase Perlongher keeps at bay the *telos* that would completely
deny the nomadic nature of this movement but seems to contra-
dict the dynamism of his earliest poems.

By stanza twenty-six, however, the lines of flight, or nomadic
deterritorializations, reappear:

Oh Padre
Ayúdenos

a correr a escapar a no quedarnos donde estamos a siempre trans-
florear cruzar la flor de este jardín por instantáneos pasadizos se-
cretos conociendo que el quedarse es morir que el no quedarse es
irse sin morir [. . .] (336–7)

This idea of stillness as death is closer to Perlongher's earlier
poetry and at odds with some of what we have read earlier in this
very poem. What is being described is a will to movement, against
the sedentary and static, in keeping with Perlongher's version of
Deleuze and Guattari's nomadology. This marks a reversal in the
values in the poem. Now Perlongher asks for and praises 'la / más
barroca confusión locura casi al borde de la locura confusa /
confusión de locuras en fusión [. . .]' (337). The celestial journey
is now a schizoid stroll, bordering on madness, like the earlier
'prisa loca' which accompanied a negative valorization of homo-
sexual cruising or queening.

However, by the thirtieth stanza Perlongher is reworking his
earlier nomadism with divine intent:

[. . .] no nos obligue a recorrer con Beba en vano distancias sidera-
les de un suburbio anterior desconocido estelas polvorientas que
dejaba el periplo de nuestro andar en pos de usted entre los ómni-
bus (337)

'Beba', 'suburbio' and 'ómnibus' are urban, mundane elements,
closely related to the drag and drift of earlier poems, now
characterized as 'vano'. Thus we have a searching for the Padre
that was worldly and pointless, associated to the city of
Perlongher's anthropology and much of his poetry. This attitude
is revealed in Perlongher's writings on Paris from the early 1990s,
where he criticized French academics who still celebrated margin-
ality and deterritorialization, despite the devastation that AIDS –
hinted at above by 'siderales' – and heroin addiction had wreaked
(Perlongher, 1999b: 56). A mystical, metaphysical searching now
supersedes this in Perlongher's work. Intriguingly, no *telos* or
purpose was stated in the earlier poetry where he highlighted
drift, so it appears that Perlongher is rewriting his own corpus
with metaphysical purpose. Again there is a seemingly insur-
mountable contradiction between the purposeless 'salir de sí' as
in stanza twenty-six of this poem, and this metaphysical intent.
The poem ends in mystery; the divine 'luz' so desperately sought
by Perlongher may in fact be only 'un efecto de luz' (1997a: 339),
a trick of the light, a will-o'-the-wisp. Searching but not finding,

revisiting former territories with hindsight and new intent, Perlongher cannot resolve the contradiction between his nomadic, purposeless earlier writing and the aspirational, ascendant mysticism here. Thus tensions remain unresolved, paradoxes abound, and an overwhelming contradiction between two types of movement prevails.

The last poem of the collection, 'Roma' places several of the key themes in *El chorreo de las iluminaciones* under the close focus of mortality:

> El extravío de los peregrinos entre los pliegues de cornalina
> mantra de mármol que se invoca por descifrar el iriseo
> de campánulas en los entretechos de donde emerge una Madona
> de la Giralda compuesta de azulejos la estirpe
> de la estampa en el desfiladero de pasillos
> cuyo espejearse mutuo revuelo les suscita
> a lo ancho de napas de furor congelado
> en la jabonosa piedra de importados jadeos
> bajo cuyas arcadas desfilan los pidientes
> no ganando sino una cinacina de espumas como aura
> y como alma apenas la evaporada pérdida
> al encuentro de acuáticos antenas que captan
> la náusea o el aullido.
> (Perlongher, 1997a: 361 [1993, New York])

Three dynamics dominate the bulk of 'Roma': searching ('peregrinos'); not finding ('extravío'); and a general air of incompletion. Appropriately for a final poem, the piece ends one line short of being a sonnet, with a number of lines that is both unlucky and associated with death in popular Western superstition (thirteen). The absence of punctuation allows the poem to drift and offers the reader significant difficulties with breathing, tempting one to stop at line-ends before starting up anew. After three very long lines, the poem settles down to near-Alexandrine form (as in a squared sonnet of fourteen fourteen-syllable lines), with a final line that stops halfway, just as the poem stops short of sonnet form.

The Christian, logocentric setting of Rome perhaps sums up the teleology in the poem, and echoes the type of teleology found in 'Padre Mario'. It should be easy to find the centre of Rome – it is a Classical city. The difference is that Perlongher's pilgrims are lost, and the *telos* – the journey to the centre of Rome, and thus the idea of purpose behind a poem – is closer in function not to a line but a maze, not a pilgrimage to a point but a lost stroll around the city. Now the city is acentric, folded and complex.[16] Perlongher imposes the multicentric pattern on the monocentric notion of a religious pilgrimage. Thus this nomadic movement radically questions the idea of purpose. Perlongher's pilgrims' loss takes place within 'pliegues', the complex surfaces that dominate many earlier Perlongher poems. This forms part of a creation of space through objects: 'cornalina', 'mármol', 'entretechos', 'desfiladera', 'pasillos', 'arcadas' – the city of the title as seen from above yet experienced from below by one lost in its folds. Perlongher's poem borrows its title from Francisco de Quevedo's Sonnet XLII, 'A Roma sepultada en sus ruinas', a poem that dealt with the impossibility of pilgrimage to the historical city owing to the intractable effects of time and decay – one of the most challenging of the many early modern poems that deal with the classical theme of *ubi sunt*. Furthermore, curious details problematize any mimetic reading, for example the 'Giralda', a minaret incorporated in the cathedral of Seville and the 'cinacina', a tree from the pampas mentioned in Güiraldes's *gaucho* novel, *Don Segunda Sombra* (1926).

There is a strong emotional charge within this complex creation of space, seen for example in 'furor congelado' – strong emotion solidified. Emotions and human action seem to crystallize, a point illustrated by the phrase 'jabonosa piedra de importados jadeos', a metaphor for human effort becoming the solid form of a building. We might suggest that here the effort of the writer is becoming solidified in the work, where writing would function as a statue to put off death.[17] However, Perlongher introduces another chemical process beyond solidifying: 'alma apenas la evaporada pérdida'. Waste, loss and escape are all expressed in the evaporation of the soul from the body, comparable to the emptying out of the body in 'El mal de sí' (1997a: 355). The soul, rather than following the pilgrimage, drifts out to sea to the 'acuáticas antenas', the unknown between – a metaphysical *murga* between belief and uncertainty, between liquid and solid, a zone held together poetically by the 'a' sounds that dominate the poem's final lines. The last line sees the escaping soul in terms of 'la náusea o el aullido'. We see the body in sickness and the howl of the most basic human self-expression that provided the title to Ginsberg's long urban poem, 'Howl' (1956). There is no convenient solidifying, no final security for reader or poet, just as there is no obvious conclusion to the pilgrims' journey. Once the human condition is pushed to its very limits, all that exists is the messy network of corporeal and sonic connections, and the suggestion of the unknown beyond.

In conclusion, Perlongher's early poetry details an aesthetic of crossing that challenges national boundaries. His exile in Brazil is accompanied by more complex movements of drift, leading to his perhaps simplified adoption of Deleuzean nomadology in his anthropology and the collection *Parque Lezama*. His later work, after the onset of AIDS and with his turn to mysticism, offers an at times problematic interaction between religious images of movement and space and his earlier, anti-hierarchical theories.

NOTES

1 Sections of this chapter were earlier published as part of the papers, 'Prolegomenon to the Political Reading of Poetry', *International Journal of the Humanities* 1 (2003), and 'Exiles and Nomads: Perlongher in Brazil', *Hispanic Research Journal* vol. 7 no.4.

2 The formation of Austria-Hungary was based on the *Ausgleich*, a compromise between the Hapsburg dynasty and Hungary. Hungary in the second half of the nineteenth century was by far the more liberal country, with freedom of expression, press and religion, whereas Austria was for much of the same period a neo-absolutist state. Under the *Ausgleich* both countries maintained their own political systems, with foreign policy defined in annual meetings. Between 1867 and 1918, Austria-Hungary became a tolerant state under the Fundamental Laws, 'whereby all nationalities in the state enjoy equal rights, and each one has as inalienable right to the preservation and cultivation of its nationality and language' (*Encyclopaedia Britannica* 2001). Thus in the empire we see a crossing of borders, doubling and a freedom of language.

3 As a reviewer for the São Paulo magazine *Leia Livros*, Perlongher assessed Jorge Schwartz's work on the connections between the avant-gardes in Brazil and the rest of Latin America, *Vanguarda e cosmopolitanismo na década de 20*. Part of Perlongher's review is a call for increased links between Argentina and Brazil: 'There is a barrier between River Plate writing (and Latin American writing in general) and Brazilian writing, crossed only on those occasions when in honour of the 'boom', a work of 'local colour' travels to the European world and then returns to these shores. In his book, Jorge Schwartz endeavours to show how these barriers were already systematically perforated' (Perlongher, 1983c: 21 [São Paulo] my translation from Portuguese). Perlongher finds in the work of his friend a project that breaks down national boundaries through a historical re-examination of the literary canon. This literary project has a

political level, 'it subverts the signifying order' (21), functioning through an attack on linguistic and literary givens. This reveals the permeability and instability of boundaries, despite appearances of homogeneity and conservative social formations. Important in this is that Schwartz's project reassesses received forms of social organization along national lines. Perlongher demonstrated the same subversive attitude to literary tradition, and a desire to rewrite the established division of literary history in both his poetry and his positive assessment of Schwartz's work.

4 Discussing the disappearance of two Uruguayan political dissidents exiled in Argentina, Eduardo Galeano observes: '[a]l día siguiente, el ministro de Defensa argentino declaró a los periodistas sin pestañear: "se trata de una operación uruguaya. Todavía no sé si oficial o no." Tiempo después, en Ginebra, dijo el embajador uruguayo ante la Comisión de Derechos Humanos: "En cuanto a las vinculaciones entre la Argentina y el Uruguay, por cierto que existen. Nos sentimos orgullosos de ellas. Estamos hermanados por la historia y la cultura"' (1981: 156–7).

5 See Bey 1991 for his description of such Temporary Autonomous Zones as alternatives to political revolution. He finds examples in pirate, buccaneer and Maroon communities, also in such counter-state uprisings as the Native American Renaissance in the USA in the 1970s, or the city of Fiume, the Yugoslav town captured by the Italian general Gabriele D'Annunzio at the end of the First World War. D'Annunzio, also a decadent poet, artist, magician and musician captured the town to give to the Italian leaders as a gift. The Italians refused, so Fiume for eighteen months existed as a bohemian independent state, funded through piracy and run as a haven for poets, artists, homosexuals and pacifists. Eventually the money ran out and the Italians received reports of the disorderly state of affairs, and threatened to attack, whereupon D'Annunzio and his putative army immediately surrendered and the experiment ended. As Bey writes, 'the TAZ is a tactic of disappearance' (1991: 128).

6 The geographer and cultural critic David Harvey suggests in his book *Spaces of Hope* that there exists 'the need for some sort of "permanent revolution" to lie at the heart of any progressive social order' (2000: 243). Harvey's utopian vision nevertheless shows the distinction between a more orthodox Marxist position and the anarcho-libertarianism of Perlongher; Harvey's utopia, while fluid and horizontal, still relies on small-scale central planning and organization and has little of the fluidity and instability of Perlongher's TAZ.-utopia.

7 See also the later poem, 'Las tías' (1997a: 82 [1985, Buenos Aires]), from *Alambres*, which alludes to the relationships between 'tías solteronas', a slang expression for older effeminate gay men, and young conscript soldiers. The same relationship, specifically soldiers who resorted to homosexual prostitution supposedly to supplement the

meagre rations and pay in the prologue to the Malvinas campaign, is
also dealt with in the essay 'El sexo de las locas' (1997b: 29–34 [1983,
Buenos Aires]).

8   The polemic is recounted in Roxana Patiño's (2003) piece on
     Argentine literary reviews in the 1980s.

9   I use the term 'exile' with caution. Perlongher's exit from Argentina
     was entirely voluntary; he returned on several occasions even before
     the fall of the military. However, Perlongher's life in Argentina, both
     as a gay man and a sociologist, had been made impossible and
     untenable by the activities of the police and military in the country. I
     do not wish to discuss the relative merits – *exileness?* – of different
     exiles. The criticism that Perlongher received for his critique of
     Argentine intellectuals from exile is recounted by Patiño (2003).

10   Key to the discussion of changes in the perception of territory in the
     recent era is the work of Paul Virilio. He suggests that 'the reduction
     of distances had become a strategic reality bearing incalculable
     economic and political consequences, since it corresponds to the
     negation of space' (1998: 46). Discussing Mackinder's world-island
     theory, Virilio asserts that today 'from any given spot we can reach
     any other, no matter where it may be' (47). Modern life then is
     characterized by 'the juxtaposition of every locality [. . .], ubiquity,
     instantaneity' (48–58). Virilio draws particular attention to the impli-
     cations of the 1947 'Inter-American Treaty of Reciprocal Assistance',
     and the politics of permanent border-crossing it implied for the
     latter years of the twentieth century (78), while the opponents of
     dictatorships 'are prohibited from abiding and prohibited from
     leaving' (79). The new world order for Virilio is one of 'dromo-
     politics', the politics of speed, from *dromo*, Greek for race, 'where the
     nation will disappear solely to the benefit of a social deregulation and
     a transpolitical deconstruction' (121).

11   The first is the four-sided maze based on the four letters of the name
     of God invented by Red Scharlach, the second is the straight line
     infinitely divided in half proposed by Eric Lönnrot, somewhat similar
     to Zeno's second paradox, expounded later by Borges as evidence
     that 'we have dreamt it [the world] as firm, mysterious, visible,
     ubiquitous in space and durable in time; but in its architecture we
     have allowed tenuous and eternal crevices of unreason which tell us
     it is false' (Borges, 1970: 243). Asterión's maze is more traditional, yet
     seemingly infinitely sized; all of them point to contradictions within
     post-Socratic philosophy.

12   Perlongher reiterates this in his chronicle of life in Paris, in particu-
     lar in his attacks on loose interpretations of Deleuze circulating in
     France (1999b).

13   '[Perlongher l]legó a viajar al Amazonas en un periplo de dos días,
     navegando por ríos de selva, hasta la comunidad que la iglesia [of
     Santo Daime] posee en la aldea de Ceu do Mapiá [*sic*]' (Baigorria,
     1996: 178–9).

14   Juan de Tarsis, second Conde de Villamediana, is as renowned for his
     colourful life as his poetry. In his introduction to the count's poetry,

José Francisco Ruiz Casanova notes that exile was a key part of his life. He was exiled in 1605 for an affair with the Marquesa del Valle, and in 1608 for winning 30,000 ducats in a card game. He was murdered by two of the king's guards in 1622. Furthermore, in a 'proceso instruido por Fernando Fariñas contra el "pecado nefando" o sodomía, proceso en el que se ven implicados varios nobles y sus sirvientes [. . . a]parece como cierto "lo que está probado contra el conde de Villamediana"' (in Tarsis, 1990: 12–20).

15 The *silva* is a verse form combining eleven and seven syllable lines, often with a mixture of rhymed and unrhymed lines (Preminger and Brogan, 1993: 1148–9).

16 Sarduy talks of the Renaissance city, based around a centre, inspired by Galileo, as in the Copernican model, as opposed to Kepler's ellipse that dominates the decentred, multiple nature of the baroque (Sarduy, 1974: 32, 51, 58–9).

17 This notion has been passed from the classics through lines such as Shakespeare's 'so long lives this, and this gives life to thee' (Hayward, 1973: 59) and has its roots in poems such as Horace's piece entitled 'His Confidence in the Immortality of his Poems': 'Exegi monumentum aere perennius / Regalique situ pyramidum altius, / Quod non imber edax non aquilo impotens / Possit diruere aut innumerabilis / Annorum series et fuga temporum [. . .]' ('I have completed a monument more lasting than bronze and more lofty than the royal memorial of the pyramids – a monument which no devouring rain, no violent northern blast can overthrow, or the innumerable succession of years or the flight of ages') (Brittain, 1964: 32–3).

Chapter 3

Perlongher and the Avant-garde[1]

Introduction

In the last chapter I examined Perlongher's treatment of the concept of territory, and argued that throughout his career Perlongher sought to create and investigate spaces for desire and communities based on desire. In this chapter I aim to examine some of the key interlocutors that he chose for this project.

Perlongher identified himself in essays and interviews through-out his career as responding to an avant-garde tradition inside and outside Argentina.[2] I aim then to identify and question this relationship with the avant-garde.[3] This involves responding to the following key questions: which writers of or associated with the avant-garde does Perlongher identify as present in his work? What does Perlongher take from their work in terms of poetics, aesthetics or thematics? In what ways does Perlongher's work differ from, diverge, or go beyond that of his stated interlocutors? Who else can I identify as clear avant-garde presences in Perlongher's work? Again, how does Perlongher's work follow these writers, and how does it differ? What then is the purpose of Perlongher's relationship with and appropriation of the avant-garde, when critics such as Bürger (1984) and Hobsbawm (1998) have denied the viability of a 'neo-avant-guard' writing?

Perlongher's Avant-garde Genealogy

Perlongher identifies a number of writers identified with various avant-garde groups as vital to his literary formation and writing. I aim here to identify these writers and examine Perlongher's poetic relationship to each of their work.

The Body and Transgression: Enrique Molina

In an interview with the review *Babel* (1988–92), Perlongher spoke of the importance of Enrique Molina to his writing: 'Pero los que me nutrieron – la poesía es un elixir – fueron los surrealistas (como Enrique Molina) [. . .]' (Perlongher, 1997b: 14 [1989, Buenos Aires]). It is unclear in the interview whether Perlongher is talking about the European surrealists – the group led by André Breton that formed in the 1920s and included at different times writers such as Antonin Artaud and Robert Desnos –, their Argentine counterpart, a group that emerged fitfully in Argentina with the publication of the journal *Que* (1928) and again in the 1940s and 50s with the journals edited by Aldo Pellegrini, such as *Ciclo* (1948) and *A Partir de Cero* (1952), or any of a number of other groups. Nevertheless, the naming of Enrique Molina (b.1910), a recognized writer within the Argentine surrealists, allows us to attempt a concrete analysis of the elements Perlongher draws from the work of a surrealist, as in the poem 'Para Camila O'Gorman':

> Con su sencillo traje de muselina blanca tijereteada por las balas,
>   rea
> La caperuza que se desliza sobre el hombro desnudo (bajo el pelo
>   empapado de cerezas)
> Como un anillo de lombriz de tierra que huye
> Así ella se levanta
> El ruedo del sencillo vaporoso de muselina blanca, sin breteles
> Los jirones del fux de vaporosa, sencilla (pero blanca)
> Como nieve de rata de la noche detrás de los altares
> Así huidiza
> [. . .]
> (Perlongher, 1997a: 77 [1987, Buenos Aires])

Perlongher's poem seems to draw on a surrealist technique found in Molina's novel *Una sombra donde sueña Camila O'Gorman* (1973, republished 1984) whereby an empty dress appears in a disquieting fashion as a premonition of death (Molina, 1984: 208). However, the situation is rather more complicated than that.

Perlongher's poem describes the body of a person who has been shot, and uses three poetic techniques to do so. Firstly, metonym sees the effects of the killing through the effects on the trappings of the body – the pierced 'muselina', muslin, of a dress, the 'caperuza', or hood, which slips down. Secondly, synecdoche takes parts of the body for the whole – the vulnerable naked shoulder – to fragment the person. Finally, rather obscure similes reinforce the effect of these techniques; the hood is like the ring of an earthworm ('lombriz'), and the twill ('sencilla') is like snow, itself a cliché, but snow 'de rata', of a rat. This multifaceted and fragmented body seems to draw heavily on the techniques of surrealism, an effect reinforced by the apparently nonsensical final simile ('como nieve de rata').

Where Perlongher's poem differs from the surrealists' work, however, is in its easily recreated sense within a certain communal environment, specifically that of those familiar with the story of Camila O'Gorman and Buenos Aires slang, or *lunfardo*. The phrase 'así huidiza' highlights two elements of that which has gone before it. Firstly, the body is fleeting, like snow, as it has been the victim of execution. Secondly, the body is one that flees; this reminds us that in *lunfardo* a *rata* is a person who runs away. This possible meaning is reinforced by the title; Camila O'Gorman was a historical figure who became increasingly well known in the 1980s owing to María Luisa Bemberg's film *Camila* (1984). She was executed in 1845, while pregnant, at the hands of the government of Juan Manuel de Rosas, for having an affair with a priest and running away to the provinces, where she and the priest founded a primary school. The subject was also dealt with in Molina's novel, which I would call quasi-surrealist, as while it includes anthropomorphic and fantastic elements – Camila and her lover gain animal body parts during sexual intercourse, for example (Molina, 1984: 183) – it is historically researched and contains a clearly defined plot. Thus unlike the surrealist juxtaposition, whereby two elements not normally found together in the world are placed together for shocking and psychically revealing effect, Perlongher's strange juxtapositions instead function as a reference for a certain community of readers familiar with his codes and practices – the type of virtual community which we saw Perlongher attempting to create space for in chapter 2.

What then is the importance of the intertextual relationship to Molina the surrealist in Perlongher's writing? I would suggest that

Molina's novel represents an opportunity for Perlongher to find validation for three thematic elements within his writing: the body, desire, and rebellion. In *Una sombra donde sueña Camila O'Gorman*, Molina focuses closely on the body of Camila, particularly during sexual scenes: 'Por las piernas de Camila corría un licor filtrado gota a gota a través de todas las estrellas de la vida animal, con el olor de caverna marina y algas de propio sexo, olores genitales como la transfiguración del horizonte y el calor y la luna' (Molina, 1984: 183). Furthermore, Molina praises the anus, and with it anal sex: 'el impulso erótico transforma en exaltación, en magia, la parte del cuerpo humano donde se cumple la función más humillante' (203). Molina, like Perlongher, takes what is conventionally considered gross and obscene, or at best only regarded in medical terms, such as genital effusions, and through juxtaposition with positively valorized terms ('licor', for sweetness and intoxicating qualities, 'estrellas' or 'luna', for their esoteric and ascendant qualities, or 'magia' and 'exaltación'), celebrates the obscene, within a specifically Argentine context and with reference to Argentine history. Furthermore, like Perlongher, Molina privileges desire and reveals how hypocrisy and violence in the (Argentine) social aim to prevent its flows and connections. As he states in the novel, 'los esplendores del erotismo nacen a la sombra de los tabúes más severos' (227). Molina's novel portrays Rosas as having a homoerotic love of whipping backsides and wearing makeup, priests who wear women's underwear and let rats crawl around in their trousers, and the secret incestuous desires that live at the heart and in the organization of the bourgeois family. In terms of transgression and rebellion, Camila, like Perlongher's *travestis* (in the poems 'Ethel' and 'Natalie' [1997a: 84; 46]) and *chongos* (in the poem 'El polvo' [31]), has a sexual relationship (with a priest and outside marriage) that is not only forbidden but also incurs the wrath of a violent dictatorship. Moreover, like Perlongher's roaming *michês* and border-crossing homosexuals, Camila is a runaway, fleeing her family and the patriarchal order; as Perlongher quoted at the beginning of his poem 'Herida pierna', 'Deseoso es aquel que huye de su madre' (Perlongher, 1997a: 47 [Buenos Aires, 1980]), a quote from José Lezama Lima (in Jiménez 2000: 473 [1945]) that underlines Perlongher's focus on desire and flight.

In terms of broad themes then, Perlongher finds in Molina a vital predecessor. However, as we have seen, at a poetic level

Perlongher does not seem overly keen on adopting surrealist techniques, such as free association or automatic writing, instead preferring writing that is more orderly and decipherable. A brief examination of Molina's poetics will perhaps allow us to suggest reasons for this discordance between Perlongher and one of Argentina's principal surrealists.

Molina's *oeuvre* is characterized by the presence of certain techniques drawn from surrealism but also by a great number of what might be termed lyrical love poems. This type of love poem often adopts a conservative form, where binaries such as man–culture/woman–nature are reinforced:

> Si apoyara en la noche mi cabeza
> como sobre algún pecho de mujer, cuando ya todo
> ha cerrado sus ojos, cuando ya todo ha cruzado las manos
> – el odio y el deseo –
> te vería llegar con tus linternas,
> vengador vagabundo cubierto de flores,
> Paraná, río mío
> ('Águila de las lluvias', 1978: 88, first published in *Pasiones terrestres*, 1946)

The poem links the experience of viewing nature – the river Paraná – with that of sleeping on a woman's chest. 'Cabeza' is placed in a dual relationship, to 'noche' through metonym and 'pecho de mujer' through simile, a position that allows access to a form of beyond, specifically the river Paraná, but also, by implication, dream. A relationship nature–woman is created through analogy between two states of repose, both assumed to be natural. Woman and night become natural means to ascend to a beyond, and with it some sort of truth or greater communion. Thus man is left in the culture position, also exalted symbolically in his status as the viewer and recorder of two natural landscapes – the woman's body and the river. Problematically, however, the river ('Paraná, río mío') is masculine in gender, so the comparison between the landscape of the woman and that of the river also creates a triangular relationship between the man, the woman's body, and the river as a macho crony. Thus the poem serves the feminist hypothesis suggested by Eve Kosofsky Sedgwick in *Between Men. English Literature and Male Homosocial Desire* (1985), that a triangular relationship often exists in literary portrayals of hetero-sexuality, whereby the man's relationship to woman is always in fact one of two men relating to an object-woman, whereby the woman serves as a disguise for 'homosocial' desire found in jealousy, macho friendliness or competition.[4]

Discussing Molina in the context of Argentine surrealism, the Argentine critic Graciela de Sola comments, 'Enrique Molina [. . .] confía a imágenes de gran belleza su exaltación de la libertad y del amor' (1967: 177). Her assessment draws out the key characteristic of love in Molina's work, a love that Sola and, I believe, Molina are careful to classify:

> Todos ellos [Argentine surrealist poets], en fin, ven la realidad como dinámica fusión de los opuestos, en marcha hacia su total unificación; al hombre como ser que tiende incesantemente a reintegrarse en el todo, y que se encamina a esa reintegración por acto de amor como enlace heterosexual (toda otra forma de exaltación del sexo viola la naturaleza profunda del hombre, destinado a fundirse en su antagónico) [. . .] (172).

The lyrical love poems to be found in Molina's collection *Amantes antípodas* (1961), described by Sola as an 'ejemplo de la nunca lograda fusión de los que se buscan desesperadamente y sin fin [. . .] contrarios que se buscan con pasión y cuya fuerza da existencia al mundo' (148), or the tragic passion of Molina's *Una sombra donde sueña Camila O'Gorman*, are all distinctly heterosexual. Indeed Molina's portrayal of sexual hypocrisy, particularly amongst the clergy – the priest who wears lingerie and enjoys letting a rat down the back of his trousers (Molina, 1984: 201–2) – and of the dictator Rosas – he of the painted lips (64) – is homophobic. Molina reveals homosexual desire in order to denounce hypocrisy but does so in a manner that unlike the practice of 'outing' is never favourable to those acts. Molina's work frequently functions through binaries; he opposes Camila and 'las virtudes de la pasión, las virtudes de la locura, el honor del amor,' to 'una sociedad donde imperan a la vez el odio y las virtudes domésticas' (19). Later we see violence opposed to love (25) and the opposition between 'vida o muerte [. . .] verdad del alma o mentiras de la convivencia social' (30). It is these binaries and barriers – between the sexes, between countries, and between time frames – that we have seen Perlongher attempting to traverse and expand in chapter 2. Thus while Molina and Perlongher coincide in the matter of free love, Molina's love is in fact rather more conservative than one might at first expect.

While Molina's work clearly exhibits the surrealist aim of reclaiming a space for love and transgression, an aim to a degree shared with Perlongher's work, closer examination reveals the practical differences between their work, fundamentally centred on Molina's insistence on heterosexuality as the true medium of love, in contrast to Perlongher's insistence on the untrammelled connections of desire.

Nonsense and Faecality: Antonin Artaud

In the same interview in which Perlongher highlighted the importance of Enrique Molina he also named Antonin Artaud (1896–1948) as a key presence in his writing, alongside '[Luis de] Góngora' and '[José] Lezama Lima' as Perlongher's 'poeta favorito' (Perlongher, 1997b: 14 [1988, Buenos Aires]). Two elements can be identified in Perlongher's poetry that demonstrate a clear presence of Artaud's poetics and thematics in his work. They are nonsense and faecality. This illustrated in Perlongher's poem '(Mamparas)':

> estentóreo vitral trizas del cuello la gorguera manchada como un
> tímpano por el eco de un flato trema crema lagartija cariosa que en
> el pecado de esa lavandina – oriental y estentórea – jala del pene
> de la anciana madre el hilo de una cicatriz. [. . .]
> (Perlongher, 1997a: 95 [1987, Buenos Aires])

Perlongher creates an active nonsense that flirts with meaning and then defies it, through lengthy enumerations (four nouns in a row in the second line) and clauses that are connected by conjunctions and prepositions without offering a logical or thematic link. Added to this poetic technique is the non-sequitur juxtaposition of words from wildly separate fields of meaning; 'estentóreo' is drawn from the classics (Hector's herald was Stentor); the 'gorguera' is drawn from armoury, a throat-piece; 'tímpano', timpani or the ear drum, is both medical and musical; while words such as 'lavandina' (bleach) and 'flato' (flatulence) suggest a toilet environment. This gives the poem a delirious and confused air. In terms of faecality, the poem centres on the 'flato'; 'estentóreo', describing its sound, frames the word, and 'flato' gains four qualifiers in the lengthy enumeration that follows it ('trema crema lagartija cariosa'). Thus the poem forces the reader to focus on the fart and, with it, the anus, as a central organizational principle. This cultivation together of the faecal and nonsense is a key technique in many of the works of Artaud, a technique he used in an attempt to shock and disgust his audiences, as in the radio play *To Have Done With the Judgement of God* (1947):

> In order to have shit,
> that is, meat,
> where there was only blood
> and a junkyard of bones
> and where there was no being to win
> but there was only life to lose.
>
> o reche modo
> to edire
> di za
> tau dari
> do padera coco
> (Artaud, 1988: 560)

Artaud represents for Perlongher an important predecessor in his attempts to renovate language so as to create space for the dirtiest and most obscene of Judaeo–Christian taboo subjects and for language that refuses to follow grammatical or conversational norms. He thus allows the poet a certain freedom of composition for the surprising connections found in the modern urban environment, or in the imaginations of persons labelled criminally perverse or insane by the state, as happened to Perlongher and Artaud.

Nevertheless, there are key differences between the uses that Perlongher and Artaud make of nonsense, particularly in relation to the issue of delirium and madness. If we look at one of Perlongher's poems which is close to the type of nonsense cultivated by Artaud, '*grades*', we will detect key differences:

> y por las gradas esa estola que
>   radas rodas, rueda, greda
> en el *degrau* – degrádase, desagradable boa, la de esa
>   moquerie, y cuyos flejos, gelatinosos, lame. losa
> la de esa escala. pues en sus ascensiones, o descensos, o
>   líneas, de laberinto, boas de fleco y
> "filipetas", botas
> lo que se pisa: paño

de "pranto", y "maquerie": machette ruinosa, lo que enella
[. . .] (Perlongher, 1997a: 93 [1987, Buenos Aires])

Perlongher's poem is reminiscent of Artaud's nonsense in many ways. Every line is dominated by sonic connections between words rather than any other relationship, for example grammatically correct syntax or lucid meaning. 'Radas' are natural bays, 'rodas' are stems, or a wrongly conjugated second person of 'rodar' (which should be 'ruedas'; in the River Plate area it would be 'rodás'), to roll or go round, or Rhodes in Spanish. 'rueda' is a wheel, so there is a connection in semantic fields, but only fleetingly, as 'greda' is clay, thematically unlinked, but perhaps metonymically connected. Similarly, 'degrádase' and 'desagradable' share identical phonemes, save the /bl/ in the latter, but do not coincide in meaning at all. The only initial constant is the movement up and down suggested by '*grades*', 'gradas', '*degrau*', 'escala', 'ascensiones' and 'descensos'. However, this is complicated by the use of different languages (French and Portuguese) and the interruption of neologisms and nonsense words in inverted commas ('"filipetas"', '"pranto"', '"maquerie"'). Furthermore, the up–down movement ceases after five lines.

This studious denial of meaning is reinforced by the constant stripping away of context. Grammatically, this is achieved through using parts of speech that suggest logical connections, only then to disappoint such expectations. For example, 'pues' suggests an explanation, but there is no clause to explain or be explained. 'Que' is not given the verb that would have completed its function. The word 'o' is used to present *unrelated* choices: 'gredas o paño', clays or cloth. Thus, rather than highlighting the difference between two similar things (even with 'black or white', both are related to colour), the suggestion of alternatives links the previously unrelated, so a part of speech is made to work against itself.

These poems represent an attempt at the purely Dionysian in language: the overflowing of sound and excessive vocabulary beyond communication or grammar, very much in the vein of Artaud. Vitally, however, among the grammatical and sonic nonsense, Perlongher's poem contains clear allusions to an aesthetic of transvestism; the 'estola', the 'boa', the 'flejos' and 'lame' all suggest a dressed-up drag performance with an excess of trappings, hairdos and make-up. The sequence 'rodas, rueda, greda' implies a 'drag', or a drift around the town, like Perlongher's wandering transvestites. For Perlongher the space the nonsense creates is less that of the madman or 'loco', than that of the 'loca' – the mad woman, but also the effeminate homosexual. Furthermore, these central points of transvestite performance within the prevailing ungrammatical nonsense of the poem suggest an experiment in *descending into* nonsense, and that the transvestite performance or drift is an escape from sense and order. In Artaud's poetry, however, nonsense seems to function in reverse. Artaud's works begin in the abyss of madness and seek desperately for moments of lucidity, as in the striking opening of *To Have Done with the Judgement of God*:

kré		puc te
kré	Everything must	puk te
pek	be arranged	li le
kre	to a hair	pek ti le
e	in a fulminating	kruk
pte	order.	
(1988: 555)		

The opening of Artaud's piece carries the same incantatory strength as the section above, demanding a certain solemnity from the audience through the visceral sublinguistic chants. However, within this, there is a plea for 'order' as a necessary precondition of the performance itself. It is clear in this piece that Artaud, the great miner of the human psyche and of the order that surrounds us, realizes that there is no possible communication from a psychopath. Whereas Perlongher's writing then celebrates the flight from rationality, Artaud's work appears to crave the ability to use the rational as a tool for exploring the depths of consciousness.

Artaud, a figure on the edge of the surrealists, who was never at ease with the doctrines of the movement or Breton's leadership, represents for Perlongher an example of literary production that privileges the taboo and the obscene, and examines the irrational and the nonsensical. However, while Perlongher finds a thematic genealogy in the work of Artaud, in some ways related to the surrealists but more closely related to more general avant-garde attempts at renovating cultural production, he takes poetic techniques learnt from the French theatre practitioner and uses them for aims more closely related to his attempts to privilege and trace desire in writing, no matter how disgusting and irrational the flights it may take.

Sex in the City: Oliverio Girondo

If Artaud provides Perlongher with certain vanguard tools for the writing of desire then perhaps the poet who most clearly provides a genealogy in Argentina for their use is Oliverio Girondo (1891–1967). Perlongher was clear in stressing the importance of Girondo's work for his own, dedicating an article to Girondo in *XUL*, entitled 'El sexo de las chicas' (Perlongher, 1984). The title alludes to two works: firstly, Girondo's poem 'Exvoto' (from *Veinte poemas para ser leídos en tranvía* [1922]), which deals with 'Las chicas de Flores', a district of Buenos Aires renowned for its prostitutes; and, secondly, Perlongher's own essay from a year earlier, 'El sexo de las locas' (1997b: 29–34 [1983, Buenos Aires]),[5] where he attacked the strange mix of homophobia and homoeroticism found in everyday life in Buenos Aires. Many of Perlongher's poems draw very directly on Girondo's work. 'Cadáveres', for example, opens as follows:

> Bajo las matas
> En los pajonales
> Sobre los puentes
> En los canales
> Hay Cadáveres
> (Perlongher, 1997a: 111 [1984, Buenos Aires])

The poem uses a slideshow effect to show the appearance of dead bodies, as Perlongher cuts between different pieces of evidence of violence. The stanza borrows clearly from Girondo's poem 'Desmemoria':

> Primero: ¿entre corales?
> Después: ¿debajo tierra?
> Más cerca: ¿por los campos?
> Ayer: ¿sobre los árboles?
> [. . .]
> ¡Son demasiados siglos!
> No puedo recordarlo.
> (Girondo, 1998: 90 [1968])

Perlongher and Girondo's poems enter into an intriguing dialogue. If Perlongher's poem, written in the early 1980s and published in 1984 represents an attempt to examine the possibility of representing the slaughter that took place during the dictatorship years, the intertextual reference to Girondo suggests the key position of experimental poetics in examining memory and inscription. Girondo's poem questions the possibility of the inscription of our perceptions and memory ('¡Son demasiados siglos!'), as the human being and the language he or she uses is flawed, while Perlongher's poem tests that assumption within the urgent socio-political confines of the end of a bloody dictatorship. The slideshow technique that allows Girondo to move from place to place while maintaining an unfragmented narrative and recording position, becomes a key tool for the opening of Perlongher's attempts to inscribe the crimes of the dictatorship.

Elsewhere, Perlongher draws on the more purely linguistic experiments found in Girondo's work, as in the former's poem 'República':

> Oh la Diosa Razón:
> las muselinas de sus amigas:
>> las cabareteras
>> las cupleteras
>> las partiquinas
>> las trotacalles
>> las meretrices
>> las vitrioleras
>> las cabezas de murga
>> las rumberas
>
> (Perlongher, 1997a: 53 [1980, Buenos Aires])

Perlongher's poem takes two liberal ideals – reason and the republic – and uses them to frame an alternative nation, a community of artists, prostitutes, dancers and singers, similar to the earlier *murga*. Perlongher creates another almost childish rhythm with five and six-syllable lines. The techniques he uses for creating an alternative community based on sensuality and art are also found in the juxtapositions and experiments with language of Girondo's collection *En la masmédula*, for example the poem 'Cansancio':

> Y de los replanteos
> y recontradicciones

y reconsentimientos sin o con sentimiento cansado
y de los repropósitos
y de los reademanes y rediálogos idénticamente
    bostezables
(1998: 179 [1956])

Girondo's technique is to take a common habit in colloquial Argentine Spanish, the addition of 're-' to a part of speech for intensifying purposes, and use it to stretch the possibilities of intelligibility. Whereas Girondo's poem is closer to a linguistic experiment, Perlongher's represents a more political project, in the sense of creating space and language for marginal groups such as streetwalkers and prostitutes, the desiring-political community of his earlier *murga*.

Another poetic technique shared by Girondo and Perlongher is the fragmentation of the body as a method of presenting the theme of sex in the urban environment. Such is the case with Perlongher's poem '*carnaval – río 1984*', taken from the 'Frenesí' series:

> El enterizo de banlon, si te disimulaba las almorranas, te las ceñía al roce mercurial del paso de las lianas en el limo azulado, en el ganglio del ánade (no es metáfora). Terciopelo, correhuelas de terciopelo, sogas de nylon, alambrecitos de hambres y sobrosos, sabrosos hombres broncos hombreando hombrudos en el refocilar, de la pipeta del peristilo, el reroer, el intraurar, el tauril de merurio.
> (Perlongher, 1997a: 105 [1985, Buenos Aires])

As well as using the types of neologisms and half-words ('tauril', 'merurio', 'reroer') we have seen in Girondo's work (above), Perlongher also displays an intriguing attitude to desire in the urban environment, characterized by the fragmentation not only of those observed – as we would expect in a vanguard poem that attempts to expand the scale of vision, in a fashion similar to the Cubist attempt to depict conceptually a place or object through uniting parts and points separated in space – but also through the fragmentation of the observer. The observed bodies are seen in parts and poses: 'enterizo de banlon' (a nylon one-piece suit), other fabrics such as velvet ('terciopelo'), parts of the body ('hombros', 'almorranas', piles) and masses of bodies. At the same time the repetition of the second person object pronoun ('te'), the rapid movement of description – faster and less unified than that found in a collage, a slide show or a cubist image – and the absence of any first person presence, show the narrative position, the observer, in similar state of fragmentation.

Girondo, a clear presence in this poem, also employs this technique of fragmentation in an attempt to portray desire in the urban environment, but with a key distinction, as we shall see, in the poem 'Exvoto':

> Al atardecer, todas ellas cuelgan sus pechos sin madurar del ramaje de hierro de los balcones, para que sus vestidos se empurpuren al sentirlas desnudas, y de noche, a remolque de sus mamás – empavesadas como fragatas – van a pasearse por la plaza, para que los hombres les eyaculen palabras al oído, y sus pezones se encienden y se apaguen como luciérnagas.

> Las chicas de Flores, viven en la angustia de que las nalgas se les pudren, como manzanas que se han dejado pasar, y el deseo de los hombres las sofoca tanto, que a veces quisieran desembarazarse de él como de un corsé, ya que tienen el coraje de cortarse el cuerpo a pedacitos y arrojárselo, a todos que les pasan a la vereda. (1996: 41–2 [1922])

In the article for *XUL* Perlongher talks of the 'fragmentación de los cuerpos' (1984: 26) in poems such as 'Exvoto'. This is clear not only in the poem's ending – the girls physically cut parts from their bodies – but also in the portrayal of the body itself as parts, such as 'pechos', 'oído', and 'nalgas' and its coverings, including 'vestidos' and 'corsé'. Furthermore, there are no individual girls, just 'las chicas' or 'ellas'. However, the fragmentation is different from that which takes place in Perlongher's work, as highlighted by the US critic Jill Kuhnheim (1996) in her assessment of Girondo's work. Perlongher's essay overlooks possible critiques of the framing of sexuality in Girondo's poetry by a relatively unchanging and innately male gaze – observing the fragmented 'Chicas de flores' for example – whereby sexuality becomes a technique that in fact stabilizes the male narrative position at the expense of the observed female bodies. Perlongher's poem, on the other hand, destabilizes such a gaze in its portrayal of sexuality in the urban environment.

Girondo represents a central interlocutor in Perlongher's dialogue with the avant-garde; he provides key tools, in particular experiments with neologisms, half-words and the fragmentation of the body. However, it is clear that Perlongher's project goes further in its attack on the narrative position and the often implicitly male gaze that stabilizes Girondo's poetry. In fact, there is another element altogether in Perlongher's use of Girondo's poetry. In the essay quoted above, Perlongher suggests that in poems such as 'Exvoto', 'por un lado [. . .] los cuerpos se despedazan. Por el otro, la sexualidad misma aparece despedazada en todos los rincones del cuerpo social' (1984: 27). Perlongher's view of sexuality in Girondo as something spread throughout society closely follows Deleuze and Guattari's statements regarding desire in *Anti-Oedipus*: 'Desire is present whenever something flows and runs, carrying along with it interested subjects – but also drunken and slumbering subjects – towards lethal destinations' (2000a: 105 [1972]). As Perlongher's piece continues he begins to echo Deleuze and Guattari almost to the word. He talks of persons in *Veinte poemas para ser leídos en el tranvía* being 'todos los sexos' (1984: 27) where the Frenchmen spoke of 'n sexes' (2000a: 296). Furthermore, he discusses how Girondo's poems privilege 'las formas, digamos, menores' (1984: 25), a term drawn from Deleuze and Guattari's book on Kafka, *Towards a Minor Literature* (1975), to describe those forms of writing that destabilize a major language, for example Kafka's use of German with its hyper-politicized content and Prague-Jewish inflection. Thus we can see Perlongher's essay on Girondo as not only popularizing the poet he found as a genealogy for his own work but also as a means to diffuse, perhaps in a simplistic manner, the theories of those writers he found useful for his own project of examining male prostitution in São Paulo.

Perlongher's final words on Girondo are equally revealing:

> El 'sexualismo' de Girondo parece proceder de una desterritorialización eminentemente paisajística [. . .], pero donde los cortes del deseo están marcados – los lugares donde el deseo rasga la mascarada social. Esta libidinización se vuelve luego contra el propio yo – la identidad – y disuelve al objeto. (1984: 27)

Deterritorialization and the attack on the 'I' or self are taken by Perlongher as the two central traits in Girondo. But they are also two key elements in the version of Deleuze and Guattari's thinking presented by Perlongher in interviews and essays: '[s]i no hay un yo – reza *Mil mesetas* –, si somos todos multiplicidades' (1997b: 139 [1988, Buenos Aires]). Thus we can detect a number of processes at work in Perlongher's appropriation of Girondo's

poetics: firstly, Perlongher is using the avant-garde as a pre-
decessor for a poetic project of writing the obscene and indecent
within the urban environment; secondly, he is inserting Girondo
into his own version of a Deleuzean framework, including terms
such as 'minor' and 'deterritorialization' drawn from Deleuze and
Guattari's work on writers such as Kafka; and, finally, he is using
this to popularize Deleuzean ideas related to his own intellectual
project of examining desire within the social – specifically at this
stage his work on male prostitution – attacking the individual and
social stratification.

Poetic Innovation and Poetic Engagement: Juan Gelman

In an essay written for the Brazilian review *Leia Livros*, Perlongher
attempted to characterize the '"Nuevo verso"' [*sic*] from the River
Plate region that was exemplified by the work of writers such as
the brothers Leónidas (b.1927) and Osvaldo Lamborghini (1940–
85) and Arturo Carrera (b.1948). These writers not only contrib-
uted to the same journals as Perlongher (*Sitio* [Buenos Aires,
1981–7], and XUL [Buenos Aires, 1980–96], in particular) but
are also of a younger generation than Jorge Luis Borges (1899–
1986), Macedonio Fernández (1874–1952), Ernesto Sábato
(b.1911) and other figures respected in Argentine letters at the
beginning of the 1980s. Thus it is fair to include Perlongher's own
work as part of the subject being assessed. Perlongher identifies
the poet Juan Gelman (b.1930) as an important forefather for
these new poets:

> Gelman incarnates a social lyricism that overwhelmed [*esmagou*]
> River Plate literature, helping to turn language into a 'national
> park'. Exile, fragmentation, dispersal would accentuate the
> tendency towards disparity and would permit the emergence of a
> 'nuevo verso'. (Perlongher, 1983b: 6 [São Paulo] my translation
> from Portuguese)

Perlongher's positioning of Gelman as a predecessor to the 'nuevo
verso' is perhaps ambiguous. While his work helped the new verse
to emerge, Perlongher also suggests that his chosen poetics and
thematics, with its tendency towards social themes ('social lyri-
cism'), overwhelmed the River Plate, an apparently unfavourable
choice of verb. However, the nationalization of language carried

out in the work of writers such as Gelman, a certain democratization of poetry that Perlongher suggests with his phrase 'national park', alongside the political circumstances of exile and political dispersal – particularly the destruction of the Argentine left carried out between 1976 and 1979 by the military dictatorship, is key for the development and emergence of the new poetry.

Perlongher's poem that perhaps most draws on the work of Gelman is his polemic and visceral piece, 'El hule':

Punto en el mar:
　　　　　　　destello en cromo
　　　　　　　(noctiluca)
Punto en el mar:
　　　　　　　o noctiluca
　　　　　　　o destello de cromo de oleaje,
　　　　　　　　　　　　　denso,
　　　　　　　de los muelles

　　　　　　　(Una niña de Quilmes
　　　　　　　perdió su monedero en unos rieles . . .)
Ahora desean que el olvido baje sus cortinillas de hule
(efecto humo) en el pantano, humor amor, y las tres moscas
(a fuer de fieras, atrapadas) dulces corroan en la mesa, recta,
de sus restos: yacencia suspendida, parentear, al paréntesis,
la biela, yela la grela el tul, quieren que baje, yo, olvidar,
el fragmento de prosa, parrafado sudor en el sudario, rastro de

ínclita musaraña
　　　　incli
　　　　nación
[. . .]
(Perlongher, 1997a: 153 [1989, Buenos Aires])

A number of features stand out from this poem as illustrative of the presence of avant-garde poetics in Perlongher's work. Firstly, the poem's layout breaks up the traditional divide between verse and prose and between different verses and stanzas. The poem experiments with drawing shapes on the page, with the tidal flow of the opening lines depicting the sea scene they suggest. Secondly, the poem experiments with different typefaces, including the italics interspersed throughout the text. Furthermore, Perlongher does not follow a recognizable scheme of rhyme or rhythm, mixing a long phrase such as 'Ahora [. . .] pantano', which has more than twenty-five syllables, with short, stabbing

phrases of as few as three, for example 'la biela' or even the
monosyllable (with a two syllable value in Spanish metrification)
'yo'. Thus the poem draws on the historical vanguards' attempts
to renovate poetic form away from strict traditional norms.

Alongside the formal elements of Perlongher's poem, it is also
interesting at the level of thematics and aesthetics. This is one of
Perlongher's most menacing and disconcerting pieces, for a
number of reasons. The very sparse, almost cinematic opening
picks out, physically on the page and conceptually, an unidenti-
fied point ('punto') against an apparently black background of
the sea ('mar') seen from the shore – the 'muelles' are the wharfs
characteristic of Buenos Aires' shoreline. The reader is left with
various options for the origin of this point of light – a firefly
('noctiluca'), or chrome ('cromo'), or also the sea, as the
'destello de cromo' is metaphorically linked to the sea ('de oleaje
denso'). This mysterious opening is juxtaposed with a childish
rhyme ('*Una niña de Quilmes*'), which, alongside the murky open-
ing, smacks of child abduction.

The bulky second section then proposes a plural third person
agent ('desean') that attempts in some way to hide certain facts.
To do this, Perlongher creates a network of phrases related to
partitioning, obscuring, hiding and disguising: 'cortinillas de
hule', the rubber curtains that separate operating theatres or
slaughterhouse floors from the outsider's gaze, '*(efecto humo)*', a
smoke screen, or 'parentear', to put in brackets, like 'paréntesis'.
In addition we also read 'parrafado', paragraphed, which owing
to the layout of the poem allows Perlongher to refer to his own
piece, itself divided into paragraphs; each is, in the poem's words,
a 'fragmento de prosa'. This process of hiding is a process of
forgetting, and one that is aimed at a 'yo', the momentary first
person singular voice of the poem. What is hidden is, as in the
opening, only hinted at but appears to be bestial and violent ('a
fuer de fieras'), yet ordered and organized ('en la mesa, recta').
Furthermore, Perlongher sets this within an Argentine idiomatic
framework, through the use of *lunfardo*, such as 'grela', used in
the 1960s for 'woman', but more generally 'dirt', and 'yela', a
lunfardo sounding mistranscription, and the kind of terms, for
example 'tul' (tulle, a fabric), that we see in earlier poems, such
as 'El polvo' (1997a: 31 [1980, Buenos Aires]), being used to
present the gender-questioning activities of transvestites in Bue-
nos Aires. Moreover, Perlongher includes a suggestion of a link at

the level of the nation-state – rather than local or microcommunitarian links – between the silencing of the poem and the proscription of memory, in the breaking up of the word '*inclinación*'. This formal device accentuates the presence of 'ínclita', renowned, previously innocently paired with 'musaraña' (a shrew), but now allowing the *nación* to become renowned. Within Perlongher's poem, there is very little doubt left for the reader as to the fact that this renowned – infamous? – nation is Argentina. The words 'musaraña' and 'rastro' both have further implications. 'musaraña' is also a speck in one's eye, an awkward, persistent presence, a piece of evidence (from the Latin *videre*, to see) that physically cannot be avoided, while 'rastro' is a trace, another small and potentially awkward presence like the sparkles and chrome of the poem's opening.

Through its presentation of an attempt to create active forgetting, particularly of what appears to be a bloody medical or surgical operation, Perlongher alludes forcibly to the contemporary debate surrounding the post-transition government's attitude to the crimes committed by the military dictatorship in the late 1970s and early 1980s. Whereas in Brazil and Chile the military engineered immunity for themselves as part of the process of handing power back to civilians – General Augusto Pinochet's status as a senator *ex oficio*, for example – the suddenness of the collapse of the military *junta* after the Falklands/Malvinas war in 1982 meant that there was no opportunity for the Generals to engineer similar assurances for themselves before the elections in 1983. The government of Alfonsín had responded to calls from human rights groups such as the Madres de la Plaza de Mayo and their campaign for information on the whereabouts of disappeared persons and prosecution of military crimes, by commissioning an investigation into the military's actions, CONADEP, or the National Commission on the Disappearance of Persons, whose report, *Nunca más*, was compiled by the writer Ernesto Sábato. However, despite initial trials and prosecutions, by 1987 the Alfonsín Radical Party government, suffering an economic crisis and witnessing the resurgence of Peronism as an electoral force, and with hard-line members of the military threatening revolt, proposed what was called the 'Law of Due Obedience', radically extending the conditions under which a soldier 'following orders' could avoid being punished for crimes. Furthermore, in 1989, in an effort to place a statute of limitations on prosecutions, Alfonsín's government declared what was called the *punto final* law, a forty-day limit, after which prosecutions could not be continued. Both laws, products of political expediency that betrayed the spirit of attempts to investigate fully the actions of the military, attempted to draw an ahistorical line under the events of 1976–83 and to create, as Perlongher's poem suggests, a parenthesis around the remembering and telling of history.

We can conclude then that Perlongher's poem represents an attempt at both innovative formal presentation and political engagement with a wider historical and social context. Such an attempt finds its most obvious Argentine predecessor in Juan Gelman, a poet who took the techniques of the avant-gardes and used them for political effect. Gelman's writing can be classed as *poesía social*, one of the schools of poetry that preceded Perlongher and his contemporaries, which was particularly dominant in the 1960s in Argentina. *Poesía social* combines the experimental poetics and social engagement of the avant-garde with a firm thematic political commitment, in particular to the organized left. Benedetti describes *poesía social* in the introduction to his collection of interviews, *Los poetas comunicantes*, as: 'Compromiso; voluntad de comunicación; sacrificio parcial y provisorio de lo estrictamente estético en beneficio de una comunicación de emergencia' (1981: 17). Thus social poetry involves a certain effort on the part of the poet: abandoning oneself as poet, committing oneself, taking sides, giving up strictly aesthetic concerns, denouncing injustice to one's fellow men, and proposing solutions. In Gelman or Perlongher's poems, we can see this effort: a commitment against central government action, such as torture or violence; siding with the victim; including prosaic, non-poetic details in the poem; and suggesting an alternative, namely solidarity against oppression, and refusing to forget or to remain silent.

In an interview, Juan Gelman comments that the constant in his poetry is 'la cotidianidad, entendida esencialmente como realidad' (Benedetti 1981: 188). Gelman is keen to point out that artistic concerns are not foremost in his mind: 'mucho más dramática que la situación del poeta que no puede ser entendido me parece la del obrero, que antes tiene problemas más urgentes' (189). The role of the poet is then to communicate everyday reality, a role that becomes even more vital during times of emergency – during a strike, or after a coup, for example.

Kuhnheim (1996) suggests that *poesía social* represents a rupture in Argentine avant-garde poetry, whereby despite the initial exchange and accommodation that occurred between the politically minded *Boedo* group and the more abstract *Florida* group in the 1920s and 30s, after the political upheavals of the 1930s and 40s, such as the military coup led by General Uriburu in 1930, and in particular after the struggles between pro- and anti-Peronist groups in the 1950s and 1960s, the gap between politically engaged or pragmatic poetry – Gelman, for example – and more artistic or metaphysical poetry – Alejandra Pizarnik, or Jorge Luis Borges – became insurmountable. Thus we can see the importance of Gelman for Perlongher's more overtly macropolitical writing, as it offers a model of using avant-garde poetics as a means to expand the scope of the poem, in terms of subjects dealt with, its political engagement, and the relationship with an implied and politically sympathetic readership.

However, there are key and revealing differences to be found between Perlongher and Gelman's work, as revealed in the former's poem 'El cadáver de la nación':

> *Por qué no entré por el pasillo?*
> *Qué tenía que hacer en esa noche*
> *a las 20.25, hora en que ella entró,*
> *por Casanova*
> *[. . .]*
>   *Y si ella*
> *se empezara a desvanecer, digamos*
> *a deshacerse*
> *qué diré del pasillo, entonces?*
> *Por qué no?*
> *entre cervatillos de ojos pringosos,*
> *y anhelantes*
> *[. . .]*
>   *Y yo*
> *por temor a un olvido*
> *intranscendente, a un hurto*
> *debo negarme a seguir su cureña por las plazas?*
> *[. . .]*
> *Ese deseo de no morir?*
> *es cierto?*
> *en lugar de quedarse ahí*

en ese pasillo
entre sus fauces amarillas y halitosas
(Perlongher, 1997a: 42–5 [1980, Buenos Aires], italics in original)

Perlongher's poem presents two situations, juxtaposed without warning. The first is that of a voice outside a corridor ('pasillo'), surrounded by threatening yet desiring figures ('cervatillos', little deer, with 'fauces amarillas', yellow teeth and 'halitosas', bad breath). The second is the death of Evita Perón, including the time she died ('20.25', when radio broadcasts stopped during the remaining years of the Peronist administration), and her funeral cortege ('cureña' is a gun carriage, as used to carry important coffins). The poem, through a juxtaposition that draws heavily on avant-garde poetics also used by Gelman, creates equivalence between the immediate access to pleasure through dangerous means, and Evita Peronism. Perlongher explained this equivalence in an interview with Guillermo Saavedra: 'Yo siempre había pensado que el peronismo era un pasillo, un atajo, una manera rápida de llegar pero con consecuencias horrorosas' (Saavedra, 1991: 2). Perlongher's poem likewise uses avant-garde poetics to suggest that the risky shortcut to pleasure found in going into the lower-class and aggressive dwelling in 'El cadáver de la nación', which in the interview with Saavedra he also links to a real house in a *villa miseria*, or slum, on the outskirts on Buenos Aires (2), is the same risky shortcut found in Peronism. This links to Perlongher's own difficult relationship with the Peronist movement, in particular the FLH's attendance at the Ezeize rally to welcome back Perón. Large sectors of the Argentine left had imagined Perón's return as a shortcut to social justice and democracy that bypassed class struggle, as recounted by Rapisardi and Modarelli (2001) and Torre and Riz (1993). However, the massacre that ensued at Ezeize as left and right-wing Peronist groups clashed and the ensuing shift to the right of Perón and his inner circle proved such hopes to be unfounded.

Gelman's work, however, clearly expresses a faithful Peronist perspective, as in the poem 'Escrituras':

la casa del administrador de la mina de wolfram
la boca de la mina de wolfram
el arroyo para lavar el wolfram y algunos ranchos
eso es todo esa es La Carolina

San Luis es chico y La Carolina está en San Luis

La Carolina es chica
treinta mineros sacan el wolfram
con sus lámparas de carburo escriben mensajes en las paredes de
cada socavón

encima de la tierra ¿se puede leer lo que hay escrito debajo de la
tierra?
¿se puede leer los mensajes de La Carolina?
'cuidado no sacar más mineral hasta que apuntalen' dice uno
'josé hay que seguir mañana por este socavón'

pero arriba ¿se puede leer?
¿hay quien lee los mensajes que escriben los mineros abajo?
¿se pueden leer los mensajes?
'Perón es nuestra única esperanza' dice uno (1980: 17)

Much of the poem functions as a slide show, cutting from one
image of the town and its mine to another, between one line and
the next. This technique draws on the influence that film and
photography had on the historical avant-gardes, and allows
Gelman to present the mine in flat and factual terms. Thus the
poem achieves the effect of documentary presentation. Within
this presentation, Gelman experiments with the difficulties of
writing for and about a perceived people. A movement down into
a mineshaft – a concentration on one point and a movement into
the deep – and across the walls of caves – not only physically out
but also into the environment of work – questions the communi-
cative ability of the lyric (the vertical axis) and epic (the horizon-
tal axis). The poem suggests that certain forms of writing are
preferred to others. The poem itself is read, while the miners'
writings, underground, are not, except in the context of this
poem. Gelman's poem then suggests the role of the poet as the
conveyor of the everyday reality of the worker, given that this
reality is excluded from the lives of most people – by distance
('encima de la tierra') or literacy ('¿se puede leer?'). The poet
thus unites the two axes, the lyric and the epic. However, problem-
atically, the poem builds up to one *graffito* that is less prosaic than
the others: '"Perón es nuestra única esperanza"'. Thus, the min-
ers' writings and the poet's presentation of the writings of the
miners are firmly inscribed within Peronism, in particular a
personalist and populist Peronism from the 1960s and 1970s,
most publicly exemplified by the Montoneros. Hence the poet's
work is firmly circumscribed within the project of organizing

Peronist resistance, often in militarized form, to the various post-
and anti-Perón governments, such as the *Revolución Libertadora*
(1955–7) or the *Revolución Argentina* (1966–73).

The possibilities of communication or intellectual leadership
that Gelman's work suggests had largely been closed off by the
time of Perlongher's writing. Perlongher's work comes after the
massacre at Ezeize, the rejection of the FLH by the Peronist Youth
in the 1970s and the purge of left-wing Peronists between 1973
and 1976. The Montonero struggle ended with an ill-fated
counter-offensive against the *proceso* that saw its numbers deci-
mated, while organized Peronism, although electorally powerful,
remained politically scattered as a party until its return in neo-
liberal, Menemist form in 1989. Perlongher's poetry emerges
from an era when the problem of organizing resistance had been
supplanted by the problem of the overwhelming nature of
certain discourses: the *proceso* dictatorship's discourse of the
medical cleansing of society and the discourse of the transition to
democracy, that full access to global market capitalism would
allow everyone to live in peace. Thus the politics that Perlongher
chooses to present, using the avant-garde elements drawn from
Gelman, is a personal and desiring politics on the margins, in
keeping with his focus on desire rather than party politics.

Perlongher's Other Genealogy

Alongside those authors who Perlongher identified as important
for his poetic project, there are two writers not mentioned by
Perlongher who I feel to be identifiable poetic presences in the
Argentine's work. Both are connected, perhaps loosely or in a
marginal fashion, to avant-garde groups in Latin America. These
writers, not to my knowledge studied critically in relation to
Perlongher, provide central techniques and tools for his poetry.

Expanding the Poetic Lexicon: César Vallejo

During the 1970s Perlongher was engaged in sexual-political
activism. In his work with the FLH, in which he led a cell known as
'Eros', and in particular in the publication of the limited circula-
tion magazine *Somos* (1973–6), it is possible to detect distinctly

vanguard activity. After abortive attempts by the FLH at vindica-
tion within Peronism, Perlongher states that *Somos* was an attempt
to reconnect the political and intellectual activities of the group
with a broader gay audience: 'A fines de 1973, el FLH consideró
llegado el momento de prestar un poco más atención a la
comunidad homosexual, descuidado entre tanto activismo
político, y decidió la edición de la revista *Somos*' (1997b: 81 [1985,
Buenos Aires]). *Somos* ran to eight editions, with a maximum
circulation of 500, was badly printed and distributed by hand. Its
aim, in the words of Perlongher, was to be 'un instrumento de
trabajo concientizador' (82). Its collection of theoretical docu-
ments, literature and information aimed to create a community,
also illustrated by their publication of the document '"Sexo y
Liberación", especie de compendio teórico-ideológico del libera-
cionismo gay argentino' (82). *Somos*, put together in secret (82),
was a sign of resistance and provocation to the government and
the police, who were both actively engaged in preventing homo-
sexual or suspected homosexual activities. Also, in true vanguard
fashion, it aimed to cause a scandal. Perlongher proudly recalls
that, 'una de sus iniciativas más brillantes – la publicación de los
términos con que se alude al coito en la Argentina (más de cien)
– fue recibida escandalizadamente por los lectores' (82). This
initiative suggests a two-pronged effort. Firstly, the publication of
such types of slang attempts to stabilize a vocabulary for talking
about a given subject, specifically sex. Secondly, such a vocabulary
attempts to create a common linguistic community of those who
understand the terms. Alongside the 'trabajo concientizador',
Perlongher and the FLH's work can be seen attempting to create
a linguistic community that coincided with and united a homo-
sexual community, similar to the type of communities we saw
Perlongher creating space for in the last chapter. In Perlongher's
earliest work there is a clear exhibition of avant-garde aims –
connecting art to society, provoking the public – with a focus on
marginal and secretive groups in Buenos Aires.

In a similar vein Perlongher assessed the circumstances of
poetic production in the late 1970s and early 1980s in his essay
'Argentina's Secret Poetry Boom' (1992, London). 'It is well
known that poetry does not sell a great deal. What fewer people
realize, however, is that it does circulate well [. . .] like a network
of stamp-collectors exchanging the typographical minutiae of

verse' (1992: 178). Perlongher's explanation is related to the political situation in Argentina:

> The end of the seventies saw the emergence in Argentina of an interesting phenomenon: the proliferation of poets. [. . .] [T]his phenomenon seemed to be attributable to the enforced fall in political activism, due to the necessarily clandestine nature – imposed by the bloody military coup of 1976 – of mass militancy typical of the seventies [. . .]. The radius of action is intense, but quite limited. There are practically no links between poetic writing and the masses, and certainly not through television [. . .]. Another important element in this current abundance is the solitude imposed by the destruction of the political and micropolitical networks of contact achieved by the dictatorship of 1976; a strong introversion which favoured the appearance of muses. In those years writing was an outlet. Writing poetry, then, favoured the cyphered and refined manner of the mannerist code. (178)

Perlongher describes a poetics of the late 1970s that, away from the overtly political poetry of Leónidas Lamborghini or Juan Gelman, tended towards the secretive, the coded, and the personal. The poets involved in this production tended to congregate around literary reviews, for example *Último Reino*. However, as we see both in Perlongher's reference to the *coup d'état* and in the other cultural manifestations discussed above, even this small and personal production is heavily informed by the contemporary political situation. What is key in this early production seems to be linguistic creation of small, almost tribal groups with a shared vocabulary.

These sorts of techniques, in particular the creation of a common lexicon, can be seen in Perlongher's early poetry, as in the poem 'Canción de amor para los nazis en Baviera':

> [. . .]
> Más acá o más allá de esta historieta
> estaba tu pistola de soldado de Rommel
> ardiendo como arena en el desierto
> un camello extenuado que llegaba al oasis
> de mi orto u ocaso o crepúsculo que me languidecía
> y yo sentía el movimiento de tu svástica en las tripas
> oh oh oh (Perlongher, 1997a: 26–7 [1980, Buenos Aires])

The poem, perhaps in rather simplistic fashion, engages in an attempt to display sexual and corporeal metaphors. Key here is the pun on 'orto'. Alongside 'ocaso' (sunset) and 'crepúsculo' (dusk), it should mean sunrise. However, the dynamic relationship with 'crepús*culo*' reminds the reader of its *lunfardo* significance, specifically 'anus'. This then provides a textual centre for a proliferation of rude slang metaphors. 'Pistola', 'camello', and 'svástica' all become crude terms for penis, while 'oasis' and, more clearly, 'tripas' are also related to the anus. Perlongher's poem takes the technique used in *Somos* for creating a linguistic community, and demonstrates the expansion of the poem's vocabulary, whereby the poem includes sexual, obscene and homoerotic elements in a perhaps crudely secretive fashion.

While it is not perhaps obviously the case at first, such a technique has a clear predecessor in the work of the Peruvian poet César Vallejo (1892–1937). One of Vallejo's great legacies to Latin American poetry is his audacious attempt to expand the lexicon available to such writing, as demonstrated in the collection *Trilce* (1922) – its very title a striking neologism drawing on *dulce, triste, tres* and so forth – and well illustrated by poem XXXVI of the collection:

> Pugnamos ensartarnos por un ojo de aguja,
> enfrentados, a las ganadas.
> Amoniácase casi el cuarto ángulo del círculo.
> ¡Hembra se continúa el macho, a raíz
> de probables senos, y precisamente
> a raíz de cuanto no florece.
> ¿Por ahí estás, Venus de Milo?
> Tú manqueas apenas, pululando
> entrañada en los brazos plenarios
> de la existencia,
> de esta existencia que todaviiza
> perenne imperfección.
> Venus de Milo, cuyo cercenado, increado
> brazo revuélvese y trata de encodarse
> a través de verdeantes guijarros gagos,
> ortivos nautilos, aunes que gatean
> recién, vísperas inmortales.
> Laceadora de inminencias, laceadora
> del paréntesis.
> [. . .] (Vallejo, 1998b: 177)

Beyond the possible esoteric and metaphysical interpretations of this most dense of poems, Vallejo's piece performs the process of literary creation *linguistically*, demonstrating the need for a new poetic vocabulary and the means by which this may be made. The problematizing of stable binary givens – 'macho'–'hembra', for example – caused by the sexual-epiphanic moment of the first stanza, where the possibility of non-existent being is revealed, leads to the need for an artistic vocabulary and symbolic archive beyond that which already exists. Hence the figure of the Venus de Milo in the second stanza – an image of beauty that is imperfect, yet thus uniquely perfect – is revealed as possibly having full arms; not only does the description of this situation require a vocabulary full of neologisms and archaisms but it also suggests a process for the creation of new vocabulary through the breaking down of the barriers between the parts of speech:'todavía' becomes a verb – 'todaviiza' – with a construction highly unusual in Spanish, a double i, while 'aún' becomes a noun – 'aunes'. Thus for the description of an imminent situation, perpetually on the cusp of being, Vallejo coins a new poetic vocabulary that expands the terms available. Importantly, this highly obscure and difficult lexicon has a very similar communitarian effect to that used by Perlongher, whereby the expansion of the poetic lexicon creates an implied audience with access to the symbolic and metaphorical sources mined by the author, in Perlongher's case the hermetic poetic and homosexual circles of Buenos Aires, and in Vallejo's a Peruvian avant-garde engaged in attempts to renew poetic construction.

Vallejo was engaged in attempts not just to renovate the language available for the poem, but also to create an abject and fragmented identity for the narrative position. Such a technique can clearly be found in Perlongher's poem 'Herida pierna':

> Debo chupar?   mamar?   de ese otro seno   herido
>   desangrado   con la pierna cortada   con la daga
>   en la nalga   ah caminar así, rauda cual ráfaga
>   montañas de basuras mágicas y luminosas
>   ser lúcida?   ahora, hoy?
> *tumbada* cual yegua   borracha cual chancha   echada
>   cual vaca   animal   animal
> No me hagas caso, Morenito: vé y dile la verdad a tus padres
> (Perlongher, 1997a: 48 [1980, Buenos Aires])

The poem creates a fragmented narrative position, between the humiliated ('Morenito') and the humiliator.[6] The humiliated is placed in the position of the abject – physically knocked down ('*tumbada*'), forced to suck something ('chupar', 'mamar'), and physically injured ('cortada', 'desangrado'). However, at the same time Perlongher alternates between two apparently distinct first person positions ('Debo' / 'No me hagas caso'). Thus the reader is left uncertain as to the identity, individuality and distinctness of the different first person positions. One is forced to question the existence of the individual in the piece, and to see the potential complicity between the parties in violent relationships, in particular in terms of the pleasure gained from committing or suffering acts of violence. Perlongher's investigation of this violence relies heavily on being able to move in and out of a childish narrative position – the nickname 'Morenito' for example, or the relationship to 'padres'. In the Latin American context, Vallejo offers a key predecessor for such a technique, as in his famous poem 'A mi hermano Miguel, *in memoriam*' (1998a: 138 [1918]).

While in his cultivation of new poetic vocabulary and the development of an abject and fragmented narrative position Perlongher follows Vallejo's work closely, there are also revealing differences between their poetics. Perlongher's 'Herida pierna' also takes an attitude towards pain that shows clear masochist elements:

Por ella (de él)   debo adorarla?   suplicarla?   adosarla?
         cultivar el jardín donde se entierra
         como liendre una mata   Oh, ensartarla!
Debo poner la cara, larga, sobre la mesa?   puedo?
No me hagas caso, Morenito, no la hagas
así, tan prominente y espantosa   la herida   lo que hiende
         la penetración del verdugo durante el acto del suplicio
         durante la hora del dolor del calor
         de la sofocación   de los gemidos
impotente como potente bajo esa masa de tejidos
(Perlongher, 1997a: 47 [1980, Buenos Aires])

Again Perlongher alternates between narrative positions, in particular adopting the child–abject position; however, phrases such as 'impotente como potente' and the active seeking of humiliation and violence by one of the parties ('adorarla', 'suplicarla', 'suplicio'), alongside the later allusion to breathless sexual activity ('sofocación', 'gemidos') suggests that the position of victim is one sought for the purpose of masochistic *jouissance* and not merely forced on an innocent party.

Vallejo's attitude to pain and suffering, however, is radically different to that presented by Perlongher. His later poems open new possibilities for suffering as a focus for political poetry, as in 'Voy a hablar de la esperanza':

> Yo no sufro este dolor como César Vallejo. Yo no me duelo ahora como artista, como hombre ni como simple ser vivo siquiera. Yo no sufro este dolor como católico, como mahometano ni como ateo. Hoy sufro solamente. Si no me llamase César Vallejo, también sufriría este mismo dolor. Si no fuese artista, también lo sufriría. Si no fuese hombre ni ser vivo siquiera, también lo sufriría. Si no fuese católico, ateo, ni mahometano, también lo sufriría. Hoy sufro desde más abajo. Hoy sufro solamente [. . .]. (Jiménez, 2000: 121 [1939])

Vallejo's poem strips away the layers of human existence to reveal an essential core: suffering. This process is amplified by repetition – of names, religions and beings – and difference, in particular the change from present indicative to past subjunctive, as both certainty and possibility consist of suffering. This suffering exists below and before religion, illness and emotional state, and seems to represent a unifying substratum for all of humanity. In the poem 'Masa', this basis of suffering gains revolutionary socialist possibilities.

> Al fin de la batalla,
> y muerto el combatiente, vino hacia él un hombre
> y le dijo: '¡No mueras, te amo tanto!'
> Pero el cadáver ¡ay! siguió muriendo.
> [. . .]
> Acudieron a él veinte, cien, mil, quinientos mil,
> clamando: '¡Tanto amor y no poder contra la muerte!'
> Pero el cadáver ¡ay! siguió muriendo.
> [. . .]
> Entonces, todos los hombres de la tierra
> le rodearon; les vio el cadáver triste, emocionado;
> incorporóse lentamente.
> abrazó al primer hombre; echóse a andar. . .
> (Jiménez, 2000: 136 [1937])

Through difference and repetition, Vallejo's poem analyses human pain. In contrast to the poems of *Los heraldos negros*

(1918), here the poem, written after the Francoist uprising in Spain and the murder of Lorca in 1936, has the pain in solitude replaced with pain and love in solidarity, a firm statement of belief in the Socialist fraternity Vallejo felt he had seen in his visits to the Soviet Union in 1928 and 1929. Vallejo's work is thus exemplary of a tradition of political reengagement and literary experiment in Latin American twentieth-century poetry.

For Vallejo, poetry could find a position of ideological certainty within the intellectual left, with its links to the socialist movement, in Peru centred on the figure of the Marxist critic and political activist José Carlos Mariátegui (1894–1930) and the review *Amauta* (1926–30), which he founded and edited. This position was given further urgency by the fascist uprising in Spain, and the dominance of the extreme right elsewhere. But by the time of Perlongher's writing, the intellectual left in Argentina had splintered into several groups, each with finely distinct political positions. In addition, the late 1970s and early 1980s had seen exile physically split the Argentine left, often involving them in bitter disputes over the relative ideological and moral merits of exile or permanence, as discussed by Patiño (2003) in her assessment of left-wing journals in Argentina in the early 1980s.[7] Thus the possibility of the type of intellectual hegemony and unity suggested by Vallejo's poetry had been removed by the time of Perlongher's writing and so, instead of implying groups of the type normally formed by avant-garde practitioners, with shared literary and political goals, Perlongher's poetry suggests groups based firmly on desire.

Poesía social: Raúl González Tuñón

The poem 'Cadáveres' owes its remarkable force, I believe, to two key techniques, as demonstrated by its opening stanzas, which I cite again for the reader's convenience:

> Bajo las matas
> En los pajonales
> Sobre los puentes
> En los canales
> Hay Cadáveres
>
> En la trilla de un tren que nunca se detiene

En la estela de un barco que naufraga
En una olilla, que se desvanece
En los muelles los apeadores los trampolines los malecones
Hay Cadáveres
(Perlongher, 1997a: 111 [1984, Buenos Aires])

The first technique is its *phanopoeia*, or casting of visual images, discussed above as a slideshow effect. Here this is particularly striking, owing to the physically distanced points united in the text by the repetition of 'en' and by the shared appearance of corpses. The poem forces the reader to view dead bodies turning up where they should not. The second technique is the poem's *melopoeia*, its musical property[8] whereby the poem mixes a childlike rhythm and the more sombre tones of the *versos de arte mayor* in the second stanza, with the constant pseudo-*anapesto* proparoxytone tetrasyllable of 'Hay Cadáveres', which through repetition becomes the poem's refrain.[9] Thus the poem develops a repetitive and sombre music, that of the appearing corpses.

Perlongher offers his own story about the genesis of the poem 'Cadáveres' in an interview from 1992:

Yo estuve en Argentina en un momento en que estaban apareciendo los cadáveres y estaba horrible todo [. . .]. Claro, la sensación era que aparecían cadáveres continuamente: era la sensación del momento que había gente que hasta ese momento no hablaban del asunto, y de repente empezaba a contar que sabían que en la casa, que en la esquina tal se fusilaba, y que en el cementerio de no sé dónde se enterraba, y empezaron a aparecer como cataratas, ¿viste?, que hasta ese momento estaban como medio enterrados. Y por todas partes aparecían cadáveres.

(Friedemberg and Samoilovich, 1992: 31)

The poem thus emerges from the last, terminal stages of the *proceso* dictatorship, when increased civil and political unrest, coupled with the *junta*'s failure in the Malvinas/Falkland's war, led to greater pressure on issues such as political process and human rights.[10] Perlongher's quotation highlights the attempt in his poetry to include the everyday and the colloquial, the secret stories about experiences of the dictatorship that owing to censorship and controls on the circulation of information had not found formal expression within Argentina. This thematics, found also in the poetry of Gelman, above, alongside the sonic and visual aesthetics of 'Cadáveres' finds an even earlier predecessor in the work of Raúl González Tuñón (1905–74). González Tuñón provides an important link in Argentine poetry from the avant-gardes of the 1920s to the social poetry of the 1960s and 70s, and in particular his work from the 1930s demonstrates the same techniques Perlongher used in 'Cadáveres'. As an example, 'Surprise Party en Doorn' creates a hauntology[11] similar to Perlongher's, as corpses invade a party for the world's leaders and celebrities:

> Pero a las 3 – quién podía imaginarlo – dos regimentos de veteranos irrumpieron en el amplio salón. Eran mutilados de la gran guerra, ciegos, mancos, cojos, dementes.
> Los personajes regios se agruparon, en medio, y ellos los rodearon, los rodearon.
> Oh, qué tristeza aquella noche en Doorn.
> Basil Zaharoff, en su coche de inválidos, hizo esfuerzos para alejarlos.
> Pero ellos no se querían ir y avanzaban lentos y espantosos y cambiando de color se tornaron amarillos, verdes, violáceos y empezaron a pudrirse bajo sus uniformes.
> (González Tuñón, 1977: 60 [1934])

González Tuñón, like Perlongher, takes a possibly factual event, in his case the interruption of war veterans at a party, in Perlongher's the discovery of a corpse, and stretches it to fantastic lengths. Perlongher does this through placing corpses every-where; González Tuñón does this by making the corpses get up and walk, then reinforcing the strangeness of this image by having the zombies visibly rot and decay. Both attempt to reinforce the brutality of the respective regimes responsible, in González Tuñón's case the politicians and business leaders responsible for the Great War and, in Perlongher's case, the military leadership between 1976 and 1983.

In another poem from the 1930s, 'Algunos secretos del levan-tamiento de octubre' (1936), González Tuñón again predates Perlongher's poetics and aesthetics in 'Cadáveres', this time through a similar creation of *melopoeia*:

> Donde el carbón se junta con la sangre
> y la ametralladora bailarina
> lanza sus abanicos de metralla.
> Donde todo termina.
>
> Ya vienen las mujeres con sus hijos

de la mano, en los brazos y en el vientre.
Dentro del gran bostezo de la mina
crece un grisú de soledad ardiente.
Donde todo termina.

Apuntad bien y sobre el barro caigan
donde el terror se junta con la sangre.
Ya están ahí los mercenarios.
Donde todo termina.
(Altamirano, 1971: 17)

The poem, which like Perlongher's 'Cadáveres' bears a strong resemblance to Paul Celan's holocaust poem 'Todesfuge' (1952), describes the massacre of a group of protesting miners that took place in 1934 at the hands of Argentine state forces. To do this, González Tuñón uses a flat, alliterative, heptasyllable refrain which, like 'Hay Cadáveres', reiterates the mortal focus of the poem. However, González Tuñón differs from Perlongher on two other fronts. Firstly, he sticks more rigidly to traditional metrics; eleven and seven-syllable lines dominate his poem. This echoes, curiously, the *silva* form used by Luis de Góngora in his *Soledades* (1613); unlike Góngora, however, González Tuñón allows himself nine and five-syllable lines, the latter being used later in the poem for speech ('Oh veteranas'), thus demonstrating the need for a certain metrical freedom when dealing with social emergencies, and anticipating the dictates suggested by Mario Benedetti, above. In terms of rhyme, González Tuñón also follows a more rigid framework than Perlongher's largely unrhymed poem. 'sangre' repeats throughout the poem, and the 'mina' / 'termina' rhyme is emphasized by further 'i-a' endings ('ceniza'). New rhymes are introduced as the poem proceeds but the same initial pairs are reiterated throughout, thus allowing the poem to suggest a historical development but also a reinforcement of the initial image of the murder of workers. This poem, as part of its attempt at political denunciation, like many of González Tuñón's poems, takes advantage of neoclassical forms that function over the whole of the poem. Perlongher, on the other hand, uses internal rhymes, alliteration and assonance, and mixes various rhythms and metres, rather than attempting a unified metrical scheme.

Poems like 'Cadáveres', with its recounting of the appearance of the victims of the dictatorship, clearly draw on the work of González Tuñón and his use of classical poetics for the purpose of denouncing injustice and violence. However, Perlongher's poetry is not as formally rigid as González Tuñón, perhaps reflecting the freedom from metrical constraints that the post-vanguard poets enjoyed in Argentina.

Post-*poesía social*: Perlongher's Project

It is apparent from an examination of Perlongher's early work (the collections *Austria-Hungría, Alambres, Parque Lezama* and *Hule*) that there is a clear presence of vanguard poetics. The German theorist Peter Bürger is quite pessimistic about the possibilities for such neo-avant-garde art. Bürger (1984: 80–3) suggests that the aim of the European avant-gardes was to reintegrate art into the praxis of life, to remove the distance that exists in bourgeois society between the two. In relation to this, the historical avant-gardes demonstrate a clear political commitment in life and art: Breton and many surrealists were members of the French communist party;[12] Dada founder Tristan Tzara was an anarchist.[13] Titles of surrealist journals – *Révolution surréaliste, Le Surréalisme au service de la révolution* – leave little doubt about political commitment. At an artistic level, works like Tzara's cut-up poems criticize not only the role of the artist in bourgeois society but also capitalist values where the art object becomes a fetish and the signature is more important than the quality of the work itself. Moreover, the movements are heuristically linked to contempt for the social organization that had led to the First World War. In the *Manifesto of Surrealism* (1924), Breton makes the social role of the movement clear:

> Surrealism is based on the belief in the superior reality of certain forms of previously neglected associations, in the omnipotence of dream, in the disinterested play of thought. It tends to ruin once and for all all other psychic mechanisms and to substitute itself for them in solving the principal problems of life. (1974: 26)

Once the avant-gardes have staged this type of attempt at renovation, revealing the distance between art and life and art's paradoxical dependence on that distance for its liberty, there is little left that the neo-avant-gardes can offer, as Bürger suggests:

> All art that is more recent than the historical avant-garde movements must come to terms with this fact [being distanced

> from social praxis] in bourgeois society. It can either resign itself to
> its autonomous status or 'organize happenings' to break through
> that status. But without surrendering its claim to truth, art cannot
> simply deny the autonomous status and pretend that it has a direct
> effect. (1984: 57)

The neo-avant-gardes are easily subsumed into the market, with
newness becoming another brand or selling point. 'The neo-
avant-garde, which stages for a second time the avant-gardist
break with tradition, becomes a manifestation that is void of any
sense and that permits the positing of any meaning whatsoever'
(61). What then could be the purpose or value of Perlongher's
reuse of avant-garde techniques?

Firstly, it is important to stress the different context and genesis
of Latin American vanguard art to its European contemporary. In
Latin America the previous major artistic movement, *modernismo*,
emerged from struggles for independence, in the case of Cuba,
and over the direction that new nations would take, in the case of
Argentina after the fall of the dictator Juan Manuel de Rosas in
1852. One of the central figures of the first *modernista* generation
was José Martí (1853–95), the Cuban nationalist who combined
Parnassian aesthetics and poetics with patriotic themes, as in the
poem 'Dos patrias' (1891). If Martí is often contrasted with Rubén
Darío (1867–1916) in terms of the Cuban's political commitment
and the Nicaraguan's more aesthetic concerns, two aspects of
Darío's work are obscured in such an assessment. Firstly, the
Parnassian splendour in *Prosas profanas* (1896) attacked the utili-
tarian domination of the word by science and what Darío per-
ceived as mediocre values coming to dominate society. Secondly,
by the beginning of the twentieth century, Darío was writing
poems such as 'A Roosevelt' (from *Cantos de vida y esperanza*,
1905), a polemical address calling for Latin American solidarity –
a directly political poem.

In contrast to the situation in Europe, the Latin American
vanguards did not represent an upsurge in literary–political activi-
ties. In Argentina, the first clear vanguard manifestation occurred
with the publication of *Prisma*, (1921–2) a newspaper initially
stuck to trees and walls in Buenos Aires by Jorge Luis Borges and
some friends. *Prisma* was the organ of young writers wanting to
break with tradition and norms in literature, influenced by new
European literary techniques. They formed the group known as

Ultraísmo (1919–23). The aims of the group are summarized in Borges's manifesto of 1921: reduction of poetry to the metaphor; elimination of surplus adjectives and connectives; abolition of all ornament, including preaching (and thus political messages); and the synthesis of two or more images into one to broaden the power of suggestion of language (Verani, 1996: 122, Salvador, 1962: 36), as displayed in Borges's earliest poems. As Verani describes, members of the group went on to publish the review *Martín Fierro* (1919–27), central to artistic developments in Argentina and concentrating on 'irreverence, aggressiveness, playfulness and caustic irony' (Verani, 1996: 122).[14] Thus the central avant-garde group in Argentina did not attempt any of the political or social engagement exhibited by its European counterpart. Conversely, the more politically minded Boedo group (1920–40)[15] did not attempt a renovation of either the status or forms of art, but instead focused on content and politics, with many members actively involved in left-wing parties and groups. In Argentina the *-ismos* did not have the same mix of literary innovation and political reengagement as their European counterparts.

In the Latin American context, it was in the post-vanguard era or artists distanced from the organized avant-garde groups where more concrete attempts at the reengagement in life through politicization of poetry took place.[16] The poetry of César Vallejo, as seen above, demonstrates an attempt in the Peruvian context to renovate art and engage it in social praxis. In Argentina, poets such as González Tuñón and Gelman, also shown above, attempted to combine poetic innovation with political purpose for their work. Thus it is important in our assessment of the influence of the avant-garde in the work of Perlongher that we acknowledge the complexity of the relationship between avant-garde writing and political engagement in the Argentine context. In some ways the situation works as the reverse of Bürger's assessment of the European vanguards and clear engagement with the praxis of life and, with it, party politics comes only *after* the literary and linguistic experiment of the avant-garde. It was left for *poesía social* in Argentina, influenced by César Vallejo and others, as exhibited by Gelman, to engage in literary experiment *and* politics, often reconsidering the role of the poet in relation to society. In Perlongher's early work then we can conclude that there is a strong influence from these neo-avant-garde techniques.

Given the distinct development of the literary avant-gardes in Argentina, the adoption of avant-garde techniques in Perlongher's work does not represent the same redundant and tardy gesture that Bürger's writing might suggest.

It is intriguing that Perlongher in his writings never attempted to define the avant-garde, or *poesía social*, and instead reserved his analysis for the 'nuevo verso' or, later, the 'neobarroco/ neobarroso' to which he felt he belonged. However, Perlongher did name certain figures from the vanguards, as revealed in the pieces analysed above. What this reveals, I feel, alongside Perlongher's at times scattergun approach to the techniques of his avant-garde predecessors, is the importance that using recognizable names held for his attempts to familiarize readers with certain common reference points for his writings, and to provide a genealogy for his writing. Hence Gelman, Molina and Girondo offer Argentine names as a synecdoche for a range of poetic practices – using everyday language, writing about sex or perversion, mixing avant-garde techniques with political denunciation – that create shared reference points between Perlongher and a community of readers also familiar with such writers, or who become familiar with certain techniques and thematics through Perlongher's namechecking. Artaud provides international validation for this project, a figure, alongside other marginal French dramatists such as Jean Genet and Alfred Jarry, increasingly respected by experimental theatre practitioners and intellectuals after his death, and a form of validation for Perlongher's attempts to include the ultraphysical and the irrational in his poetry. Meanwhile Vallejo and González Tuñón provide concrete techniques for experimental poetry related to its political circumstances but in which Perlongher is allowed a certain artistic freedom. Perlongher's early poetry draws on those figures who while having links to the vanguard groups were also to a certain degree outsiders, as in the case of Artaud, who was expelled from the surrealists, Vallejo, who was never directly part of a vanguard group, or Molina, linked to the rather disparate surrealist group in Argentina. In many ways this offers another validation for Perlongher's own political position. In the 1970s, as mentioned above, Perlongher was involved in sexual–political activism, with the FLH; in the late 1970s Perlongher was part of the 'secret poetry boom'; both represent the kind of group activity associated with avant-garde art. However, one must also consider the links between this activity and the rock music subculture of Buenos Aires in the 1970s. The sociologist Juan José Sebreli details the practical links between rockers, hippies and gays:

> La maquinaria policial tenía que justificar su existencia manteniéndose en permanente actividad [in the 1970s]. Las comisarías tenían su 'cuota' diaria de sospechosos a detener [. . .]. [N]o quedaban otros blancos en las calles que los drogadictos – que en realidad eran escasos –, los hippies, los alcohólicos y los homosexuales, quienes se convirtieron de ese modo en las víctimas obligadas de las razzias. (1997: 326)

The links between homosexuals, hippies and rockers, most often the victims of police raids and violence in the 1970s, had, according to Sebreli, an influence on the constitution of Perlongher's sub-section, or 'cell', within the FLH, 'Eros':

> Este grupo tenía una tendencia más literaria y una orientación irracionalista – influencia del surrealismo y de Georges Bataille – que lo hacía más atractivo para la afluencia a él de los hippies, y llega a participar en 1973 con los rockeros del grupo Parque, que se reunían en el Parque Avellaneda. (334)

Sebreli makes the link between Perlongher's artistic leanings towards surrealism, his political activism and the hippy and rock movement. In fact, rock music in Argentina exhibits several key traits of vanguard activity. Its production is almost always communal; it is constantly engaged in processes of renovation; it is self-aware in terms of its relationship to an audience, society and consumers; it is often directly political, as in the anarchism of punk; and it runs the same risk of becoming institutionalized as Bürger detected in the change from vanguard to neo-vanguard art. Furthermore, both the FLH and the writers of *XUL* and *Último reino* were linked through personnel, such as Perlongher, and marginal position, to the underground of rock music and hippy activity that had appeared in Buenos Aires in the late 1960s and 1970s, as described by Anguita and Caparrós (1997: 133–4; 391–9). In Perlongher's early poetry we find a strong influence from musical vanguards, less in terms of poetics but more perhaps as an ideal of marginal rebellion, a form of cultural production linked to urban vagrancy, marginal groups, and drug taking, as described in the short story 'Evita vive', dealt with in chapter 1.

For much of the 1970s rock represented a key space of marginal resistance. The first hippies appeared in Buenos Aires in

1967; as early as 1968 'extraños de pelo largo' were being arrested (Puente and Quintana, 1988: 23). They had thematic and ideological links to the Beats and Ginsberg, Romantic rebellion, and, particularly in the lyrics of Alberto 'Flaco' Spinetta, the techniques of surrealism.[17] Rock provided a popular space for the treatment of sexuality, for example the frequently censored band *Polifemo* (51) or Spinetta's 'Me gusta ese tajo' (51). Furthermore, there was a space for alternative ways of thinking to conservative rationalism: 'las causas de la locura [in 70s rock lyrics] pueden ubicarse en situaciones de marginamiento' (59). These features, as we have seen, are closely linked to Perlongher's adoption of avant-garde poetics. Perlongher's early poetry and literary activity can be seen engaged in an attempt to reengage art with life, an attempt that is linked to groups such as the hippies and the *rockeros*. Perlongher commented on the importance of rock to the 'new poetry', and by implication his own early work, in Argentina in the late 1970s and early 80s in an article co-written with Alberto Nigro (1980), where the authors stated that 'las fuentes tradicionales de provision de poetas – estudiantes de letras, lánguidos adolescentes introvertidos – se ven enriquecidos por el bullicio de roqueros' (1980: 64). However, Perlongher later abandoned rock as an influence – the article with Nigro was not included in his authorized bibliography and he never mentioned the subject again in his essays, except to deny its importance (D. Molina, 1988: 17). Furthermore, he began later in his career to dismiss surrealism, as in an interview with Friedemberg and Samoilovich (1992).[18]

Perlongher's friend and literary executor, Roberto Echavarren, a writer greatly interested in the sexual politics of rock, makes a telling observation in his introduction to the 1999 Spanish edition of Perlongher's prostitution thesis: 'El *punk*, el *rocker*, el *hip-hopper*, son "espontáneos", en principio no están hechos para que los miren los adultos, sino para mirarse a sí mismos dentro de un grupo joven. El prostituto, señala Perlongher, se contamina de rasgos musicales' (1999: ix). Echavarren's words suggest styles of music and relevant dress as a narcissistic method of community building. If we can see Perlongher's interest in rock subculture as linked to possible homosexual liberation, and then later in its links to his anthropological research, we can suggest that this interest would disappear along with his interest in homosexuality itself as a topic, as outlined below in chapter 4. Perlongher mentioned the possible negative effects of drugs as a form of ecstasy – a typical technique of rockers and hippies – as demonstrated by the films *Drugstore Cowboy* and *Sid & Nancy* (1997b: 163–4 [1990, Paris]), which both betray the bohemian's descent into self-destruction, which he called '*éxtasis descendentes*, destructores del cuerpo físico' (163). Furthermore, Perlongher's words in his essay 'La desaparición de la homosexualidad' (1991c), where he suggests that homosexuality had become just another option in society, strongly echo Puente and Quintana's words on rock: 'hoy [1988] usar el pelo largo o teñido de verde escandaliza a unos pocos; los pantalones ajustados y las minifaldas son moneda corriente' (1988: 13). Both, then, have become diluted in the market place. Malcolm Cowley (2002: 313–16) points out that the marginal and offensive, in particular the bohemian lifestyle, can easily become mainstream with the course of years, while Thomas Frank (2002: 316–27) studies the relationship between 1960s bohemian US art – the work of Ginsberg or the Yippies – and the punk ethos – Henry Rollins in particular – and argues these rebellious elements are innately recuperable to capitalism. Vitally, the lyrics of Charly Garcia, 'Flaco' Spinetta et al. had popularized a certain version of surrealism and avant-garde literary techniques such as neologisms and shocking juxtapositions, which perhaps for Perlongher made the literary vanguard less interesting as a tool for his poetic project. The later marketing of a form of drug-inspired surrealism within *rock nacional*, as illustrated by the lyrics of Soda Stereo,[19] which after the banning of British rock during the Falklands/Malvinas conflict became a standard commercial expression of Argentine youth culture, exhibits the process whereby the marginal is ghettoized within the market, as discussed by Perlongher in an interview with Ulanovsky (1990: 11). This, alongside the increasing dissipation of the marginal groups to which Perlongher had belonged in the 1970s, I believe is an important factor for Perlongher's move away from avant-garde techniques. Nevertheless, the avant-garde represents a key source of poetics in Perlongher's early poetry, key both to his poetic practices and his construction of a community of readers.

NOTES

1   Some of the material in this chapter was dealt with in a different form in my papers, 'Perlongher and Surrealism: Opposites and the Individual Self', *Arara* (Winter 2001); 'Evitá hablar de la política: Multiple critical readings of Perlongher's "Evita vive"', *Tesserae: Journal of Iberian and Latin American Studies* vol. 9 no. 1 (2003), available at *www.tandf.co.uk/journals*; and 'Perlongher and the Avant-garde: Privileged Interlocutors and Inherited Techniques', *Hispanic Review* vol. 73 no. 2 pp. 157–84. In the last case, I am grateful to the University of Pennsylvania Press for their permission to reuse some of this material.

2   See, for example, Perlongher, 1997b: 14 [1989], 97–100 [1991], 1984, 1983b, 1983c, Perlongher and Nigro, 1980, Friedemberg and Samoilovich, 1992: 32.

3   On the European avant-gardes, see in particular Bürger, 1984; on the Latin American avant-gardes see Verani, 1996; Salvador, 1962; Vich, 2000; Unruh, 1994; for a broad introduction to Latin American surrealism, see Baciu, 1974.

4   Kosofsky Sedgwick's (1985) central example is Manet's painting *Déjeuner sur l'herbe* (1863), where the nude woman between the two men represents both the gift and the subject of conversation. It is the woman who looks straight at the painter, but the men who make the decisions. José Amícola illustrates Sedgwick's argument with a *cordobés* joke: a man is on a desert island with Claudia Schiffer. Fearing they might be the last two people alive, the two have sex to continue the species. After the act, the man asks Schiffer to pretend to be another man. It's one thing making love to the most beautiful woman in the world but the real pleasure, Amícola concludes, is having another man to brag to (Amícola, 2000: 19n).

5   This essay, published in *El porteño* in 1984, was originally presented as a paper at a conference held by the Centro de Estudos e Assistência Sexual, São Paulo, in 1983.

6   The poem also draws on Osvaldo Lamborghini's short story 'El niño proletario', from *Sebregondi retrocede* (1973), which details the rape and murder of a proletarian boy by three upper-class boys. Like much of Lamborghini's work, the story revels in both political allusions and sexual violence.

7   Patiño (2003) suggests a splintering between four groups: politically independent reviews such as *El Porteño* (1982–92), to which Perlongher contributed frequently, voicing pro-democratic and human rights based concerns; the more politically nationalist reviews such as *Sitio* (1981–7), to which Perlongher also contributed, but with whom he broke over its apparent support for the military during the Falklands/Malvinas conflict; progressive, pro-democracy left-wing reviews such as *Punto de vista* (1978–), which saw themselves as post-Marxist and pro-democratic and supported many of Alfonsín's liberal policies; and the more left-wing, Marxist publications such as

Pie de página (1983–5) and *Praxis* (1983–6), which criticized those who believed that only 'possible utopias' could be sought. Perlongher's position as an exile in Brazil further removed him from the possibility of contributing to organized intellectual politics.

8   See Pound (1954: 15–40) for an explanation of *melopoeia, phanopoeia,* and *logopoeia,* which he regards as the three modes of poetry.

9   See Quilis (1969) chapter 1 for an explanation of these metrical forms.

10 The Argentine psychologist Hugo Vezzetti is clear in linking the change in public opinion regarding the dictatorship to the failure of the Malvinas campaign. He remarks that, 'the emergence of human rights discourse as the public sphere emerged after the defeat in the Malvinas' (2002: 164). 'The defeat in the Malvinas also produced its street demonstrations as reactions against humiliation and deception. This was effectively when the *desaparecidos* were discovered, and it was then that justice and rights were reintroduced into society' (164–5). Perlongher's words are echoed in vaguer fashion by the linguist Lucrecia Escudero Chauvel: 'había también muchos argentinos que se resistían a la guerra y se ponían en duda la información que recibíamos. Pero curiosamente estas voces encontraban poco eco en los medios. [There was also] una "información de afuera", que circulaba entre todos pero de la que ninguno quería hacerse cargo' (1996: 25). The information about which she speaks includes the existence of concentration camps in cities (25) and the disappearance of thousands of people; these whispered rumours became the 'catarata' of shocking revelations after the conflict that Perlongher mentions.

11 See Derrida (1994) for an analysis of the concept of 'hauntology'. Derrida suggests that haunting points to the excess uncontained by any binary or dialectical logic. His *Spectres of Marx* is framed by a quote from Stirner: 'Mensch, es spukt in deinem kopfe'.

12 In the Second Surrealist Manifesto Breton stated his revolutionary commitment: 'I really fail to see – some narrow-minded revolutionaries notwithstanding – why we should refrain from supporting the Revolution, provided we view the problems of love, dreams, madness, art, and religion from the same angle as they do' (1974: 140 [1930]). He confirmed his 'allegiance to the principle of historical materialism' (142). Despite his problems in gaining acceptance from the French Communist Party, he committed the surrealists to the revolution: 'we shall prove ourselves fully capable of doing our duty as revolutionaries' (142).

13 Commenting on the genesis of the Cabaret Voltaire, Tzara observed: 'we proclaimed our disgust [...] This war [WW1] was not our war [...] Dada was born from an urgent moral need, from an implacable desire to attain a moral absolute, from the deep feeling that man, at the centre of all creations of the spirit, must affirm his supremacy over notions emptied of all human substance, over dead objects and ill-gotten gains [...] Honour, Country, Morality, Family, Art, Religion, Liberty, Fraternity, I don't know what, all these notions had

once answered to human needs, now nothing remained of them but a skeleton of conventions, they had been divested of their initial content' (from 'Introduction', Tzara, 1975). In 1929 Tzara, like Vallejo, visited Russia. In 1935 he joined the French Communist Party. He was involved in the Spanish Civil War on the side of the Republicans, and worked as secretary of the Madrid Committee for the Defence of Culture in 1937.

14   Other magazines in the Argentine vanguard included *Proa*, concentrating on literary renovation (three editions between 1922 and 1923) and *Inicial*, running to eleven editions (1923–7).

15   Roberto Mariani, involved in *Boedo* publications such as *Claridad* and *Extrema Izquierda*, produced the following taxonomy of the *Florida/Boedo* divide: *Florida/Boedo; vanguardismo/izquierdismo; ultraísmo/realismo; Martín Fierro, Proa/Extrema Izquierda, Los Pensadores, Claridad;* la greguería/el cuento y la novela; la metáfora/el asunto y la composición (Salvador, 1962: 68). While the *Boedo* group were interested in reengaging literature and politics, they did not demonstrate a distinct approach to the techniques of writing.

16   An exception is the *Amauta* group surrounding Mariátegui in Peru, committed from an ideological basis of socialism. Mariátegui saw art as very much a social activity, writing that '[n]o aesthetics can reduce artistic creation to a question of technique [. . .] And formal conquests are not enough to satisfy an artistic revolution' (from 'Arte, revolución y decadencia' [Verani, 1996: 129 (1926)]).

17   Spinetta recorded an album in 1973 called *Artaud*. Puente and Quintana (1988: 27) draw attention to Spinetta's surrealist-tinged lyrics, such as from the song 'Muchacha (ojos de papel)' (79). Similarly, Charly García's piece 'Serú Girán' adopts certain vanguard literary techniques, such as neologisms and portmanteau words: (113 [1978]).

18   Perlongher, questioned about the connections between his more delirious works and the surrealists, was keen to stress the 'diferencia de que yo intento, con esa especie de inclinación barroco, darle un poco más de rigor, y no dejar un puro flujo donde valga todo' (Friedemberg and Samoilovich, 1992: 32).

19   See, for example, 'En la ciudad de la furia', with its drug-inspired flights and cityscapes (from the album *Comfort y música para volar. Soda Stereo Unplugged* [1996]), or 'Un misíl en mi placard' and its surprising image of domestic space under threat.

Chapter 4

Perlongher and the *Travesti*[1]

Introduction

In the chapters so far I have examined Perlongher's poetic creation of space and the development of his poetics of border-crossing and nomadism; I have also examined the avant-garde writers Perlongher identifies as literary predecessors or upon whose techniques and poetics he draws in his attempts to trace desire in the social; in this chapter I aim to examine a concrete subject in Perlongher's poetry, specifically the figure of the *travesti*.

I choose the term *travesti*, a term that appears frequently in Perlongher's poetry and essays, as an umbrella word to describe and connect a number of different but closely related themes and aesthetics: cross-dressing, or wearing the clothes socially appropriate for the opposite sex to one's own; drag, or the performance of dressing up as a member of the opposite sex, often as part of a theatrical show; and transvestism, the medical term for those who feel compelled to wear clothes more appropriate to the opposite sex. The *travesti* in Perlongher's work, and more generally in Argentina, is a figure closely related not only to local sexual practices and identity politics, but also to economic necessity and class issues. Thus I am not discussing here the transvestite as described by Lesley Gordon in his/her *Aspects of Gender*: 'Homosexuals are rarely transvestites and only the rare transvestite is homosexual. Homosexuals, after all, are men looking for other men as love objects, not women, or ersatz women'. The difficulty of such an essentialist approach is apparent in Gordon's assertion that transvestites 'in general terms [. . .] are genuine males who function as such, are generally heterosexual and do not necessarily or inevitably or are even likely to want abandon their male lifestyle' (1995: 4–7).

Perlongher initially used the figure of the *travesti* in his short story 'Evita vive' (1975) to question the unity of individual identity, human body and sex and, thus, explore the at times dangerous and persecuted space of those whose sexual identity is excluded by laws such as the Buenos Aires *edictos policiales* against cross-dressing, vagrancy and homosexuality. To a similar effect Perlongher's early poems mount grammatical attacks on fixed and binary models of gender and sexuality, and create a thematics of bodily adornment and change that questions any stable relationship between one's biological sex and one's gender. In the first half of the 1980s, Perlongher's *travesti* figures take on an increasingly political edge, closely related to Perlongher's anarchism. However his poems written after the emergence of AIDS as a serious threat in Argentina and Brazil (around 1985) are marked by an association of transvestism to mimesis – pretending to *be* a woman, rather than using *travesti* techniques to question the stability of the terms 'man' or 'woman'. Later in his career Perlongher abandoned the theme of sexuality and turned towards mystical themes. We find, however, in poems from his mystical phase, a return to the gender-crossing aesthetics of the earlier poems and an attempt to create a poetics of the in-between – as we saw in chapter 2 – using both mystical and transvestite elements. This return reveals the continued importance of *travesti* aesthetics in Perlongher's work.

Three key stages can thus be outlined in Perlongher's work with regard to the *travesti*, the stages that provide the titles for the sections below. Firstly, in the 1970s, there is a relationship and dialogue with feminism; secondly, in the early 1980s, Perlongher's poetry offers an examination of the politics of desire. It is important here to reassert the significance of desire for Perlongher. For Perlongher, desire, 'deseo', was an umbrella term that included but was not exclusive to homosexuality, sexuality, perversion, and pleasure. Desire for Perlongher, throughout his career, was that which made human beings connect, create and move. Desire is for Perlongher that which escapes, flows, runs and connects, and is perhaps the key trait of his early portrayal of *travestis*. The third and final stage in Perlongher's portrayal of the *travesti*, dating from the late 1980s and until Perlongher's death in

1992, is the mystical phase. Although strictly speaking the *travesti* is thematically absent, it is important to assess the degree to which the *travesti* still informs Perlongher's poetics and aesthetics.

I aim then to answer a number of questions in this chapter. How does Perlongher define the *travesti* poetically? Why is the *travesti* important for Perlongher's poetry? How does his portrayal of the *travesti* develop? Why do any changes occur?

Becoming Evita: Perlongher and Feminism

In chapter 1, I outlined Perlongher's story 'Evita vive', in which Perlongher describes Eva Duarte de Perón's fictional reappearance, several years after her death, amongst marginal groups in Buenos Aires linked by illegal sexual practices, drugs and police harassment. In the story's three sections, in which Evita exists as a sexual and physical ghost, Perlongher uses *travesti* aesthetics and thematics in order to question the division of human beings along sex and gender lines. This questioning demonstrates clear similarities to the efforts of contemporary feminists inside and outside Argentina, who also, amongst other aims, sought societal change that would allow human beings to follow desire – through extramarital or homosexual relationships, for example – without legal or personal harassment.

In 'Evita vive' Perlongher's use of *travestis* to question the stratification of gender operates in three key areas. Firstly, he describes characters who alter their gender through language or behaviour, and demonstrates how this challenges binary sex and gender. In the first section, Perlongher's narrator describes herself throughout in the feminine and is addressed in the feminine by others ('preciosa', 'querida', 'puta') but also calls herself 'una marica' (1997b: 191–2) and is thus, by implication, a homosexual and effeminate man. However such attempts to describe the narrator as masculine sit awkwardly with the apparent comfort with which she adopts the feminine gender. Furthermore, there is a formal subversiveness in certain ungrammaticalities in her narration: 'se las cortó [her nails] para que el pedazo inmenso que tenía el marinero me entrara más y más, y ella entretanto le mordía las tetillas y gozaba, así de esa manera era como más gozaba' (192). Not only does the section describe perverse sexual intercourse – purely for pleasure, non-reproductive, homosexual on two counts (a woman with two men, one of whom describes herself as a woman) – but it also leaves the reader with no obvious solution to the question of who is enjoying ('gozaba') the sexual activity. Evita, the narrator and Jimmy could all be the subject of the verb 'gozaba'. It is also very hard to envisage exactly what position the bodies are adopting. Thus the individual body, individual identity and fixed sexual identity are all called into question in the presentation of *travesti* characters in 'Evita vive'.

Secondly, we see how attempts to assert rigid distinctions in terms of sex, sexuality or gender fail. In the third section we see Chiche, a 'chongo' – a lower-class male stud who has sex with men, sometimes for money, but who insists on his own hetero-sexuality – who is intent on asserting such gender divisions. Grammatically, he divides male and female ('todos – y todas', 'nos[otros ... viejos y viejas' (194)) where Spanish grammar would happily allow an undifferentiated group of 'viejos' even if the group consisted of men and women, thus demonstrating a desire to maintain the divides between the sexes. Furthermore, he attempts wherever possible to label homosexual characters – 'Alex el putito', 'el puto Francis' (194) – through nicknames that stress the male and the homosexual. As Acevedo suggests:

> [E]l taxiboy – generalmente un ser que, como todo machista, se identifica demagógicamente con la heterosexualidad y aspira a casarse con alguna 'noviecita buena' – puede servir de ejemplo para ilustrar una posible – y poco auspiciosa – evolución de la actitud erótica del conjunto social: el objetivo del acto sexual, que desde la moral tradicional es centrada en la procreación, se desempeña – sin pasar por el placer en sí – hacia la ganancia económica. (*Somos* 1974, in Acevedo, 1985: 208)

In both the above cases, the homosexual is designated through a term that is derogatory but also clearly intended for a person who is masculine in gender, as opposed to the term 'marica', described immediately above. In one case the diminutive ('el putito') reasserts the physical inferiority of the effeminate homosexual. Moreover Chiche is proud of his manhood (concentrated in 'el pedazo que tengo', the big penis he boasts about throughout the third section) and his sexual prowess, particularly his repetitive skills, a valuable commodity for a male prostitute ('con tres polvachos la dejé hecha') (194). However, even he cannot stop the sliding nature of sexual identity. His attempts to clarify the gender of Evita, by calling her 'mina [. . .] mujer, mujer' (193–4), only accentuate the prevalent uncertainty, as they smack of over-protestation. His own name, Chiche, sits uncomfortably mid-gender, while even his organ takes on a grammatically feminine gender ('la chupaba'(193)): the very symbol of masculinity is feminine. Thus Perlongher demonstrates how even the most extreme displays of machismo and masculinity cannot exclude the uncertain nature of sex, gender and sexuality.

The third area of Perlongher's sexual subversion in 'Evita vive' is that the version of Eva Duarte de Perón is very much like a *travesti*. If we take the narrator of the first tale as Perlongher's presentation of a *travesti* ethos and aesthetic, then a number of key techniques characterize the *travesti*. Firstly, the narrator uses clothing to perform gender and identity. Secondly, s/he creates a public scandal through provocative and wild behaviour. Thirdly, the narrator is sexually proactive, picking up men and instigating sexual intercourse. On all three counts Perlongher's Evita fits: throughout 'Evita vive' she is described through clothes and accessories such as her 'bretel' (strap), her 'rodete' (bun), her long green nails, her make-up, and her 'trusa' (underwear). Secondly, in the second section Evita's scandalous provocation of the police ('"Pero pedazo de animal, ¿cómo vas a llevar presa a Evita?"' [193]) or her quasi-political speech ('"Grasitas, grasitas míos, Evita lo vigila todo, Evita va a volver por este barrio para que no les hagan nada a sus descamisados"' [193–4]), Evita creates the same type of embarrassing public scene as the *travesti* narrator of the first section creates in her fight with la Lelé (191). Thirdly, Perlongher's Evita undertakes a fully participative role in sex. This is not to say that she occupies the supposedly 'macho', insertive role so often (symbolically) sought by those exercising political power in Argentina,[2] simply that she initiates and appears to relish sexual activity as an exercise of desire and bodily intensity. In the first tale she seems to have picked up Jimmy of her own initiative. Chiche notes that 'era una puta ladina', a backhanded compliment to Evita's (oral) sexual prowess (194). As Mexican sociologists Alonso and Koreck (1993:116) point out, whereas the active/passive, *chingón/chingada* framework stages anal or vaginal intercourse as exercising superiority over the recipient, oral sex suggests a degree of equality and confuses notions of activity and passivity. Perlongher extends this by offering a depiction of oral sex within a deeply confused gender framework. Moreover and, perhaps, most importantly, Evita looks like a *travesti*; she is mistaken for a *travesti* by Chiche, as he asks her '"Seguro que no sos un travesti, preciosura [. . .] Dejame tocarte la conchita, a ver si es cierto"' (194). Thus Perlongher demonstrates the similarities between the most important woman in Argentine politics in the twentieth century and the *travesti*.

'Evita vive' thus reveals the importance of desire to the functioning of politics. If the relationship between a cruising *travesti* and a macho *chongo* or sailor on shore leave, as described in 'Evita vive', might be seen as an example of desire in its purest form, uncontrolled by social mores or the law, Perlongher's story draws parallels between such clear displays of desire and the functioning of politics in Argentina, in particular the relationship between the Argentine public and Evita. Not only does the love expressed by the Peronist masses for their 'standard bearer' become sexualized and desiring but also the hatred of Evita and Juan Perón expressed by the various anti-Peronist revolutions, such as the *Revolución Libertadora* (1955) or the *Revolución Argentina* (1966), is displayed as sadistically desiring, as exemplified by the brutal beating that the police officers give to Chiche as they order him to forget about Evita (1997b: 195).

These two effects of Perlongher's use of the *travesti* in the text – questioning binary divisions between sex and gender, and linking desire to politics – draw important parallels with contemporary Argentine feminism, a socio-political movement which like the FLH was campaigning against the violent patriarchy operating in Argentina in the 1970s. Leonor Calvera's *Mujeres y feminismo en la Argentina* (1990) charts the 'new wave' of feminism in the 1970s working with the radical North American feminism of Kate Millett's *Sexual Politics* (1970) or Shulamith Firestone's *The Dialectic of Sex* (1970). Importantly the Argentine feminists of the 1970s, like Perlongher's friend Sara Torres, a member of the Grupo Política Sexual, linked desire to politics, and brought the use and control of the body overtly into debate. There was an overlap between the feminists and homosexual rights activists like Perlongher; the Unión Feminista Argentina, the most prominent Argentine feminist organization in the 1970s, campaigned with the Grupo Política Sexual, the sexual rights group founded by Perlongher and feminists such as Sara Torres in 1972, and the Frente de Liberación Homosexual against the Peronist anti-contraceptive laws of 1974. All the groups had close ties to poets, for example the poet and children's writer María Elena Walsh (b.1930), who wrote a number of poems and songs in support of the feminists. Furthermore, all the groups were disbanded under the dictatorship. Perlongher found a space for his politically and sexually provocative writing within feminism, for example publishing essays in feminist reviews like *Persona* or *Alfonsina* in the 1970s and early 1980s. Not only did Perlongher overtly address a female and feminist audience, but he also adopted a common practice among turn of the century writing by women in his adoption of a pseudonym of the opposite sex, Rosa L. de Grossman.

The historian and gay rights activist Zelmar Acevedo highlights these links between gay rights and feminism, and shows more generally how the FLH found space for the campaign for homosexual rights in the 1970s within feminism. He quotes an essay from *Somos* [Dec 1973], in which the campaigners for homosexual rights, including Perlongher, who wrote for the newspaper, described how the frequent depiction of feminists as women who wanted to be men and the concomitant denigration of lesbians, formed part of the same pattern of discrimination and stereotyping as that carried out against homosexual men. The article from *Somos* describes how the terms of abuse 'tortillera' and 'maricón', while obviously signifying different types of social stigma, both pointed to the same problem, specifically the patriarchal need to define women, a need that demonstrated 'el desdén que se tiene a la mujer [. . .]' (184). Acevedo, who had worked with Perlongher on *Somos*, and to whose book *Homosexualidad: Hacia la destrucción de los mitos* (1985) Perlongher contributed a section on 'La prostitución masculina',[3] makes clear the link between the projects of homosexual and women's liberation. He argues that homosexual rights campaigners and feminists have to work together, as both are faced with the same problem:

> La problemática de ambos es la misma: destruir la denigración clásica de los elementos denominados 'pasivos' dados en los *símbolos* anal y vaginal sobre el papel preponderante del símbolo fálico, estandarte de toda sociedad machista. (1985: 270–1)

For Acevedo 'anal' and 'vaginal' are both denominated as passive by the ruling *machista* values of society, in relation to the phallic symbol, which is powerful and active. This need to attack the binary, judgemental and violent striation of society into male/masculine/active/powerful/positive/phallic vs female/feminine/

passive/weak/negative/anal–vaginal is the uniting factor between feminists and gay rights activists and, vitally, it is the same striation that Perlongher attacks in 'Evita vive'. Furthermore one of his key tactics, that of displaying the functioning of desire in politics, is also drawn from contemporary feminism. The feminists in 1970s Argentina were campaigning to be allowed to follow and express desire, to define themselves outside of patriarchal terms, and for human rights that did not discriminate on the grounds of sex or sexuality; Perlongher though goes even further in his gender politics, following desire no matter how perverse or shocking the result may be, as revealed in the orgiastic and drug-fuelled carnivalesque of 'Evita vive'. It is this insistence on following desire no matter where it may lead that takes us into Perlongher's next phase, exceeding feminist-based gender politics, and inhabiting a more radical politics of desire.

The Politics of Desire

The story 'Evita vive' demonstrates how Perlongher uses the *travesti* to question the patriarchal organization of society. This project displays clear links to contemporary feminism. In his poems after 1980, Perlongher's writing continues to use *travesti* aesthetics. A shift can be charted from attacks on grammatical gender to increasingly radical aims, particularly in an attempt to use desire for political ends.

Grammar and Gender

One can find in Perlongher's first collection *Austria-Hungría* (1980, Buenos Aires) a poem that uses *travesti* aesthetics to deconstruct binary gender divisions in language, 'El polvo'.

> En esta encantadora soledad
> –oh claro, estabas sola!–
> en este enhiesta, insoportable inercia
> es ella, es él, siempre de a uno, lo que esplende
> [. . .]
> o esos diálogos:
> '*Ya no seré la última marica de tu vida*', dice él
> que dice ella, o dice ella, o él

que hubiera dicho ella, o si él le hubiera dicho:
'*Seré tu último chongo*
[. . .] '
(Perlongher, 1997a: 31)

The poem challenges the normalization of gender through grammar, what the theorist Brian Massumi calls 'standardized contexts within which every word spoken echoes those spoken in all others' (1999: 33), through a number of techniques. Firstly, Perlongher adopts ambiguous vocabulary, for example, the title ('polvo'): dust, powder, sexual intercourse, ejaculation, cocaine and make-up, or '*marica*': a male homosexual and a magpie. Perlongher also uses ambiguous pronouns. 'él' and 'ella', taken simply, are the binary opposites on which gender is stratified and functions in language. However, through juxtapositions and undecided alternatives ('ella, o dice ella, o él / que hubiera dicho ella, o si él le hubiera dicho') this binary is expanded into a blurry and vague space between the genders. If we saw in chapter 2 how Perlongher crossed and expanded the space between nations, here we can see how he carries out the same with grammatical gender. Furthermore, Perlongher uses dialogue to problematize stable gender; in the 'diálogo' section, the 'él' voice is at times a '*marica*' and at others a '*chongo*', at once a homosexual man and a stud like Chiche, above. Similarly, subjunctive verbs among the masculine and feminine pronouns ('hubiera dicho') suggest degrees of possibility rather than stable being, movement rather than fixed positions. These techniques unite to create the effect of messing up grammatically stable gender, one of the tenets of correctly written Spanish. As the theorist Judith Butler suggests in her book *Gender Trouble*, '[i]f gender itself is naturalised through grammatical norms [. . .] then the alteration of gender at the most fundamental epistemic level will be conducted, in part, through contesting the grammar in which gender is given' (1999: xix). Thus we can detect in Perlongher's poem an attack on the type of divide detected by Cixous and Clément in *The Newly Born Woman*: 'activity/passivity, sun/moon, culture/nature, day/night, father/mother, mind/heart, intelligible/palpable, logos/pathos, man/woman' (1993: 43). This early poem then continues the use of a *travesti* aesthetic as a grammatical attack on gender divisions.

The unanthologized poem 'Cántiga' further demonstrates this
approach to linguistic stratification and exhibits a call for nuances
and dynamism in portrayals of sexuality and difference:

> cantigas   cántigas
> provócome   como   mujer, como   hombre
> provo   co   me
> provócome
> vómitos, voluptuosidades
> de la vuelta, vultos:
> vulvartubula
> cántigas
> [. . .]
> canta conmigo:
> como mujer   como hombre
> mujer de todas las
> marido de todos los
> mujer/marido:
> [. . .]
> chilla   como   ballesta en el silbido   chilla
> como   mujer, como   hombre
> en las cantigascántigas
> provócome:
> como   en   mujer en   hombre
> (Perlongher, 1981b: 27 [Buenos Aires])

Perlongher uses a number of techniques to question the stability
of gender as presented in grammar. Firstly, he employs three
double similes, ('provócome como mujer como hombre', 'canta
conmigo: / como mujer, como hombre', 'chilla / como mujer,
como hombre') to place the first, second and third persons as
equally related to both man and woman. Thus the poem's narra-
tive voice, implicit reader and subject matter can all be man or
woman. Secondly, he includes a punctuation mark not common in
poetry, the bar between 'mujer/marido'. The bar posits a division
between woman and husband and thus represents the standard-
ized family unit as a tool of separation and exclusion. However it
also suggests the possibility of alternating between these two
positions, to be *woman or husband*. This alternation allows the
disjunction between male and female to be non-exclusive, in that
one can be either man or woman, rather than either be man or be
woman. The distinction is fine but critical, in that the former
questions the distinction between the sexes in a radical linguistic

and existential fashion. Perlongher explores the bar itself as a territory, just as we saw him exploring the border itself as a territory. In addition, Perlongher uses misspellings, wordplay and tongue twisters that generally destabilize and play with grammar, such as 'vuelta, vultos: / vulvar', or the alternation between 'cantigas' and 'cántigas'. This reasserts the focus on forms of language and expression not tied to rational communication that are included in the poem: songs, chants and the multichannel concept of provocation, a communication that is linguistic but importantly also corporeal. Thus we can see in Perlongher's early poetry the use of the dynamics of those whose sexual identity cannot be contained within legally permitted models as a means of attack on prevailing conservative models of sexuality.

The *Travesti* as Micropolitical Resistance

In the collection *Alambres*, published in 1987 but containing poems that were published elsewhere as early as 1981, Perlongher uses three *travesti* techniques to question received gender structures: naming; a 'boudoir' effect; and cutting. The first technique is exemplified in the titles of some of his poems, such as 'Ethel' or 'Daisy'. Both are feminine names. However the names not only clearly describe *travesti* characters (see below) but also are neutral in grammatical gender, and the type of names used by *travestis*, as discussed in chapter 2, being imported, exotic and not Spanish. The names and titles of Perlongher's poems thus cross geographical borders and cross the boundary between the sexes on two counts.

The boudoir effect is traced in *Alambres* in details, the paraphernalia of feminine adornment on the body:

> Como en ese zaguán de azulejos leonados
> donde ella se ata el pelo con un paño a lunares – y sobresale un pinche
> como un punto: en el bretel donde el mendigo gira
> las huellas de los hombros embarrados en la gasa desnuda
> ('Ethel', 1997a: 84 [1981, Buenos Aires])

> > si al follaje ebrio lames, no es ese rouge que dejas pringar
> > en el pescuezo, como una boa nacarada?
> ('Daisy', 1997a: 85 [1983, Buenos Aires])

Three processes contribute to the poems' boudoir effect: firstly, the juxtaposition of items, such as fabrics ('paño'), hairpieces ('pelo'), straps ('bretel') and make-up ('rouge'), that in almost cubist fashion unites the elements required for the *travesti* performance and, furthermore, places us in an environment of adornment and disguise. Secondly, the poems stress performance and dressing up through the many body parts, poses and positions that occur, at the expense of individual characters. The person is not stable but is instead dependant on context, specifically what he or she is doing and how he or she is dressed. Finally, 'Daisy' and 'Ethel' make unexpected physical and vocal demands of the reader. The use of half sets of question marks questions the way we read: the reader can either skim ahead, realize there is a question mark and then alter tone accordingly, see the question mark and then turn back, suddenly raise pitch, or ignore it altogether. Either way, the poem insists on shuttle movements backwards and forwards not in keeping with the normal direction in which one reads and directly affects the reader's body. The rich sound of the poem, full of /s/, /r/ and /l/ phonemes creates a text that is almost sticky to read, particularly with the *porteño* accent demanding many /zh/ or /sh/ sounds. These two effects demand a parsimonious, luxuriant reading that moves in directions not expected in poetry. The ensuing luxuriant slowness is similar in its non-productive pleasure to the dressing-up aesthetic of the *travestis* present in the poems. Perlongher's poem thus utilizes *travesti* performance in order to call into question received gender structures.

The third element of Perlongher's early *travesti* poetics is found in the notion of the cut. In 'Daisy' we read of 'tajos del corte', 'el tajo', 'un corte', 'navaja', 'la "heridilla"', 'llagas', and 'heridillas'. This density of cutting has two effects: firstly, it calls to mind the very real process of cutting involved in what Deleuze and Guattari call 'the prodigious attempts at a real transformation on the part of certain transvestites' (1999: 275) and which the Chilean writer and theatre practitioner Pedro Lemebel graphically describes in his chronicle, 'Los diamantes son eternos', where a *travesti* describes performing her/his own breast implant operation with a knife, silicone, some *pisco* and a needle and thread (2000: 79). As a subset to this form of cutting, we must also remember the sartorial efforts above, whereby cutting fabric, particularly in the alteration of clothes, forms a central part of the *travesti* performance. Both surgical operations, such as breast implants or gender reassignment (extremely rare in Argentina in the late 1970s and early 80s), and the use of clothes and adornment, show how the link between the body, the individual, sex and identity is socially constituted, and also how it can be questioned by the *travesti*. Secondly, the poem displays the cut as an attack on the individual and the limits of the body; Judith Butler talks of 'the boundary and surface of the body as politically constructed' (1999: xxxi). That is to say that what constitutes the limits of one's body, where the individual starts and ends, is a political matter. Butler goes on to suggest, in keeping with what we read in Perlongher's poem, that the questioning of such natural limits can have radical potential for questioning the political status quo: 'just as bodily surfaces are enacted as the natural,' she states, 'so these surfaces can become the site of a dissonant and denaturalised performance that reveals the status of the natural itself' (186). *Travesti* techniques then form a radical attack on received gender and identity structures.

What then of those who might see Perlongher's *travestis* as merely an exercise in camp, regarded by Susan Sontag as resolutely apolitical in her 'Notes on Camp' (1967)? An Argentine theorist closer in both time and geography to the circumstances of Perlongher's writing offers a key response to Sontag's piece. José Amícola, in his book *Camp y posvanguardia* (2000: 54) suggests that, 'el camp es una forma nueva de ver la realidad; su aparición coincide con una corriente que hace de la sospecha sobre la tradición – incluidas las propias vanguardias – su piedra de toque'. Amícola's argument, against that of Sontag, is that camp and transvestism have a resolutely political function: 'al imitar las diferencias sexuales, este travestismo o *drag* pone en tapete la estructura imitativa de esas diferencias, produciendo una resignificación de las imposiciones sexuales creadas por la sociedad' (55). Responding to Sontag, Amícola suggests that events in the years after the US critic's essay have demonstrated that which she did not predict, specifically that camp would go from being unique to the North American gay lifestyle to providing 'operativos' to attack the dominant signifying order around the world (137). In terms of language Amícola offers a potential reading of Perlongher's use of puns and sound games: 'La ambigüedad semántica pasa su fuerza al significante. Y en este sentido, podemos decir que el camp es el reino del significante, tanto textual como gestual' (200). Hence Perlongher's poems might be seen as politically provocative games, while the many proper names that title his *travesti* poems are closely related to Perlongher's anarchism: an attempt to gain the maximum possible freedom despite politically repressive circumstances during the military dictatorship that lasted from 1976 until 1983. I shall explain this link to anarchism in greater detail below.

In these political circumstances, it is important to re-examine the terminology that we have been using so far. The Argentine sociologists Rapisardi and Modarelli include in their study of the gay scene in which Perlongher had been involved in the 1970s an intriguing testimonial from Jorge Divain, who, like 'Ethel' or 'Daisy', was engaged in gender provocation. In fact, the issue of the *travesti* is complicated by Divain:

> *Nosotros no éramos travestis. Este término si bien es bastante viejo no siempre quiso decir lo mismo. Por ejemplo, las travestis de los años 70 vivían, como las de hoy, siempre vestidas de mujeres, y con actitud de 'femme fatale', pero no tenían tetas, cosa que ahora es como una condición necesaria. [. . .] Lo que nosotros éramos no hay con que compararlo hoy en día. No se puede decir que fuésemos* drag-queens *de tiempo completo, porque no nos dedicábamos a un arte real del transformismo, ni actuábamos un papel de divas en el que, además, creyésemos. Vestirse de mujer era, antes que nada, como una fiesta, una broma, un desafío a tanto rechazo. Decir, por ejemplo, estoy orgulloso de lo que hago y me cago en el pendejo macho de la esquina que me hizo la infancia tan difícil.*
> (Rapisardi and Modarelli, 2001: 105–6)

There is a contrast here between Dionysian and performative dressing-up as a provocation to conservative values and another, more stable and essential form of transvestism that aims at *being* a woman rather than *becoming-woman* ('devenir mujer'), the term that Perlongher (1997b: 33 [1983, Buenos Aires]) draws from Deleuze and Guattari to describe the questioning and indeterminate process of liminal *travesti* performance, as opposed to *travesti* identity. Another of Rapisardi and Modarelli's interviewees, Marcelo Acosta, suggests that a different figure was important for Perlongher, specifically the *marica*, the 'pansy' or 'queer': 'La marica para el Perlongher de entonces [the 1970s] era el verdadero desafío a los roles sexuales estereotipados y la más auténtica ruptura con la cultura machista' (Rapisardi and Modarelli, 2001: 166). This contrast between the *marica* and the *travesti* illustrates a key feature of the becoming-woman in Perlongher's early poetry: the dressing up, camping and make-up of the *marica* is a key individual form of libertarian resistance, whereas the relatively stable lifestyle of certain *travestis* living *as women* (100) does not necessarily offer such oppositional alternatives.

Perlongher uses both terms in his early poetry and essays, and does not discriminate in his writing to the degree that Acosta suggests he did in his activism and private life. However, it is important to draw attention to the use Perlongher makes of *travesti* aesthetics and techniques, rather than suggesting that men trying to be women are in themselves oppositional or problematic for the dominant social order. What I think is important here is to attempt to situate Perlongher's desiring-politics within the contemporary political milieu in order to clarify my earlier suggestion that Perlongher's use of *travesti* aesthetics and techniques is related to anarchism.

'A Painful Relationship': Perlongher, Left-wing Politics and its Alternatives

Throughout his life Perlongher held a certain attitude towards politics, which can be characterized as a form of anarchism. He rejected party politics, in particular the division into minute factions that characterized the left-wing opposition parties in the 1960s and 1970s in Argentina, many of which he had belonged to, and aimed to join factions together. The poem 'Siglas', displays this in burlesque fashion, with its proliferating list of increasingly complicated party-political names:

> Entonces confías en el FRP, junto a los restos de la ARP, nostálgica del PVP, del FPL y, por qué no, de la UP
> Pero no conseguías olvidar las deliciosas reuniones del MALENA
> – eran los tiempos en que el FRIP se fusionaba con Palabra Obrera para formar el PRT – Secesiones sionistas fundarían PO
> (Perlongher, 1997b: 211–13 [1985, Buenos Aires])

The danger this highlights is of the ideological splintering as groups split, reformed, came together and then split again. Each party fuses, divides, harks back to another, or aims to join with a third. As a real-life example, Perlongher had belonged to Política Obrera, later Partido Obrero, both listed in the poem, and not to be confused with Palabra Obrera, also in the poem, Partido Obrero (Trotskista), or Partido Obrero basado en los sindicatos.

Almost all of these groups were disbanded under the *proceso*
dictatorship, and the late seventies and early eighties were marked
by a general feeling of the impossibility of organized socialist
resistance given the shift to the right in *justicialismo* and the
violent oppression of the late seventies. This compounded the
problems that Perlongher had experienced with groups such as
Política Obrera, who refused to pronounce favourably on the
question of homosexuality in 1971, and with Peronism after the
publicity campaigns waged by the Peronist right against 'homo-
sexuales, hippies y drogadictos' in the late 1970s. Thus Perlongher
found his interests doubly unrepresented in this period. As
Rapisardi and Modarelli write, '[l]a relación de Perlongher con la
izquierda no podía ser sino doloroso'. Curiously, Perlongher had
insisted on the FLH's participation in the demonstrations to wel-
come back Perón at Ezeiza airport in 1973:

> En el debate entre los miembros del Frente sobresale, como
> siempre, la Rosa [Perlongher]: 'Hay que ir'. En el calor de la
> bienvenida las locas levantan sus consignas. No son más de treinta.
> '*La verdad es que no estábamos convencidos de ir, ya se percibía un clima
> de sangre. Pero Perlongher insistió. No éramos Peronistas, pero sabíamos
> que todo en ese entonces pasaba por la izquierda del movimiento. Era
> nuestra técnica trotskista clásica. Apenas llegados a Ezeiza, nos metimos en
> la columna de la JP* [Peronist Youth] [. . .] *La JP intentaba mantener
> una distancia considerable entre ellos y nosotros. Que se viera claramente
> dónde terminaba la columna. Nadie nos disputaba el espacio.* (Héctor
> Anabitarte [in italics]; Rapisardi and Modarelli, 2001: 157)

Perlongher had attempted to find validation for homosexual
rights within the organized ranks of Peronism; however, Peronism
did not want to have anything to do with homosexual rights. This
was perhaps due to the general *machismo* in Argentine politics, or
to suspicion about homosexuality as being bourgeois decadence
or a possible weak link in political activism, making a party
member potentially subject to blackmail or coercion. Thus in the
dictatorship years Perlongher was beginning to seek alternative
forms of political resistance, linking his earlier anarchism to
sexuality. As his friend Sara Torres outlines in an interview with
Rapisardi and Modarelli, after Perlongher's time in jail in 1978,
marginal figures became increasingly important to his early
career as a poet and anthropologist:

En el orden académico, por esos años decide aplicar la teoría en la que ha ido creciendo, desde la corriente sociológica norteamericana hasta el deleuzismo, para investigar un grupo humano específico: el prostituto callejero. (Rapisardi and Modarelli, 2001: 181)

The *travesti*, the *miché* and the lumpenproletariat prostitutes represented figures in active opposition to the state but in a way not linked to formal political organization, figures whose marginality can become a source of revolutionary freedom. Perlongher's position echoes the development of the New Left in Europe and the United States, whereby figures excluded from the traditional party system were increasingly seen as the fountain of popular revolution. This position is outlined in Herbert Marcuse's *One-Dimensional Man*, a theorist Perlongher had read and studied in the 1970s:

> [T]he 'people,' previously the ferment of social change, have 'moved up' to become the ferment of social cohesion [. . .] However, underneath the conservative popular base is the substratum of the outcasts and outsiders, the exploited and persecuted of the other races and other colors, the unemployed and unemployable [. . .] Thus their opposition is revolutionary even if their consciousness is not. Their opposition hits the system from without and is therefore not deflected by the system; it is an elementary force which violates the rules of the game and, in doing so, reveals it as a rigged game. (1991: 256–7)

For Marcuse, critical theory – the type of work Perlongher was engaged in as an anthropologist – could provide the link between intellectuals and the exploited, extra-legal classes whose position outside the political system means they are more difficult to channel into the system. If Marcuse ignores the sexual politics of what he terms the 'Great Refusal', the link is made in another text key to Perlongher's work, Georges Bataille's *Eroticism*:

> I am not thinking of the working-class of today but of Marx's *Lumpen-proletariat.* Extreme poverty releases men from the taboos that make human beings of them, not as transgression does, but in that a sort of hopelessness, not absolute perhaps, gives the animal impulses free rein. (Bataille, 1987: 135 [1964])

For Bataille, the lowest classes have a moral freedom not found in the working or middle classes. Thus Perlongher found the revolutionary freedom needed for liberation in absolute social marginalization and subjection by the law. His essays from the early 1980s represent an attack against state attempts at social stratification, particularly the semi-legal and selectively applied police edicts used to clear the streets, thus clearly identifying his political position in support of those classed as vagrants and petty criminals by the law. In the 1983 essay 'Nena, llevate un saquito', published in the feminist review *Alfonsina*, Perlongher wrote:

> No todos saben que si las chicas de Flores [a reference to the poem by Oliverio Girondo and an area famed for its prostitutes in Buenos Aires] arrojaren hoy en día su seno a pedazitos, antes que un caballero se inclinare a recogerlos se haría presente un patrullero. Del mismo modo, quien se atreviere a ir en deshabillé al mercado, no sería apenas condenado por el cotorreo de las vecinas: caería sobre ella el peso azul del Estado. (Perlongher, 1997b: 25 [1983, Buenos Aires])

He recounted in this essay the pseudolegal arrest of 'los gays y las prostitutas' that was occurring in Buenos Aires at the time, the subjection to 'internación curativa' or 'examen médico venéreo' and the use of the excuse of 'averiguación de antecedentes' to take alleged suspects into custody without trial or charge.

For Perlongher then, the dressed-up *marica* or streetwalking *travesti* embody in his early work the victim of patriarchal stratification as well as an attack on it from an anarchist and libertarian standpoint that defends the right to difference and the position outside legal frameworks and stratification. An approach such as Perlongher's is explained by the US theorists Ekins and King, who suggest that 'conceptualizing gender in terms of "performance" – as opposed to category or identity – places cross-dressing and sex-changing [. . .] at the forefront of contemporary challenges to gender oppression' (1996: 3). Similarly, Judith Butler explains:

> *In imitating gender, drag implicitly reveals the imitative structure of gender itself – as well as its contingency* [. . .] the 'normal', the 'original', is revealed to be a copy, and an inevitably failed one, an ideal that no one *can* embody [. . .] That gender reality is created through sustained social performances means that the very notion of an essential sex and a true or abiding masculinity are also constituted as part of the strategy that conceals gender's performative

character and the performative possibilities for proliferating gender configurations outside the restrictive frames of masculinist domination and compulsory heterosexuality. (1999: 175–6, 180. Italics in the original)

It is important to note here that while these theorists stress the importance of cross-dressing as a challenge to received gender structures, Perlongher's early work takes the dressing-up and sex-changing of the *travesti* and *marica* and creates a radical political position, opposing not only the conservative political factions but also excluded by opposition political groups.

Mysticism and the *Travesti*

Perlongher's writing from the late 1980s however does not seem to follow the same political tack as his earlier work on desiring politics. Two key changes occur. Firstly, Perlongher appears overtly to lose interest in the earlier *travesti* subjects of his poem. Secondly, he shifts his attention to mysticism. However, I aim to argue that despite this apparent change of theme, Perlongher still draws heavily on *travesti* aesthetics and dynamics for his mystical poetry.

Becoming-woman/Becoming-stuck

I contend that there are three factors in Perlongher's change of position with regard to the *travesti*. These are the political changes in the post-dictatorship era, the spread of AIDS, and Perlongher's reading of Deleuze and Guattari. The poem 'Devenir Marta', for example, from the 1989 collection *Hule*, is much less optimistic than earlier poems about the *travesti* as a politically provocative figure:

A lacios oropeles enyedrada
la toga que flaneando las ligas, las ampula
para que flote en el deambuleo la ceniza, impregnando
de lanas la atmósfera cerrada y fría del boudoir.

A través de los años, esa lívida
mujereidad enroscándose, bizca,

en laberintos de maquillaje, el velador de los aduares
incendiaba al volcarse la arena, vacilar

en un trazo que sutil cubriese
las hendiduras del revoque
y, más abajo, ligas, lilas, revuelo
de la mampostería por la presión ceñida y fina que al ajustar

los valles microscópicos del tul
sofocase las riendas del calambre, irguiendo
levemente el pezcuello que tornando
mujer se echa al diván
(Perlongher, 1997: 139 [1989, Buenos Aires])

While the great amount of detail, for example the fabrics, make-up, cutting and stitching that we also saw in 'Dolly' and 'Ethel', above, the focus on the body and its adornment, the clothes, the fabrics and interiors are all characteristic of Perlongher's earlier *travesti* poems, and the title itself ('*Devenir* Marta') describes that process as 'becoming-woman', there are a number of discordant elements. Whereas the earlier *travesti* poems showed the body connecting and defying limits, here the body is stuck in the 'atmósfera cerrada y fría'; age is signalled 'a través de los años' as the aged *travesti* becomes less provocative and dynamic than the youthful counterpart of the earlier poems; and the 'maquillaje' is also a potentially fatal 'laberinto', as described in chapter 2. While the final verse traces a proud movement up, 'irguiendo / levemente el pezcuello', and the becoming-woman reaches a form of completion in the past participle, 'tornado / mujer', the movement down, onto the 'diván', further closed off by the oxytone stress, suggests a dead end.

I believe that this reflects Perlongher's later misgivings about the *travesti* and, with it, other camp tactics, as aspiring to status as an individual identity inside the new sexual politics of 'coming out', rather than an intense process, and as reinforcing the two-sex model that dominates Western society. Whereas the *travesti* had earlier represented a subversive and provocative figure, by the late 1980s, through repetition within the market, it no longer held such a radical position. In pop music, trash documentaries and tabloid newspapers in the 1980s, the *travesti* became a widely disseminated and discussed figure in Latin America. This is closely related to political changes in the post-dictatorship period. With the Presidency of Raúl Alfonsín (1983–9) there had been a change in policy in Argentina regarding sexuality and police intervention in private activities. As Acevedo (1985) recalls, political attempts to distance Argentine politics from the violence and discrimination of the *proceso* period offered a new space for minority groups. In 1982, the Coordinada de Grupos Gay, which had protested in front of the Casa Rosada against the dictatorship, became the Comunidad Homosexual Argentina, a group that Acevedo calls 'menos radicalizado' (1985: 279) than the earlier FLH, which Perlongher had helped found and then dissolve. Acevedo outlines the public and political acceptance of the group, in significant contrast to the FLH; the group gained the status of 'Asociación Civil', the first officially recognized homosexual rights organization in Argentina. By November 1984, the CHA had its own bulletin; by 1985, they had offices in the centre of Buenos Aires. *Travestis* and other sexual rights activists were present at human rights conferences related to the *Nunca más* proceedings and were greeted favourably.

The post-dictatorship climate of openness was clearly influenced by changes in the political situation relating to the shock defeat of the military's campaign in the Malvinas, which had been widely supported by all colours of the political spectrum, except Perlongher and a few other radicals; in the 1980s the organized left offered little space for a thinker like Perlongher. Hence while writing *Hule* (1989) Perlongher found himself in a political environment radically different from the world of alliances and Trotskyite insertion tactics that had characterized the circumstances of the writing of *Austria-Hungría* and parts of *Alambres*. Furthermore, as an exile in Brazil, he was physically distanced from the limited opening up afforded to the gay rights movement in Argentina. Nevertheless, this opening up in fact meant that the revolutionary and marginal position of the *travesti* or *michê* was becoming increasingly channelled through the market.

The second and perhaps most important factor in Perlongher's change of position is the spread of AIDS in Brazil. Although Perlongher had spent much of the period 1982 to 1985 in São Paulo researching homosexual street prostitution for his 1986 Masters thesis, by 1987 he suggested that the mass eruption of AIDS in the city had turned his work into a 'piece of archaeology' (1997b: 57 [1987, São Paulo]).[4] In an essay in *Lua Nova*, Perlongher noted how in Brazil, at least, the appearance of AIDS had led to a number of paradoxes. AIDS and greater public acceptance of homosexuality, what he terms the 'desbunde' or coming out, had coincided with the removal of homosexuality from the official list of mental illnesses in Brazil. Perlongher argued that the acceptance and legalisation of homosexuality was in fact a means of controlling sexual activity:

> With the excuse of combating AIDS, there is an attempt to establish a new sexual order, in which homosexuality can be tolerated at the price of its discipline and self-control. Thus, previously unthinkable intimacies like anal intercourse with ejaculation gain public space.
> (Perlongher, 1985: 35 [São Paulo] my translation from Portuguese)

For Perlongher, homosexuality that is no longer transgressive and publicly confrontational is as powerful a tool of control as its policing and criminalization. AIDS had led to the spread of a new medico-judicial discourse of sexuality, specifically that of safe sex, with the practice of anonymous liaisons now subject to a massive public information campaign and, through local council measures against saunas and nightclubs, new forms of legal censure in Buenos Aires and São Paulo. While AIDS made the previously taboo a suitable subject for very public discussion – one cannot imagine an Argentine chat show discussion of the techniques of anal sex before the mid eighties – it did so at best within quite strict parameters.

'Dolly', also from *Hule*, offers a clear portrayal of the eruption of AIDS amongst River Plate homosexuals, and demonstrates how AIDS violently shut off the possibility of sex as an attack on patriarchal stratification:

> La telaraña de jeringas
> diestros cintazos pernoctaba
> el *pernod* junto al jarabe
> que en el vaho de alcohol
> cierne la pierna,
> [. . .]
> La cantarera, a pedacitos.
> Desabrochada en la camilla,
> atada a la máquina de ojear
> que regula las disfunciones
> de los órganos, en el
> dolor arqueante de ese vieja
> [. . .]
> Pues desplegando el nervio herido, hendido

aullaba el cocoliche los fastos de una regia
victoria en el canal, cisco tortuoso
reducido al vidráceo por la faca
de dos filos, legumbre
sanguinolenta lentejuela tuesta
a su rispidez el estertor de un chancro religioso[. . .]
(Perlongher, 1997a: 146–7 [1989, Buenos Aires])

The body, apparently that of a *travesti*, given the use of the name 'Dolly', is still shown defying the binary divisions of gender, as in the confusingly gendered phrase 'ese vieja'. The new element in the poem, however, is the medicalization of the body, which is shown full of syringes and tied to machines. These are not positive connections when compared to the physical connections between people and organs presented in earlier poems; the poem mentions 'opilaciones', an illness whereby menstrual fluid does not flow. This has a double significance; firstly, it identifies Dolly by analogy as a *travesti*; secondly, it shows the ways out of the individual body being shut off. I stated earlier that Perlongher's poetry privileged desire as that which flows and connects; this poem shows how AIDS blocks these flows and connections. The reference to River Plate slang ('cocoliche', a theatrical Italianate style of Spanish from Buenos Aires) sets this within an Argentine context. Thus the poem shows the sexual attacks on patriarchal stratification of Perlongher's earlier poems being violently shut off as the body is tied to machines and enclosed in the clinic. This reflects the new aesthetics of gay rights politics in response to AIDS: as many older homosexual men very visibly died of AIDS, an occurrence portrayed in the mass media as evidence of the dangers of promiscuity and lack of self-control, the 'gay–gay' couple became a symbol of sexual responsibility and individual self-control in Brazil (and, to a lesser extent Argentina) while the *michês, chongos, maricas escandalosas* and *travestis* continued to be harassed not only by the forces of law and order, but fashion and the mass media in both countries.

Rapisardi and Modarelli (2001) argue that neo-liberal market forces were the key factor in changing the patterns of homosexual behaviour in Buenos Aires in the 1980s – for example the commercialization of discos and androgynous marketing – more than AIDS. However, it is worth remembering that Perlongher wrote his anthropological thesis in Brazil, a country which witnessed a much more significant impact from AIDS and HIV. In fact, Perlongher himself acknowledged that AIDS was of less importance to studies on Argentina:

> En Argentina hay más incidencias en SIDA de drogadictos que de homosexuales. Tal vez esto sea un síntoma de que la Argentina sea una sociedad en la que la orgía no existe. [. . .] No hay orgías, no hay carnaval.
>
> (Ekhard and Bernini, 1991: 86 [Buenos Aires])

The reference to 'carnaval' makes the contrast obvious: in Brazil there is *carnaval*, there are orgies and, most importantly, the effects of AIDS were felt significantly in the sexual sphere. Thus, while the *travesti* and the *marica* had represented a form of micropolitical resistance in Perlongher's early work, AIDS and the ensuing public reaction closed off many of its possible openings. In relation to this medical change and media saturation, Perlongher himself observed the need for a change in his writing after the collection *Hule* (1989):

> Empecé a percibir en la gente una suerte de hastío en relación a la liberalidad sexual. La hipersexualización de los medios y de todos los mensajes terminó por bloquear la posibilidad de trance a través del sexo [. . .] Tengo que buscar otro trance para mi escritura [. . .]
>
> (Saavedra, 1991: 3 [Buenos Aires])

For Perlongher, political and medical factors had made sex and, with it, the *travesti* characters of his earlier work, no longer provocative or interesting. There is, however, another factor in his change of position, specifically his reading of Deleuze and Guattari, on which he based the course on urban anthropology that he taught in the mid 1980s at the University of Campinas in Brazil. As the French theorists wrote, '[b]ecoming is never imitating' (1999: 275). Despite their interest in becoming-woman, the process identified above as key to the *travesti*, they were at times ambivalent to becoming-woman in itself:

> A kind of order or apparent progression can be established for the segments of becoming in which we find ourselves; becoming-woman, becoming-child; becoming-animal, -vegetable, or -mineral; becomings-molecular of all kinds, becomings-particle. (1999: 272–3)

This suggests that becoming-woman is only worthwhile as a starting point, rather than as an end itself. With the spread of transvestite figures in the mass media and the development of surgical techniques for gender reassignment, it became more and more possible in the 1980s for the becoming-woman of the *travesti* to turn instead into *being a woman*. As Deleuze and Guattari write in *Kafka: Towards a Minor Literature*, and as Perlongher seemingly came to believe in the 1980s, one must be wary of 'the suspect temptations of resemblance that imagination proposes' (2000:14). If dressing-up is either just that, or part of an attempt to switch from one side of a binary to the other *permanently*, for Perlongher, following Deleuze and Guattari, the dynamism of the process of becoming is lost. Thus Perlongher was in the late 1980s wary of *travesti* identity as a possible goal in itself, part of his general wariness over the very concept of identity as borne out in his assessment of the multiple names for sexual roles and transactions in São Paulo, about which he commented 'no interesará tanto la identidad, construida representativamente por y para el sujeto individual, sino las intersecciones del código que se actualizan en cada contacto' (1993:72–3 [1987, São Paulo]).

Perlongher characterized this change in his interests, in Deleuzean style, as a movement from the marginal to the minor. In an interview from 1990 he stated:

> A esta altura del partido ya no soy marginal. Soy un nómade, a la manera del nómade de Gilles Deleuze, me siento el que hace pasar todos los flujos, el nómade de los mil planicies. La marginalidad encarnó un ideal de la década del '70 [. . .] Era mi vida. Pero ese partido ya no se puede seguir jugando. Soltar flujos es fascinante, pero hay que tener cuidado, porque al menor descuido todo puede desgobernarse y precipitarse a aguas ajenas. En estos años aprendí a hacer una búsqueda de la condición humana, en el sentido sartreano. En las últimas décadas aquella condición se hizo descendente, a través del delirio de las drogas o del sexo [. . .] No digo: soy un marginal arrepentido. Digo: estoy en otra cosa.
> (Ulanovsky, 1990: 11, Buenos Aires)[5]

For Perlongher then, the marginal politics of the *travesti* that he had used in his earlier poetry and writing had become both personally dangerous and potentially conservative. As a result, in 1991 Perlongher signed off completely on the subject of male homosexuality with the pointedly titled essay *La desaparición de la homosexualidad*. Perlongher does not deny the real repression of those practising homosexuality, but rather suggests the danger of normalization through identity politics, as 'gay rights' becomes just another committee within the apparatus of state power:

> [E]l movimiento homosexual triunfó ampliamente, y está muy
> bien que así haya sido, en el reconocimiento [. . .] del derecho a la
> diferencia sexual, gran bandera de la libidinosa lidia de nuestro
> tiempo. Reconozcámoslo y pasemos a otra cosa. (1997b: 89 [1991,
> Buenos Aires])

Perlongher seems to suggest then that other, more radical and
newer themes are required. Perlongher's turn away from sexuality
accompanies an apparent disillusionment with the treatment of
sexuality, not only by the state but also by the promoters of gay
rights themselves. He continues:

> ¿Qué pasa con la homosexualidad [. . .]? Ella simplemente se va
> diluyendo en la vida social, sin llamar más atención de nadie [. . .]
> Al tornarla completamente visible, la ofensiva de normalización
> [. . .] ha conseguido retirar de la homosexualidad todo misterio,
> banalizarlo por completo. (88)

The phrase 'ofensiva de normalización' allows Perlongher to link
disparate elements of the sexuality debate: both state power
normalizing through medical and disciplinary measures and the
protestors trying to present homosexuality as not deviant but,
instead, *normal*. The effect is equal on both sides: homosexuality is
accepted, but no longer interesting. And with the introduction of
the condom and the Anglo-style gay–gay couple, we have what
Perlongher calls, borrowing his terminology from Deleuze and
Guattari and Foucault, a replacement of the 'sociedad de disci-
plina' with a 'sociedad de control' (88): equally individualistic
and, for Perlongher, another dead end.

Becoming-mystic

I shall deal more fully with Perlongher's poetics of mysticism in
chapter 6; here I wish to examine the continued presence of
travesti aesthetics and techniques in Perlongher's later poetry.
Perlongher's response to the emergence of AIDS, safe sex and the
ensuing end of widespread orgiastic sexual practices, is another
line of flight, worked out with reference to the French philo-
sopher Georges Bataille's work, *Eroticism*: the mystical. In the essay
quoted above Perlongher proposes that: 'Abandonamos el cuerpo
personal. Se trata ahora de salir de sí' (88). One might offer the
taxonomy: coming out ('cuerpo personal')/coming out of oneself

('salir de sí'). The first, which is related to the new politics of gay identity and publicly accepted but self-controlled homosexuality, Perlongher interprets as essential, identity-based, individual and sedentary. The second, which Perlongher finds in the mystical experience, is verbal, non self-identical, non-individual, and nomadic. The first poem from the collection *Aguas aéreas* illustrates the poetics of this new line of flight:

[. . .]
Recio el cantor, bruñidas las guedejas,
dejo de mambo inflige al modular
intensidades en el cieno,
                          plástica
porosidad de la materia espesa.

En el dejo de un espasmo
contorsionaba los ligámenes
y transmitía a los encajes
la untuosidad del nylon

rayándolos
en una delicada precipitación.
(Perlongher, 1997a: 248 [1991, Buenos Aires])

The poem was 'inspired' by the Santo Daime church in São Paulo (Perlongher, 1997a: 293 [1991, Buenos Aires]), a religion that believes that a vision of the divine can be achieved through ritually imbibing the hallucinogen *ayahuasca* or *yagé*, and accompanying the ensuing visions and physical purging of the body with ceremonies, songs, prayers and dances. In Perlongher's poetry, the *ayahuasca* ceremony seems to offer a way out of individuation, as an example of the 'salir de sí' described above. In the first poem of *Aguas aéreas* Perlongher describes the ceremony through the depiction of four areas. Firstly, he describes a quasi-spastic Dionysian dance ('el dejo de un espasmo'); secondly, he describes the song that accompanies the ceremony and its singer ('el cantor'); thirdly, Perlongher details the sickness induced by the drug, the 'purge' that *ayahuasca* users experience, closely related to the dance ('contorsionaba los ligámenes'); and, finally, the mystical experience itself, the visions of lights and flashes that precede the appearance of the divine, are described ('una delicada precipitación'). Thus Perlongher details an experience that appears to offer a way out of individuation and the division between persons, instead creating a communal intensity within the religious framework of the ceremony that allows the subject to stretch beyond itself and join with others and the divinity. This is in keeping with Perlongher's writings on the subject of São Daime: 'la experiencia dionisíaco [. . .] asegura, en lugar de la individualización, justamente una ruptura con el *principium individuationis*' (Perlongher, 1997b: 153 [1991, Buenos Aires]).

However, even as Perlongher attempts to write poetry that captures the *ayahuasca* ceremony, a spiritual experience, he seems drawn to the physical side of the ceremony. This is manifested in two areas. Firstly, Perlongher focuses formally on the corporeal, for example the rhyme that moves down from 'nylon' to 'precipitación', or the line-end focus on 'encajes' and 'ligámenes', both drawing attention to the body and its adornment, or 'precipitación', which could be a dive into the unknown, a stream of lights, a gush of vomit, or simply a ladder in one's nylons. Secondly, and vitally, we have elements drawn from the portrayal of the *travesti* of earlier poems: 'encajes' and 'nylon', both part of the *travesti* aesthetic of dressing-up we saw above. What this reveals is that Perlongher's mystical line of flight is still very much linked to the vocabulary and aesthetics of his earlier *devenir mujer* poems and that to deal with the force of the spiritual – exemplified by the bodily contortions and hallucinogenic lights above – without falling into the abyss of madness or death, Perlongher is reliant on forms from these earlier poems. The intensity of the *travesti*'s becoming-woman is both a starting point and a source of vocabulary for his mystical writings.

The importance of physical elements drawn from his earlier *travesti* poems is further drawn out in Perlongher's other attempts to theorize the *ayahuasca* experience. In an essay published posthumously but similar in theme and content to a number of essays written around 1990, Perlongher draws on the ideas of Deleuze and Guattari , describing the ceremony as exhibiting a 'plano de los cuerpos' and a 'plano de expresión' (1997b: 163 [Buenos Aires]). The former consists of the lights, visions, and physical experiences of the ceremony, as described in the poem (the contortions or lights, for example); the latter contains the songs and dances of the ceremony, echoed in the poem through formal tropes and repetitions. What is interesting is the curious oversimplification that Perlongher commits, whereby he replaces Deleuze and Guattari's terms in *A Thousand Plateaus*, drawn from the linguist Louis Hjelmslev, '*plane of content*' and '*plane of expression*' (Deleuze and Guattari, 1999: 43, 88), with 'cuerpos' and 'expresión'. While Deleuze and Guattari's *plane of content* does include the body, it is not just that, but also actions and passions.[6] So it would seem that even as Perlongher attempts to theorize intellectually a spiritual experience, he is drawn again to the very physicality of the ceremony.

The fifth poem in the series is thus formally intriguing, as it clearly adopts an aesthetic of crossing thematically linked to Perlongher's *travestis*:

SI LA DIVINIDAD LIQUIDA AHÓGASE [*sic*]
o bulla, en el calor carnal,
su playa látex – antes
que promontorios, grutas –

gránulos de negrura
oh noctiluca enardecida yergue
en la onda de conchas y cangrejos
el anillo de espuma

en la piel tensa y tenue
muelle el despeñadero en remolinos
el simulacro de su frenesí
huecos estampa en el alud coral
para que halague su volcán el ala
de un camoatí libélulas libando.
(Perlongher, 1997a: 255 [1991, Buenos Aires])

The poem is obviously a sonnet (fourteen lines). Traditionally sonnets have uniform line lengths. However a syllable count here reveals another famous verse form: the seven and eleven-syllable lines of the *silva*, the form used by Góngora in his *Soledades*. There are other clear Góngoran elements: the 'si' opening; the comparison form 'antes que x, y'; and the vocabulary ('promontorios', 'grutas') in lines three and four.

Before we can classify this poem as an attempt to marry two of the most important verse forms for innovation in Hispanic poetry, the sonnet and the *silva*, there is an element that does not fit. The oxytone ending of line two, 'carnal', leaves us with a line length of nine syllables. Thus Perlongher performs an attempt to be both *silva* and sonnet at the same time, the becoming-sonnet of the *silva* and the becoming-*silva* of the sonnet, but with the awareness

of corporality and physicality, embodied in the two-syllable oxy-
tone of 'carnal', that does not fit received forms such as the
sonnet or the *silva*. Thus on the macroscale the whole poem is
between a *silva* and a sonnet, whilst on the microscale, line two is
between a heptasyllable and a hendecasyllable. This contradictory
aesthetic of chiasmus, whereby accentuated physicality crosses
between pre-established boundaries, is the same as that demon-
strated above by the *travesti*; as Butler suggests, the outside says
female – women's clothes and make-up – with the body inside
being male; conversely, this outside also proclaims its masculinity
– broad shoulders, large hands – with a feminine inside, a 'woman
trapped in a man's body' in vulgar terms (1999: 174). The *travesti*
dresses up, disguises him/herself, and then, as Perlongher states,
defies expectations through potential active–insertive sexual par-
ticipation, thus committing a *double crime* (Perlongher 1993: 49
[1987, São Paulo]). This movement is never stable, the essence
always false. Thus Perlongher's mystical poetry still draws on the
travesti aesthetic and the techniques used in his earlier poetry; his
Dionysian dancer is wearing tights.

   In conclusion, Perlongher's earliest work, the short story 'Evita
vive', uses the *travesti* in order to question received gender
structures in a manner that draws on feminist gender politics. In
his early poetry Perlongher develops from this feminist position,
from a radical attack on the grammatical structures of gender
towards a consideration of the political implications this holds.
While Perlongher's earlier *travesti* figures might be seen almost as
case studies of *travesti* becoming-woman used as political resist-
ance, Perlongher's work from the second half of the 1980s seems
to suggest that the *travesti* aesthetic has become conservative, and
he thus abandons the *travesti*. However Perlongher does not
abandon the body in his spiritual poetry; even as he attempted to
escape the limits of bodies wracked by illness and censured by the
state, he continues to use the becoming-woman of the *travesti* and
the *marica* and the sexual positioning of the body as a central
trope in his writing.

NOTES

1   This chapter began as a paper given at the 2002 Birkbeck College/
     Journal of Latin American Cultural Studies summer conference. A

version was published in issue 12.1 of the *Journal*. Part of the section on Evita was also included in a different form in the paper '"Evitá hablar de la política": Multiple critical readings of Perlongher's "Evita vive"', published in *Journal of Iberian and Latin American Studies*, 2003. Both papers are available at *www.tandf.co.uk/journals* .

2   As an example of the use of the active–insertive position as a symbol of power, the *cono sur* expression 'mazorca', a group of thugs or a despotic government, is derived from the word for a corn cob, the object used by the nineteenth-century dictator Rosas's 'patota' gangs to rape victims.

3   This essay is not included in the Perlongher's "established bibliography" (Ferrer, 1996a), perhaps because it is not credited directly to Perlongher. This is curious, as Perlongher's essay, 'Historia del Frente de Liberación Homosexual en la Argentina', also in Acevedo's study, is included by Ferrer.

4   As with his importation of Deleuze into Argentina, Perlongher was at the forefront of theorizing on AIDS; the Biblioteca de Congreso, Buenos Aires, does not list in its catalogues any mention of AIDS in newspapers before 1990. That is not to say that the syndrome was not mentioned – it was, by Perlongher, for example – but rather that it was not front-page or headline news.

5   Rosi Braidotti (2000) offers a critique of Deleuze's becoming from a feminist perspective on a number of grounds: the privileging of certain becomings, the lack of 'empirical women' in the theory, the refusal to accept non-post-gender theories of sexual difference and specificity: 'llegué a la conclusión de que Deleuze queda atrapado en la contradicción de postular un "devenir mujer" general que no tiene en cuenta la especificidad histórica y epistemológica del punto de vista feminista femenino' (139). Braidotti insists that sexual difference must be recognized as basic to any discussion of sex and sexuality. Her critique of Deleuze is intriguing as it offers certain inroads into Perlongher's possible blindness to the continuing problems faced by *travestis* in Argentina, as detailed by Álvarez (2000), and the distinctly market-led opening up to androgyny as a fashion statement.

6   Of course even here I am oversimplifying Deleuze and Guattari's formulation, taken from 'Postulates of Linguistics', plateau 4 of *A Thousand Plateaus*. Here they distinguish between a horizontal and a vertical axis. The first relates to Perlongher's formulation, whereby 'an assemblage comprises two segments, one of content, the other of expression' (1999: 88). There is also, however, a vertical axis, on which 'the assemblage has both *territorial sides*, or reterritorialized sides, which stabilize it, and *cutting edges of deterritorialization*, which carry it away' (88).

Chapter 5

Perlongher's *Barroco*[1]

Introduction

I do not intend in this chapter to add to the already cluttered field of theorizing on the *barroco* and *neobarroco* in recent Argentine poetry and, in particular, in relation to Perlongher's work. Instead I argue that what Perlongher and theorists commonly identify in his work by the term *barroco* or the related terms *neobarroco* or *neobarroso* is more accurately described as a form of avant-garde kitsch.[2] The *barroco* of the Golden or Early Modern Age, as in the writing of Luis de Góngora (1561–1627) or Francisco de Quevedo (1580–1645), and the writing classified by Perlongher as *neobarroco* or *neobarroso*, for example that of Emeterio Cerro (b.1952), is more complexly related to Perlongher's work than is often acknowledged. These works and Perlongher's theorizing on them represent a source of poetic tools and operating strategies for Perlongher's work. These tools allow Perlongher to validate certain sexual practices and kitsch phenomena by creating analogies to commonly respected literary and historical phenomena. I use the term 'kitsch' because Perlongher cultivates an aesthetic that dynamically relates high art and low social classes and the attendant cultural manifestations and valorizes what one might call feigned good taste, while calling into question the value of good taste itself. This kitsch can be regarded as avant-garde because, firstly, it attempts to investigate the metaphor in a way similar to certain historical avant-garde groups, secondly, it allows a focus on secretive and marginal groups, and thirdly, it highlights and valorizes irrational behaviour.

Perlongher's Retrospective *Barroco*

In many ways the close association between Perlongher's work
and the term *barroco* is a retrospective critical operation. For
example, *Prosa plebeya* (1997), Perlongher's collected essays, con-
tains a section consisting of literary essays (as opposed to his
works on politics, sexual rights, drugs, the Falklands/Malvinas
Islands, or Evita Perón). Such is the centrality of the *barroco* in
criticism on Perlongher that the editors Christian Ferrer and
Osvaldo Baigorria entitle the section 'Barroco barroso'. This title
predetermines the subject matter of Perlongher's literary essays to
the *barroco* and concomitantly limits the selection to essays written
after 1986, when Perlongher started seriously considering the
barroco as an operating strategy for his poetry, as revealed by the
emergence of the term, previously infrequent, as the title and
main subject in many of his essays. The first essay Perlongher
dedicated to the *barroco* and the *neobarroco* is from 1986 but the
bulk of Perlongher's essays on the subject date from 1988, a date
that is significant as it represents the beginning of Perlongher's
public recognition as a writer and also coincides with important
political and socio-sexual changes in Argentina and Brazil.

By 1988 Perlongher had become recognized as an important
poet in Argentina, receiving the Boris Vian Prize in 1987 for
Alambres, which ran to a second edition in 1989. Two more of his
collections (*Hule* and *Parque Lezama*) had been accepted for
publication. Perlongher was also beginning to be regarded as a
respected columnist in Brazil. Moreover, Perlongher had com-
pleted his thesis on male prostitution in São Paulo and had begun
teaching at the University of Campinas. Furthermore, Perlongher
had acknowledged that AIDS had led to a significant change in
the field of sexuality, especially in Brazil among the subjects of his
thesis, the prostitutes, clients and *entendidos* of the *bocas* in São
Paulo (Perlongher, 1997b: 57 [1987, São Paulo]). By 1988 the
Alfonsín government in Argentina was floundering, with rising
inflation, threats from the military and stalled attempts to pros-
ecute the members of the armed forces involved in torture and
murder during the *proceso* era.

Two early essays not included in *Prosa plebeya* offer other
presences than the *barroco* in Perlongher's considerations of
writing. The first essay, written in collaboration with Alberto Nigro
for the Buenos Aires review *Mutantia* is intriguingly not listed in

Perlongher's official bibliography in *Lúmpenes Peregrinaciones* (Ferrer, 1996a). The essay relates the emergence of a new 'poesía argentina subterránea' to rock lyrics, small groups of aficionados, literary workshops and 'la ausencia de verdaderos maestros' owing to the generation gap between Jorge Luis Borges, Enrique Molina, Edgar Bayley et al. and the younger poets (Perlongher and Nigro, 1980: 64–5 [Buenos Aires]). The essay does not mention the *barroco*, except in a rather curious fashion towards the end of the piece, almost as an afterthought. In relation to certain existential tendencies in Argentine letters, exemplified by the work of Alejandra Pizarnik, they remark:

A ello debe agregarse, como influencia más reciente, la recuperación del barroquimo [*sic*] – de la literatura, del lenguaje – puesto en circulación tanto por la 'moda' estructuralista como por la difusión de escritores estilo Lezama Lima o Severo Sarduy, no tan bien conocidos como respetados; esta corriente toma a la poesía más como una experimentación con la palabra que como una expresión de sentimientos. (66)

Three elements stand out here. Firstly, 'barroquismo' is effectively dismissed, as a trend or a fashion statement. Secondly, its diffusion has not been accompanied by a *reading* ('no tan bien conocidos') of the poets said to be of influence. Finally, the apparently defining trait, that of 'experimentation with the word', is so vague as to be meaningless. However, the latter does point to a certain quasi-vanguardist self-perception of experimentalism.

In terms of a social origin for this 'new poetry', the authors suggest a ghettoization of poetic production and reception: 'La producción poética deviene así en una especie de rito iniciático, de intercambio entre adeptos: literatura para y entre literatos, que difícilmente llega a conmover quien está "afuera del mambo"' (64). Thus the new poetry is secretive, subterranean and presents a language for the few who are in the know. Perlongher also commented on this closed circulation of poetry in his essay, 'Argentina's Secret Poetry Boom' (1992), where he related the phenomenon to the necessarily secretive practices of oppositional and cultural groups during the political repression of the 1970s and early 80s.

Perlongher and Nigro's essay thus draws attention to two key points. Firstly, the new poetry is secretive and marginal, related to the rock and hippy subculture. It is secretive in that it talks about

that which decent society may know takes place but chooses to
ignore or condemn – the consumption of drugs or homosexual
activity – but also as it uses a language understood only by a small
few. Secondly, in the divorce from earlier generations, Perlongher
and Nigro draw attention to the *adanismo*, or pioneer spirit,
common among avant-garde groups, which the 'new poetry'
displays.

In another essay by Perlongher on the subject of the 'nuevo
verso', written three years later, he again attempts to characterize
the new poetry of Argentina, this time for a Brazilian readership.
Perlongher abandons comment on the link between the new
poetry and rock music. Nevertheless, the trait of being politically
subterranean is still important to the new poetry. As Perlongher
writes, '[t]he new River Plate writing carries the marks of terror
and pleasure. And in the "new verse" from Argentina we detect
the influence of exile, fragmentation and dispersal' (Perlongher,
1983b: 6, my translation from Portuguese). Perlongher draws
attention to the threat of political censure or violence, against
which small groups emerge whereby textual pleasure can be
enjoyed. Thus the 'new verse' represents a form of linguistic
political resistance, as Perlongher suggests. In this vein, the poetry
demonstrates another key trait, a trait also dealt with in the article
with Nigro: 'they [the poets] refuse to put poetry at the service of
a message – seeking instead a "passage", the reverberations of
certain linguistic keys, the multiplicity of signifieds' (6). Thus in
refusing to follow common sense or convey meaning, the new
poets represent for Perlongher a form of political opposition to
the social order.

There is, however, an important difference between the two
articles. Whereas before, in the article written with Nigro,
Perlongher suggested an absence of 'masters', here Perlongher
highlights the influence of writers such as Oliverio Girondo,
Macedonio Fernández and Enrique Molina. These writers were all
associated with avant-garde groups in Argentina, the *Martín Fierro*
group in the case of Girondo and Fernández and, in the case of
Molina, the surrealists. Thus again Perlongher highlights the link
to the avant-garde for *neobarroco* writing. Despite his insistence on
the importance of Lezama Lima and the *neobarroco cubano*,
Perlongher returns to names and tropes from local avant-garde
groups. Furthermore, Perlongher opposes certain traits in the
Argentine 'new verse' to its Cuban equivalent: 'the writing of

Osvaldo Lamborghini is of a radical perversity: it opposes writing as a cut to the "writing as tattoo" of the Cuban Severo Sarduy' (6). While Perlongher stresses the importance of the Cubans, it is very hard to see from his essay what the 'new verse' has in common with the Cuban *neobarroco* except again in the most vague terms – experimentation with language, for example. It seems that Perlongher is more concerned to divulge a set of terms such as the variations on *barroco* or the proper names 'Lezama' and 'Deleuze' for the readership of the popular São Paulo magazine *Leia Livros*, a set of terms that are key to his own writing and theorizing, than to engage in a fully coherent and detailed investigation of the subject matter. Nevertheless, his writing on the *neobarroco* again closely highlights its links to the historical avant-garde and the emergence of small, largely private groups of poets against a background of political and personal risk.

Hence it is interesting to see Perlongher's later attempts to identify the *barroco* traits in his own work. In particular, Perlongher used the formats of the newspaper cultural supplement and the small literary review, both of which enjoyed a boom in the Argentine post-dictatorship era, to comment on his *barroco* poetics. In an interview with Guillermo Saavedra for the Buenos Aires newspaper *Clarín*'s 'Cultura y nación' section, Perlongher spoke about the *barroco* processes at work in the writing of *Alambres*. Although many of the poems were ready for publication in 1981, almost a seven-year wait occurred before Perlongher could publish the book: 'empecé a pulirlo, a agregarle, a barroquizarlo, digamos' (Saavedra, 1991: 3). Two operations are at work here: first, Perlongher retrospectively identifies his work as *barroco*. Secondly, he justifies this by offering his own definition of *barroco*: polished and added to. What is curious here is the paradox, seemingly unnoticed by Perlongher, between polishing – *removing* imperfections from a surface – and *adding* to it. One might visualize Perlongher's contradiction by imagining folding an object with great force. Thus one could add to it and complicate it, yet make it smaller. Visible on the surface would be points and parts of content, like isolated words or letters on a piece of paper written on then screwed up. Hence for Perlongher the *barroco* is not necessarily a definable era, or a given set of poetic structures – the chiasmus or the squared metaphor, for example – but certain operations of *aestheticizing* a text. Again Perlongher seems keener to publicize his terms than to specify precisely what they mean.

In another interview, with Carlos Ulanovsky for *Página 12* of
Buenos Aires, Perlongher further discusses his *barroco* operations:

> Yo, hasta ahora, elegí rescatar las refulgencias íntimas, *menores*, de
> la lengua. Sacar a relucir aquello que las literaturas *mayores*
> condenan al silencio. En este sentido, cierta poesía ofrece la
> posibilidad de realizar esta tarea. [. . . S]oy un *barroco plebeyo* [. . .]
> O un barroco de trinchera, de barrio. Pienso, por ejemplo, en mi
> poema 'Cadáveres'. Sacar palabras de la *jerga cotidiana* y
> incrustarlas en una *operación complicada y sofisticada*. En un sentido
> más profundo, sería como tratar de provocar pequeñas mutaciones
> que afectan directamente en el interior de la lengua. Acaso si lo
> que escribí tuvo alguna repercusión es porque, en el plano de la
> expresión, esto provoca movimientos y cambios. (Ulanovsky, 1990:
> 11, my italics)[3]

Perlongher insists on the *barroco* as a process of aestheticizing the
everyday ('jerga cotidiana', 'una operación complicada y sofisti-
cada'). At the same time he demonstrates a certain will to use,
perhaps even to popularize, terminology drawn from Deleuze and
Guattari ('plano de la expresión', a key term in the two volumes
of *Capitalism and Schizophrenia*). Again, Perlongher gives the
impression of forming a critical discourse, identifying its sources
and training readers in his terminology. The text, as highlighted
by the italics (above) creates a dynamic relationship between high
and low cultural references, between the literary or academic and
the everyday or street. The *barroco* operations Perlongher claims
characterize his poetry are similar to those he observed in his
anthropological work on homosexual practices, as both cast a
critical gaze on street and minority practices from a relatively
distanced position – an academic treatise, or poem, for example –
and attempt to immerse themselves in and portray that environ-
ment or those practices. The Ulanovsky piece is interesting in that
although a significant part of the interview is dedicated to
Perlongher's poetry and poetics it is entitled 'El SIDA puso en
crisis la identidad homosexual'. I feel that, ironically, the emer-
gence of AIDS offers greater space for thinkers like Perlongher
and also for Perlongher's reappraisal of *barroco* operations, par-
ticularly given the new mass-media interest in those groups per-
ceived to be most at risk from AIDS and those groups perceived as
the greatest risk for spreading HIV, for example *travesti* prostitutes
having sex with nominally heterosexual men, or 'bisexual' or
'active' male prostitutes. Perlongher's turn to the *barroco* after

1986 and the concomitant rereading of his earlier work then must be seen in the light of contemporary socio-sexual developments in Argentina and Brazil.

Neobarroco/Neobarroso/Barroco

Perlongher's clearest statement on the *barroco* was his introduction to the bilingual anthology *Caribe Transplatino* (1991, São Paulo) and this piece is vital for understanding his interpretation of the *barroco*.[4] Here Perlongher insists on the *barroco* as an operation of folding but one which owes its recent re-emergence to Lezama Lima: 'Es precisamente la poesía de José Lezama Lima, que culmina en su novela *Paradiso*, la que desata la resurrección, primeramente cubana, del barroco en estas landas bárbaras' (Perlongher, 1996: 19[5]). For Perlongher the *barroco* is not limited to a historical era: 'Deleuze ve, con propiedad, trazos barrocos en Mallarmé' (19). His terms, however, are frequently confused: '[E]l barroco consistiría básicamente en cierta operación de plegado [. . .] Es en el plano de la forma que el barroco, y ahora el neobarroco, atacan [. . .]' (20). The problem here is that if the *barroco* is an operation, then the *neobarroco* is not different from the *barroco*, and so does not need a separate name, except in order to create an artificial historical division which Perlongher's insistence on the *barroco* as an operation would preclude. It is almost as if Perlongher is double staging the *barroco*: the *barroco* (historical artistic period) exhibits the *barroco* (folding), as does the *neobarroco*, which is both a historical artistic period and a name for the *barroco* as an operation of folding *in recent years*. For much of the essay Perlongher makes no distinction between the *barroco* and the *neobarroco*. There are, however, distinct examples of the *neobarroco*, according to Perlongher, for example art nouveau's *neobarroco*, which differs from Severo Sarduy's use of the term in his theoretical work (25).

In another essay from 1991, a review of Tamara Kamenszain's *Vida de living*, Perlongher characterizes the *barroco* by the technique of folding. This he explains, as one might expect, with terminology from Deleuze: 'el plegado [. . .] que Deleuze consideraba la operación barroca por excelencia' (Perlongher 1991d: 8 [Buenos Aires]). Perlongher talks of 'cierta épica de impersonalidad barroca' (8). He continues, '[n]o se trata, insistamos, de los

grandes espacios de la épica, sino de los espacios íntimos, meno-
res, en los pliegues y repliegues de la superficie' (8). This process
of folding and refolding is *barroco* par excellence for Perlongher.
The paraphrase from Deleuze, which Perlongher does not source,
is very similar to an early paragraph from *The Fold: Leibniz and the
Baroque*:

> The Baroque refers not to an essence but rather to an operative
> function, to a trait. It endlessly produces folds. It does not invent
> things: there are all kinds of folds coming from the East, Greek,
> Roman, Romanesque, Gothic, Classical folds . . .. Yet the Baroque
> trait twists and turns its folds, pushing them into infinity, fold over
> fold, one upon the other. (Deleuze, 1993: 3, ellipsis in original)

Deleuze also insisted on folding as the dominant characteristic of
the baroque. However he also distinguishes two types of fold,
those related to 'the pleats of matter', and those related to 'the
folds in the soul', two folds differentiated as they refer to 'two
infinities' (3). What is interesting here is that Perlongher does not
offer such a differentiation in his readings of the *barroco*, rather
he simplifies – might we say popularizes? – Deleuze's theorizing to
one operation, the fold pure and simple, thus making available a
set of vocabulary and tools for discussing the *barroco* that are
drawn from Perlongher's own intellectual background.

Let us examine this work of folding with Perlongher's poem
'Cadáveres':

> Bajo las matas
> En los pajonales
> Sobre los puentes
> En los canales
> Hay Cadáveres
>
> En la trilla de un tren que nunca se detiene
> En la estela de un barco que naufraga
> En una olilla, que se desvanece
> En los muelles los apeadores los trampolines los malecones
> Hay Cadáveres
> (Perlongher, 1997a: 111 [1984, Buenos Aires])

The phrases are like short snippets of conversation; one could
imagine overhearing phrases such as 'bajo las matas' or 'en los
canales'. As snippets, they are isolated from the rest of a sentence,
lacking the grammar or the punctuation to connect them, except

through enumeration and proximity, and from context. The operation of folding can be imagined then as if one were to write everything one heard ('en los pajonales', 'sobre los puentes') on a huge piece of paper, and then fold forcefully so that certain phrases were on the surface and thus connected where previously they were distanced. However, the phrases are also places. Thus places that are distanced in geography are brought together by this operation, not unlike the Futurist attempt to portray the speed of modern technology. Hence Perlongher's poem exhibits the characteristic that *he* identifies as key to the *barroco*. At the same time, as we saw in chapter 3, the poem draws almost directly from Oliverio Girondo's poem 'Desmemoria', from *En la mas-médula* (Girondo, 1998: 90 [1968]). Perlongher does not mention Girondo as an influence on the writing of 'Cadáveres', however the effect is clear: Perlongher's formulation of the *barroco* as simply folding allows him to include almost any other writer as exhibiting the *barroco* trait and as a source of genealogical valida- tion for his poetic project.

It is worth then comparing Perlongher's formulation of the *barroco* as folding with the work on the baroque of, for example, Walter Benjamin in *The Origin of German Tragic Drama*.[6] Although Benjamin's assessment of *Trauerspiel* has certain similarities with Perlongher's and his poems, for example Benjamin's suggestion that baroque authors must tread in the footsteps of respected teachers and established authorities, but produce 'variations'; that an attempt is made at Classicism, but 'exposing the undertaking to highly baroque elaboration'; and that the work exhibits a certain 'wildness and recklessness' (1977: 160), it differs in key respects. Firstly, his taxonomy, which distinguishes *Trauerspiel* from other baroque writings, for example Calderón's plays, is much more complex than Perlongher's. Secondly and, perhaps vitally, '*Trauerspiel* operates with a stock of requisites' (231). Thus it is always readable, always engages didactically with its audience, in keeping with its proselytizing Christian aims. Perlongher's operation of folding does not require a stock of requisites; indeed his radical importation of authors into his *barroco* canon would positively abhor such a limiting strategy. Again, Perlongher's *barroco* is clearly a strategy for creating poetic genealogies, rather than a strictly applicable literary taxonomy.

Perlongher's genealogy for the *neobarroco* in the River Plate region is complex and complicated. He states that after the devaluation of Góngora's work in the neoclassical era, the Spanish Generation of 1927 – particularly García Lorca – rediscovered his *oeuvre*. This influenced Juan Ramón Jiménez, whose journey to Cuba took the influence to the *Orígenes* group, of which Lezama Lima was a member. However, the members of the *Orígenes* group were also influenced by European vanguards (Perlongher, 1996: 24). He suggests that the *barroco* is not natural in Argentina; indeed Argentina had no *barroco* poets of note and Borges 'ya había descalificado el barroco con una ironía célebre' (25).[7] However, Perlongher states decisively:

> Ello no quiere decir que el impulso de barroquización no estuviese presente en las escrituras transplatinas – y de un modo general, en el interior del español –. Ya Darío había artificializado todo, y algún Lugones lo seguiría en el paciente engarce de las jaspeadas rimas. Por otro lado, el neobarroco parece resultar – puede arriesgarse – del encuentro entre ese flujo barroco que es, a pesar de los silencios, una constante en el español, y la explosión del surrealismo. (25)

The roots of the *neobarroco* in Argentina are thus found in the work of the *Modernistas* and the avant-gardes of the 1920s and 1940s, and their followers. As discussed in chapter 3, by 'surrealism' Perlongher is perhaps implying more a general avant-garde tendency that would include authors as chronologically, thematically and poetically diverse as Enrique Molina and Macedonio Fernández. Indeed Perlongher names these two and Oliverio Girondo as key figures in the *neobarroco*. Their enemy is 'los estilos oficiales – el realismo y sus derivaciones, como la poesía social' (25–6). It is worth also highlighting another connection here, not mentioned by Perlongher, specifically the shared influence and cultivation of the irrational in these poets. The problem here is that the influence of Vallejo, a clear link between the tardy Argentine surrealists and the historical avant-gardes, as discussed in chapter 3, is ignored by Perlongher. Furthermore, he contradicts his earlier essay (1983b, above), where Gelman – perhaps the social poet par excellence in Argentina – is listed as key to the new poetry.

This combination of historicized movements and non-historicized operations allows us to make a distinction. For Perlongher, there is an operation, folding, which is the essential trait of the *barroco*, a tendency that has appeared over the centuries and across continents. There are also examples of this tendency, all with a historicity, such as the Golden Age *barroco*, the Cuban *neobarroco*, and the Argentine *neobarroso*.

For Perlongher the *neobarroco* differs from the Golden Age *barroco* in one key respect:

> Hay, con todo, una diferencia esencial entre estas escrituras contemporáneas y el barroco del Siglo de Oro. Montado a la condensación de la retórica renacentista, el barroco áureo exige la traducción: se resguarda la posibilidad de decodificar la simbología cifrada y restaurar el texto 'normal', a la manera del trabajo realizado por Dámaso Alonso sobre los textos de Góngora. Al contrario, los experimentos neobarrocos no permiten traducción, la sugieren – estima Nicolás Rosa – pero se ingenian para perturbarla y al fin de cuentas destituirla. (Perlongher, 1996: 26–7)

Perlongher is drawing attention to a key distinction between the classical and the modern, specifically the cultivation of plurisignification in the modern, whereas the classical tends to resort to set formulas, as highlighted by Benjamin above. However, this is also Perlongher's genealogical masterstroke, acknowledging the Golden Age but simultaneously downgrading it. The new poetry is freer to fold and experiment because it is not based on Petrarchan frameworks. Thus the *neobarroco* in Argentina is more *barroco* than the *barroco* itself.

Perlongher complicates matters with another formulation: the *neobarroso*. He attributes this to Osvaldo Lamborghini: 'su obra puede considerarse el detonador de ese flujo escritural que embarroca o embarra las letras transplatinas' (27). Now, dirtying and 'baroquing' are one and the same, their equivalence suggested by the 'o' in Perlongher's formulation. Perlongher is suggesting that the operation of folding in the River Plate region tends specifically towards the low, the dirty and the sexual, dirtying literature and dragging classical tropes through the mud. Again, a *barroco* formulation by Perlongher privileges the hidden and the low through academic or literary work.

Moreover, Perlongher insisted on a further distinction between types of *barroco* in a review of the Portuguese translation of Lezama Lima's *Paradiso*: 'it wears its roots, its origin, the point from which it flourishes, as opposed to the neoclassical *barroco*, which is purely exterior, as in the case of Alejo Carpentier' (1987c: 38 [São Paulo] my translation from Portuguese).[8] There is an obvious irony here as the Deleuzean Perlongher praises a writer for displaying roots and origins, a Platonic anathema to the French philosopher. Carpentier is held up as an example of the academic, state-sponsored *barroco*, rather than the rogue spirit found in Góngora and Lezama. Two ironies occur here. Firstly the *barroco* and *gongorismo* achieved in the Latin American colonial era a contradictory status as both a state style and a source of new artistic freedom and notions of genius, as suggested by Peter Bürger (1984: 41), particularly within the cloisters of religious orders, where the *barroco* style flourished, as in the writings of Sor Juana Inés de la Cruz, or in the spectacular religious art of Minas Gerais. Secondly, Argentina itself has almost no *barroco* literary tradition. Thus to speak of an opposition between a state *barroco* and a rogue, independent version is both contradictory and historically inaccurate. It is as if Perlongher is attempting to write out the existence of the Latin American *barroco* tradition and its theorists, including for example Sor Juana, Carpentier or Andrés Bello.

Perlongher finds the key *barroco* trait of *Paradiso* in its excess – obviously – but more importantly, in its in-betweenness: '*Paradiso* should be read as a long poem, or, better still, as a point of passage between poetry and the poem, between the flow and its incarnation' (1987c: 38, my translation from Portuguese). Perlongher offers another example of this betweenness: 'from the union of a cat and a marten, there is born not a cat or a marten, but a flying cat' (38). Problematically, these elements are not radically different from Carpentier's theorizing on the *barroco*, as in his essay 'Lo barroco y lo real maravilloso' (1975), despite Perlongher's claims. Thus I consider Perlongher's constructions of the *barroco* and the *neobarroco* to be complex strategies of poetic self-vindication and alliance-forming, closely related to developments in the mass media and politics in Argentina in the 1980s and the emergence of small, loosely linked and international late avant-garde groups in Latin America.

The *Neobarroco* as a Movement

Many of Perlongher's contemporaries, particularly the so-called *neobarroco* authors, differed from Perlongher in that they stripped all overt political references from their poetry. One such example is Emeterio Cerro, whose *Las Mirtilas* was published by Último Reino (like three of Perlongher's collections), in 1989. Cerro's trajectory is exemplary of Perlongher and his peers: born in 1952 in Balcarce, province of Buenos Aires, *licenciado* in psychology, a psychoanalyst and a trained stage manager who has studied linguistics at the Sorbonne. He has published poetry, theatre and novels with *XUL* and Último Reino, and runs a theatre company called 'La Barrosa'. *Las Mirtilas* is a highly ludic, non-communicative collection that uses short, disjointed phrases, words and parts of words, distributed in patterns around the page that create an experimental feel, as if elements have been thrown together to see how they will accompany each other.

The collection's opening poem '*El caigan a manos de*', an *ars poetica* for the collection, exhibits the playfulness that character-izes Cerro's work; it has a lightly humorous tone and flirts with rhyme, like a children's song. Coupled with this there is a certain *use* of the Golden Age *barroco*: '*no son de Poesía su Escuela / allí donde nacen dramática gramática mata*' (7); the twisting of syntax (hyperbaton) is characteristic of Góngora and his *Soledades*. The Golden Age *barroco* is used to offer a literary space for the sexual. We read a metaphor for the sexual gaze that includes a playful neologism: '*parra / donde ojo parsimohoso pierde calzón*' – '*parsimo-hoso*' suggesting both lingering (*parsimonioso*) and moist (*mohoso*). The poem links the high and the low, like Perlongher's work (above); the *Mirtilas* are described as '*colgajes / luciérnagas, serpen-tinas*' (7): dangly bits ('*colgajes*'), the genital, combined with the high register adornment of '*serpentinas*' and '*luciérnagas*'.

What is even more noticeable about the collection and where there is a key difference to Perlongher, is in the absence of politics or history from Cerro's collection and the focus on the purely ludic and metapoetic. *Las Mirtilas* suggests that the *neobar-roco* as a movement or school is one that is united less by strict poetics than by a certain career trajectory and by a desire to privilege ludic, often sexual experimentation in poetry.

Much of Perlongher's work involved reviewing such work by other River Plate artists and intellectuals. The risk this sort of activity presents for the artist is becoming conservative and stuck: writing for a predetermined audience, being 'understood' by a select crowd and engaging in intellectual review swapping. Raquel Ángel talks of the shift from 'Prometheus' to 'Narcissus' that affected many intellectuals in the 1980s, an end to stated political

commitment and an embracing of the new 'social democracy';
many left-wing and former exiled or censored intellectuals were
employed by the Alfonsín and Menem governments (Ángel 1992:
9–14) in an unprecedented *rapprochement*. As Eduardo Grüner
remarked: 'intellectuals and leaders from the 1970s – I don't
mean all of them, but the majority – have become more or less
part of the official political class; some with Alfonsinismo, even
Menemismo or FREPASO' (Moreno 2002c: 157).

This allows us to situate *neobarroco* theorizing in Argentina as in
many ways linked to new aims for artistic openness and pluralism
in the post-dictatorship era, where values such as artistic freedom
are opposed to the censorship and exile of artists under the
proceso regime. Conversely, such freedom may obscure exclusion-
ary and controlling changes that result from neo-liberal economic
and social policies in Argentina. From this situation arise the
irony and the necessity of the exclusion of political themes by
many successful writers within the *neobarroco*.

The Argentine critic Omar Chauvié links the *neobarroco* to the
emergence of new publications such as *El Porteño*, *XUL* and *Último
Reino*, which offered new spaces for debate and polemic in
Argentina. Thus there existed in the 1980s a more solid academic
and commercial base for poetry and debates over poetry. There
exists at the same time however uncertainty, particularly with
regard to literary tradition and the relationship with the past, part
of a process of self-examination in the wake of the dictatorship.
Old certainties – the classical literary values of clarity and har-
mony, for example – break up but, at the same time, there is a
resistance to this break-up. The *neobarroco* is thus a tendency, a
vanguard without manifesto in the 1980s in Argentina (Chauvié,
1998: 112), where excess is the norm and various indetermina-
tions prevail: what is said becomes assimilated to phrasing, follows
the rhythm of verse and forgets meaning; the signifier is raised to
the maximum possible value, words are governed by opacity, and
speech becomes a musical game (113). In Perlongher, the *barroco*
is opposed to the idea of a core or dominant social meaning, and
decentring and fragmentation dominate (113). Nevertheless, with
the existence of new commercially distributed magazines for
poetry, such as *Diario de Poesía*, the *neobarroco* offers a certain
strategy to 'construir poder' (114) for these vanguard groups.

The sociologist Pierre Bourdieu critically assesses this type of
situation in his work *The Field of Cultural Production*. While

Bourdieu's classification of different types of art and his charac-
terisation of the 'field' may seem at times rather too general for
practical critical application, some of his observations about
practices within the artistic field are highly revealing for our
assessment of the work of self and mutual-validation that occurs
within the *neobarroco* movement. Bourdieu observes that:

> In the present stage of the artistic field, there is no room for
> naïveté, and every gesture, every event, is, as the painter nicely put
> it, 'a sort of nudge or wink between accomplices'. Never has the
> very structure of the field been present so practically in every act of
> production. (1993: 109)

Bourdieu insists that individual creativity is never the only factor
in artistic creation and that the conditions of the field are vital in
determining artistic content, reception and success. The modern
era, then, for Bourdieu, with the increasing commodity status of
cultural capital, is one where the field dominates ever more. This
leaves the artist in a position of increasing dependence on his or
her peers: 'the artist's work [is] closer to that of the "intellectual"
and [this] makes it more dependent than ever on "intellectual
commentaries"' (109). Thus mutual reviewing, introducing and
editing are all part of a process whereby the *neobarroco* poets
follow what Bourdieu calls the 'autonomous principle' of those
who seek relative independence from the economy. Within the
autonomous sector, argues Bourdieu, a new phenomenon
emerges:

> Tiny, 'mutual admiration societies' grew up, closed in upon their
> own esotericism, as, simultaneously, signs of a new solidarity
> between artist and critic emerged. This new criticism, no longer
> feeling itself qualified to formulate peremptory verdicts, placed
> itself unconditionally at the service of the artist. (116)

In the case of Perlongher and his fellows, this situation is
complicated when the writer is also the critic, a dual role not
assessed by Bourdieu. However, his suggestion of 'solidarity' still
holds true. Within these 'mutual admiration societies' – the
process of mutual reviewing, editing and so forth that many of the
self-identified *neobarroco* writers engaged in – we can also identify
the privileged space occupied by the act of quotation. Bourdieu
suggests that the quotation is aimed at other informed readers.
The authors quoted – in the case of the *neobarroco*, Lezama Lima

and Góngora obviously figure most prominently – are called
'privileged interlocutors', those whose work is implicit in the
writings of a member of the field, whose work an author has
internalized, and whose reading is expected from the other
members of the field. Here then we find one of the many
ambiguities of the so-called *neobarroco*. Despite the privileged
interlocutor status predominantly of Golden Age *barroco* authors,
as revealed in reviews and interviews, the Latin American avant-
garde writers are also vitally important for the writings of the
neobarroco. Furthermore, the radical difference between the level
of political content in writing – a quality which I feel sets
Perlongher apart from a writer such as Cerro – reveals the
extreme difficulty in supporting through critical analysis many of
the claims made by these writers about their work. Perhaps what
we can be sure about in our assessment of these writers is their
engagement in a particular career path, namely a mutually
dependent creation of an autonomous artistic space in which the
term *barroco* functions as a privileged reference point, but in
which other writings, in particular the Latin American avant-
gardes are also of significant importance, especially for the tech-
nical and poetic aspects of their writing.

Ghetto Slang and Metaphors

An analysis of Perlongher's exploration of the metaphor reveals
several aspects of his perception and utilization of the *barroco*: the
complicated relationship with the Golden Age *barroco*, which
while apparently intimate in his pronouncements seems more
distanced under analysis; attempts to create a literary pedigree for
his and others' experimental writing; an examination of the risks
of the metaphor as a conservative trope; and the ever important
links between Perlongher and the avant-garde.

   Key to the early work of Perlongher is a certain representation
of the homosexual 'ghettos' of Buenos Aires, and later São Paulo,
and their attendant slang. Perlongher draws analogies to
respected cultural manifestations in order to positively validate
the ghetto and its language. This is illustrated by '(Estado y
soledad)', the final poem of *Austria-Hungría*, with its play between
classical Greek references and the streets of Buenos Aires:

Aquí, por Zeus os digo, Patroclo fue cubierto por Aquiles
(según un inscripción descifrada en los baños de Nouvelle
	Pompéi)
Aquí, en verdad os digo, yació Líber penetrado por Arce:
en ese tuco

Caminamos Lavalle, por la Alemania espesa
donde se yerguen las escolopendras y
silban, por Laprida, por Pasteur
silban las balas de las pistolas, huele a gas
donde antes olió a lim
(Perlongher, 1997a: 61 [1980, Buenos Aires])

Perlongher presents mimetic details from the streets of contemporary Buenos Aires: Lavalle (a popular street for homosexual cruising), Nouvelle Pompéi (a XXX cinema), and the military violence of the *proceso* ('balas', 'pistolas'). 'Lim' is a brand of detergent, appropriate for the setting of a cinema toilet. At the same time, Perlongher uses what one might call crude or vulgar metaphors, euphemisms from everyday speech that start as metaphors but become banal. 'Tuco' metaphorically suggests semen ('tuco' is to spaghetti as semen is to a penis – a white, sticky substance found near a tubular object), while the 'escolopendras', a centipede, is perhaps a crude metaphor for the penis, particularly appropriate as it suggests the provocative pose of Buenos Aires *taxi-boys* who would be present in such a location (the standing up motion of a centipede is equivalent to the rising of a penis becoming erect). Meanwhile, the classical Greek references – Liber, Arce, Zeus and Achilles – aestheticize this street setting and language in unexpected ways. An analogy is created whereby homosexual behaviour and illicit sex is identified in Buenos Aires, but with an overlap – the type of movement in space and time described in chapter 2 – to classical Greece. In this early poem Perlongher not only identifies the stifling prison environment of the military dictatorship but also a type of poetry, the crude metaphor, which he identifies as equivalent to the classical beauty of ancient Greece.

The later poem 'Leyland', from *Parque Lezama*, written during Perlongher's research in São Paulo, exhibits the use of such simple, translatable metaphors, for example, 'El cobrador empina su cachimbo' (Perlongher, 1997a: 194 [1990, Buenos Aires]), where 'cachimbo' translates as penis. This is not an attempt on my part to supply an interpretation of the poem, rather that the poem, through its own contextual markers, seems to limit the interpretation of certain tropes. In the example above, 'cobrador' is the key factor, inserting the mercantile element (the relationship between one who charges, the prostitute, and a client) that determines the meaning of the trope. The 'metaphorical' nature of Argentine slang is signalled by one if its foremost researchers, José Gobello: '[lunfardo] es un idioma cargado de metáforas' (1958: nn). Perlongher spoke of these types of metaphors, translatable within a given social context, in essays written on the subject of male prostitution from as early as the mid 1970s: a term that is initially metaphorical but with use over time within a certain group becomes a cliché.

Elsewhere in Perlongher's poetry from the early 1980s, there is a more complex form of metaphor that complicates this representation and vindication of ghetto activity and codes. In the early poem 'El polvo', from *Austria-Hungría*, metaphors for sexual perversity are key to the aestheticization of the obscene; faeces is shown in metaphors where the obscene is juxtaposed with the precious: 'Ella depositaba junto al pubis cofres de oro amarillo, joyas / de las piratas / fruto de sus deposiciones' (1997a: 31 [1980, Buenos Aires]). These metaphors are rather complicated, in that the excess of detail on the referential side ('joyas de piratas', 'cofres de oro', 'frutos') outweighs the metaphorical reading: there is more weight for the description of jewellery than the metaphor for faeces. Thus we have a metaphor that goes beyond the squared Petrarchan metaphors of Góngora and drifts into excessive description of the referential side. Rather than just the formula, 'depositions are to her as jewels are to pirates', the description of the jewels and the pirates dominates, so phrases like 'frutos de sus deposiciones y repuestos' (line thirty-six) are very difficult to interpret.

The poem 'Para Camila O'Gorman' from *Alambres* deepens this experimentation with metaphor, and allows us to suggest a classification of the types of metaphor found in Perlongher's work:

> Con su sencillo traje de muselina blanca tijereteada por las balas,
> rea
> La caperuza que se desliza sobre el hombro desnudo (bajo el pelo
> empapado de cerezas)
> Como una anilla de lombriz de tierra que huye

Así ella se levanta
(Perlongher, 1997a: 77 [1987, Buenos Aires])

The poem is organized around the repetition of logical introductory phrases, for example a two-line phrase, followed by 'como', then a 'que' to introduce a long subordinate but drifting clause. The formula 'w como x que y así z' (for example 'como una anilla de lombriz de tierra que huye / asi ella se levanta') is used three times elsewhere in the poem. It allows Perlongher to experiment with increasing levels of obscurity and decreasing levels of mimesis. The first line *refers* to a verifiable historical character – Camila O'Gorman, executed by Rosas's troops – and the movement proposed by 'como' can be seen as a traditional simile: 'w is like x'. The addition of 'que' and 'así', however, shows a double movement away from simply describing that character: 'that y', 'so z'. This reaches its greatest intensity in the use of isolated words and phrases, stripped of obvious context or semantic position further on in the poem: 'Así huidiza', 'Blanca', 'Blanco' (77). The poem thus traces a number of metaphors in the broadest sense of the word (Greek for 'transference', thus the movement of a word from one context to another). The first is the simile ('como'), the translatable comparison of w to x. The second is the metaphor as in the Golden Age *barroco* tradition, for example the phrase, 'la infantería colorada partió en persecución de las infantas' (Perlongher, 1997a: 77), where Camila and her lover Ladislao are to Rosas's army as the innocents are to Herod's troops. The third type of metaphor is found in the long, drifting clauses, not translatable, in the sense of something that can be restored or semantically fixed to a metaphorical referent, as for example the classical references in Góngora's *Soledades* can be. This is found in particular in the sonically driven and stammering parts of the poem where the verbal signs of simile or metaphor are defied by the breadth of sonic and sensual connection: 'Jala la nieve de las guaridas de la noche que se disuelve como un humo / Blanco / Que desbordaba' (Perlongher, 1997a: 77). Hence an element like 'anilla de lombriz' is initially a simile for Camila's hood, but is also a worm, and later, teasingly, an 'anilla de vaselina', suggesting another persecution altogether, that of homosexuals.[9] Rather than x being like something else, Perlongher creates points and parts in constant movement in a molecular space between any possibility of unified, molar beings: what might be termed a (non) metaphor, where while the possibility of decoding is suggested, the weight of extra sonic and sensual detail creates a constant tension between the desire to translate or decode and the work the poem performs to complicate this possibility.

For Perlongher, the last type of metaphor was key to his work; his refusal of the possibility of translation for the *neobarroco* (1996: 27 Buenos Aires [1991, São Paulo]), as discussed above, is in keeping with the long, sensuous, drifting clauses that dominate much of *Alambres* and *Hule*. Amícola (2000: 167–8) links another *barroco* trait, that of anamorphosis, or the picture that only looks realistic from a certain point of view or when seen in a distorting mirror, to modern sexual marginality and its codes, as in the work of Genet or Sarduy. One could relate this to the ghetto codes and vulgar metaphors found in Perlongher's poems that deal with homosexual communities. Importantly then, the *barroco* possesses traits linked to the keeping of secrets within a fixed community, such as the small marginal communities discussed above, as well as the small community of an avant-garde group. Perlongher though, as his career progressed, became increasingly wary of ghettoization as a way of limiting oppositional groups to small, contained spaces within state apparatus (Ulanovsky, 1990: 11; Perlongher 1997b: 88 [1991]; Ekhard and Bernini, 1991: 84, all Buenos Aires).

Thus the metaphor, as ghetto slang limited to a socio-geographical zone, can be turned into a fixed and conservative stock of requisites and exchanged and channelled within state apparatus. This then is perhaps the reason Perlongher aims to extend the scope of the metaphor beyond the Golden Age *barroco* schemata. It is therefore worth comparing Perlongher's meta-phors with those of Girondo, the avant-garde poet Perlongher regarded as so important to the *neobarroco* in Argentina. In the poem 'Otro nocturno', from the collection *Veinte poemas para ser leídos en el tranvía*, Girondo creates a set of similes and metaphors related to night:

> La luna, como la esfera luminosa del reloj de un edificio público.
> [. . .]
> Noches en las que nos disimulamos bajo la sombra de los árboles,
> de miedo de que las casas se despierten de pronto y nos vean pasar,
> y en las que el único consuelo es la seguridad de que nuestra cama
> nos espera, con las velas tendidas hacia un país mejor. (1996: 49
> [1922])

The poem displays both simple similes and more complex, even experimental metaphors. The first simile shows the poet using the city as protagonist ('un edificio público') to create equivalences that raise the artificial ('el reloj') to the level of nature ('la luna'), in keeping with the urban focus of many avant-garde writers. The second section is a fully functioning metaphor: sheets are to bed as sails are to boat. Girondo's development here – the experimentation – is the addition of a third term, 'a better country' ('un país mejor'), so the formula reads sheets to bed to dream as sails to boat to better country. Thus we can see how Perlongher moves from an innovatory basis already founded by his vanguard predecessor Girondo to advance the metaphor away from possible stagnation and conservatism.

In her analysis of avant-garde authors, Cynthia Vich pays significant attention to the position of the metaphor in their writing. She suggests that:

> Tanto en Europa como en América Latina los vanguardistas estaban convencidos de que la re-creación de la realidad que querían efectuar sólo podía darse tras la renovación del lenguaje; del lenguaje poético específico [. . .] Por esta razón la metáfora se convirtió en el eje de la estética vanguardista, no sólo a nivel creativo, sino también a nivel teórico, proponiéndose como el elemento clave de la ruptura frente a la tradición estética [de] la identificación de dos elementos en base a algún tipo de característica compartida por ambos [. . .] Para oponerse a este concepto, los vanguardistas elaboraron la 'imagen múltiple' (Gerardo Diego) o la 'metáfora excepcional' (Jorge Luis Borges). (2000: 109–10)

With the aim of changing the world, the vanguardists changed the metaphor. What they did was very similar to Perlongher's work: 'la combinación de elementos cuya semejanza resultaba muy difícil de descubrir [. . .] el irrealismo de comparación' (110) or 'la prolongación excesiva de las imágenes' (110). This allows connections where traditionally none would be found: 'Consecuentemente, la metáfora vanguardista se definió a partir de una lógica que ante todo proponía la libertad asociativa como principio creador fundamental' (111). Thus while Perlongher's work may have a convoluted relationship to the Golden Age *barroco* and displays a problematic and testing attitude to the metaphor, one cannot understate the links, both in broad technical terms and in terms of the creation and validation of small socio-cultural groups, between Perlongher's supposedly *barroco* or *neobarroco* work and the historical avant-gardes.

The Observational and Abstract *Barroco*

The collections *Hule* (1989, Buenos Aires) and *Parque Lezama* (1990, Buenos Aires) are central to any theorizing on Perlongher's interpretation of the *barroco* as they emerge from the years in which he dedicated a significant number of essays and reviews to the subject, and clearly illustrate attempts at *barroco* writing. They include titles such as 'Formas barrocas' and 'Preámbulos barrosos'. In fact, their years of publication are deceptive. As Perlongher states, *Hule* 'fue escrito después que *Parque Lezama* pero, a esas jugarretas editoriales, salió antes' (Saavedra, 1991: 3). Reversing the order in which the collections are usually anthologized (see Perlongher, 1997a: 371, 379), so that instead *Parque Lezama* precedes *Hule*, allows the reader to identify a point of tension and development that may otherwise go unnoticed. The key tension between the two works is between what I would call the *observational* and *abstract barroco*. Perlongher creates an *observational barroco* in *Parque Lezama*. Here he describes sexual practices amongst marginal figures and lumpenproletariat classes either using the word 'barroco' and its variants, or techniques drawn from the poetry of the *barroco*, without a direct macropolitical content, and includes functioning metaphors for sexual actions. *Parque Lezama* reflects Perlongher's investigation of zones of homosexual sex-commerce as possible micropolitical resistance to state power, given the failure of macropolitical left-wing projects in the late 1970s and early 80s and Perlongher's disappointment over the left's support for the dictatorship's campaign in the Malvinas/Falkland islands.

In *Hule*, instead, we see the creation of an *abstract barroco*. This entails creating Golden Age and architecturally baroque forms such as swirls, folds and relationships of unresolved tension between objects. This is mixed with macropolitical developments in Argentina in the late 1980s. Furthermore, *Hule* demonstrates the presence of the law in bodily contacts. In *Hule* the (non) metaphor (see above) dominates, in an apparent attempt to avoid ghetto interpretations. The second collection sees the spread of AIDS and the medico-judicial response it provoked, closing off

sex as a form of micropolitical resistance, alongside a certain
nostalgia for anarchist political resistance, given the spread of
convenient discourses of forgetting and *rapprochement* towards
military criminals and the spread of neo-liberal free market
economic policies in Latin America. *Hule* also contains poems
that respond directly to political developments in the late 1980s,
for example the *punto final* law stopping legal cases against *proceso*
crimes and the attempt to relocate the capital of Argentina to
Viedma in the south.

The Observational *Barroco*

Much of Perlongher's early use of *barroco* as a descriptive term was
confined to his anthropological work, where he used the term to
describe several phenomena in the business of masculine prosti-
tution, for example the many names given to sexual roles:

> *Bicha bofe, michê, travesti, gay, boy, tía, garoto, maricona, mona, oko, eré,
> monoko, oko mati, oko odara*, y sus sucesivos combinaciones (¡un total
> de 56 nomenclaturas en sólo algunas manzanas!); estos nombres
> barroquizan hasta tal punto el sistema clasificatorio que resulta
> válida asociar esta inflación de significantes a la proliferación de
> divinidades [. . .] en el paganismo de Bajo Imperio Romano [. . .]
> (1997b: 47 [1987, São Paulo] Italics in the original)

As in Perlongher's poetry, elaborate naming can be used to
aestheticize illegal sexual practices and marginal figures. However
the shift from *barroco* to another historical periodization, in this
case Roman paganism, is highly revealing: Perlongher is either
uncertain about his terminology, or is trying to extend the field of
action of the term 'barroco'. He does this with his description of
the sociability among *michês* as 'familias más exóticas que entrete-
jen corsets barrocos' (50). Here *barroco* is neither a historical
period nor a literary genre. Instead, it is a cipher for 'complex',
'manifold' or 'connecting in different ways' and, perhaps, 'spon-
taneous', or 'irrational'. It offers, therefore another link to
Perlongher's avant-garde predecessors. Importantly, too, the term
is used to identify a minority sexual group.

The poem 'Leyland', from *Parque Lezama*, is most notable for
its play between two types or fields of language. The first is
everyday language that mixes slang and terms from languages

other than Spanish, and which appears to describe a pavement
scene: 'Leyland', 'Liverpool', 'pedal', 'manopla', 'volante',
'papelotes', 'sucia', 'taburete', 'rapaz' (Perlongher, 1997a: 194–5
[1990, Buenos Aires]). The second is higher register or more
limited language taken from horse rearing, biology, jewellery,
tailoring and the exotic: 'jaspea', 'burilando', 'zafiro', 'felpan',
'pasamanerías', 'orla', 'esmaltada', 'cocuyos', 'estribo', 'ané-
mona', 'cobra', 'cristalina', 'pulpo' (194–5). This proliferation of
terms supplies the details for a presentation of sex as mercantile
exchange. What is interesting is the way that the poem, through
creating a close proximity between words separated by register,
allows dynamic similarities between the two sets to stand out, for
example the physical and practical links between 'pedal' and
'estribo'. This sees Perlongher presenting and problematizing the
relationship between high and low culture.

The poem is largely close in content to the practices described
by Perlongher in *O negócio do michê*: a play of looks and signs
between potential partners preceding anonymous sex in the back
of a car. In the essay, 'Avatares de los muchachos de la noche' (a
trial run of his thesis) he stated:

> Las relaciones de la prostitución viril están marcadas por una
> exacerbación de las diferencias [. . .] Las grandes oposiciones
> binarias que codifican el *socius* aparecen siendo ellas mismas
> deseadas; revelan así su reverso intensivo. Si el encuentro entre
> jóvenes y viejos remite a la vieja tradición occidental de la
> pederastia, se da también un peculiar cruce de clases, que se
> manifiesta entre algunos de los clientes como un deseo de salir de
> su clase social [. . .] El *michê* ha de deslizarse, así, por las fisuras de
> la jerarquía social [. . .] circunstancia presente en algunos
> discursos, donde expresiones de *argot* de los bajos fondos se
> mezclan con términos cultos e incluso psicoanalíticos (Perlongher,
> 1997b: 52 [1987, São Paulo])

The poem and the anthropological observation identify the same
bipolar processes and movements. The play in language between
different fields, a bipolar movement between high and low poles,
can be taxonomized thus:

Client:	More	Effeminate	Older	Richer	Higher class	Whiter	Suburban-dwelling
Michê:	More	*Macho*	Younger	Poorer	Lower class	Darker	Working in Centre

This relationship has an obvious predecessor in the Golden Age *barroco*. Foster and Ramos Foster detect in Góngora a similar bipolar movement:

> For Góngora, the peasants with their simple lifestyle are the real heroes of life [. . .] Góngora turned away from the classical standard norm whereby only noble subjects and themes were treated with the sublime language of the *stylus gravis*. Instead, his humble characters appear as they are [. . .]; yet they speak and are treated with dignity, complexity, and subtlety. (1973: 139)

High style is used to elevate characters from the popular and rural classes. The effects of this are characterized as the presence of 'barbarians on Parnassus'. They argue that this is part of a project by Góngora to destabilize received perceptions of the world, to create a new poetic world 'far superior in its complexity to the trite, mimetic *loci amoeni* of the previous age'. This includes 'the extravagant, the unusual, and the unknown' (25). They talk of 'the poet's goal of interrelating as much as possible and proving to his reader that reality is neither static nor linear, but rather shifting, recursive, plurivalent in significance, and, above all, dramatic' (27).

Perlongher, in his anthropology and poetry also describes 'barbarian' or lumpenproletariat criminals and prostitutes with high culture language, avant-garde sound patterns and experimental metaphors. In his thesis for example he spoke of the 'preámbulos barrocos' to sexual transactions. He added that:

> El fenómeno [the many names for sexual roles] se presenta, literalmente, como barroco: [. . .] una proliferación de significantes que capturan el movimiento pulsional, bajo una multiplicidad de perspectivas, sofisticando las codificaciones y haciendo cada vez más oscuro, hermético, obsesivo, el sistema. (Perlongher, 1993: 71–2 [1987, São Paulo])

This is the observational *barroco* discussed above, an attempt to find forms and patterns from the Golden Age in illegal, marginal and lower-class sexual practices, echoing Góngora in an attempt to find a respected literary predecessor for his project.

The description of a group of lumpenproletariat prostitutes as *barroco* is clearly an example of high language being used to describe the low.[10] Perlongher sees this sort of meeting as characteristic of masculine prostitution in the 1987 essay (above) and in the poems of *Parque Lezama*. A year after the essay, however, this movement of high to low can also found in Perlongher's critique of his own poetry, part of a discussion of the relationship between the body and writing. He observed an 'elemento que está presente en mis poemas: la conexión de lo más bajo con lo más alto' (D. Molina, 1988: 16). What this indicates is a shift of terms from anthropology to criticism and poetry: tropes or definitions that were formulated in Perlongher's anthropology find relevance in his assessments of his poetry. With the radical changes in the position of sexuality that accompanied the emergence of HIV/ AIDS, the terminology that he had used for sexuality no longer functioned in that sphere, indeed that sphere had changed radically. However, the connection that he had developed between sex and poetry in *Parque Lezama* offered the possibility of a translation of sexual discourses, specifically this popular *barroco* he detects, into literary ones. Sex, as revealed by AIDS, can turn completely destructive, or be reterritorialized by the state. So poetry represents a means of following intensities without risking death.

What is especially intriguing here is that Perlongher's observational *barroco* contains a remarkable blind spot. In Perlongher's work on the *barroco* he never once mentions Francisco de Quevedo, preferring instead Góngora as his privileged interlocutor, as revealed in his essays and interviews from the period. While Góngora indeed described idealized lower-class and rural figures using high-register techniques and elaborate poetics, Quevedo's late-picaresque novel *La vida del Buscón llamado Don Pablos* (1626) provides a model much closer to Perlongher's work, as described by Michael Alpert (1969: 15) when he talks of 'the wealth of violent descriptive imagery, the puns, the conceits, and of course the scatological sordidness of the hero's misfortunes'. Quevedo's work, whilst sneering at the pretensions of its autobiographical narrator, Don Pablos, allows him to aestheticize the most unpropitious material. His mother, a prostitute, becomes a 'zurcidor de gustos' (Quevedo 1977: 43), while his father, a barber and pickpocket, is described as a 'tundidor de mejillas y sastre de barbas' (41). The father's activities as a pickpocket are described through elaborate metaphorical euphemisms, for example, 'mi padre metía el dos de bastos para sacar el as de oros', a card-playing metaphor to describe two fingers ('dos de bastos') removing a coin ('el as de oros'). Perhaps the most remarkable element of Quevedo's presentation is found in the most scatological section of the text, where Don Pablos discovers that he has been the victim of a cruel practical joke, whereby a fellow guest at the inn where he is staying defecates in his bed: 'al alzar las sábanas, fue tanto la risa de todos, viendo los recientes no ya palominos sino palomas grandes' (74). The section works on a brilliant implied augmentative. 'Palominos' were at the time faeces stains on clothes, so by shifting from the diminutive to the root, 'paloma' is implied as the augmentative of 'palominos' and, thus, means stools. Quevedo displays the *barroco* skills of *genio* and *destreza* to describe faeces. What is interesting for our study of Perlongher is that the more recent poet ignores Quevedo's *El Buscón* and his many other scatological, obscene and raucous pieces, a direct *barroco* predecessor for Perlongher's work, instead focusing on folding, Góngora, and avant-garde writers in his genealogies and theories.

The Abstract *Barroco*

Hule is coloured by a different interaction with the world than *Parque Lezama*, specifically through the presence of macropolitical themes. 'El hule', discussed in detail in chapter 3, returns to the territory dealt with in Perlongher's most famous poem, 'Cadáveres': military violence, the control of the body, and memory in the light of official attempts to draw a line under the military violence with the laws passed by the Alfonsín government such as *punto final* and 'due obedience'. Alongside 'El hule', other poems in *Hule* that similarly interact on a macropolitical scale include 'Lago nahuel', a poetic obituary to Nahuel Moreno that nostalgically laments the passing of Argentina's foremost anarchist historian and activist; 'Viedma', a burlesque of the Alfonsín government's plan to move the capital of Argentina to the south; and 'El cadáver de la nación', a voodoo ceremony performed with the corpse of Evita Perón that draws heavily on the memoirs of her embalmer, Pedro Ara, and which politicizes desire in a similar fashion to 'El hule'.

In parallel to such overtly political poems, accounts of the closure of political options or new forms of repression, in *Hule* Perlongher also creates forms without an overt political aim: artifice rather than testimony. If folding in the work of Mallarmé and Lezama Lima was characterized by Perlongher as *barroco*,

Perlongher's creation of abstract folded shapes in *Hule* is perhaps best seen as an abstract literary *barroco*, particularly as the key movement is one that creates folds and shapes without a specific relation to identifiable real-world details.

This is illustrated in the poem 'Superficies paganas':

Forúnculos de paja en la gomosa superficie del surf:
                                        deslizamiento:
ondas de argento transmarino encabalgadas en jaeces
de índigo, cuyas correas o meandros
ataban confundían del yerrar las huellas en la arena,
                                        evanescentes.
[. . .]
(Perlongher, 1997a: 128 [1989, Buenos Aires])

The abstract literary *barroco* is created here by a number of means. Although the poem superficially suggests a seascape, it also draws shapes on the page ('ondas', 'huellas'), while its content is of a greater intensity – in colour ('argento', 'índigo') and in sound (el surf') – than the real world. The language is often archaic or obscure ('argento', 'jaeces'), yet is also extremely self-referential: 'encabalgadas' also describes the enjambment that occurs on many of the poem's lines. The twenty-one lines of the poem are distributed in three visually distinct sections, the central seven lines ebbing like a receding tide. There is also a *chiaroscuro* effect of sun against darkness:

desquitar
del sucio estambre de la marca,
                                        sucursales del sol
abría en el negro
                        crujir de las cutículas
[. . .] (128)

The *chiaroscuro* functions here through the play between bright light ('sol') and darkness ('negro'). This is a Golden Age *barroco* trope and causes a movement in and out on the part of the spectator. To reinforce this, the poem employs a similar effect in its syntax. Isolated phrases draw the reader in, before the larger effect of the poem's spatial arrangement and syntactical movement draws the reader out in a cultivation of instability and tension.

This instability has interesting effects for the possibility of metaphoricity in the poem:

                                        (peli-
canes furiosos disputando
en lo hondo de la huella, incandescentes pizcas del strass,
                                        polvillos
flatulentos, haces de mirra entre las cañas líquidas.)
                                        Erguías,
en el sublime transparente, los andariveles
                    de una joya que ríe al irisar
de pegajosa piel ébano chirle.
(128)

Whereas mercantile or genital elements were the master tropes
that could overdetermine other poems (above), leading to the
possibility of translation as sexual metaphors, here that possibility
is less likely, largely because the consistently high-register lan-
guage ('strass', 'mirra', 'sublime', 'joya', 'irisar', 'ébano') creates
its own texture, its own luxurious network of sound and image
between whose points the reader is encouraged to move. Thus the
body is a much less obvious presence than in the observational
barroco poems. Pleasure is found in textual games and patterns,
rather than in the depiction of sex.

This pleasure in abstract shapes and connections is amply
illustrated by the first short poem in the 'Formas barrocas' series,
which is included in full:

Las volutas de los anteparos mineralizan el desarraigo
de los volúmenes voluptuosos, en claroscuros de cim-
breos. Pasa una sombra por la cascada artificial.
(Perlongher, 1997a: 129 [1989, Buenos Aires])

Perlongher's poem places in movement various nouns that
describe movements – swirls, spirals, swaying ('volutas', 'cim-
breos', 'cascada'). Added to this there is the *chiaroscuro* effect,
both of the shadow – black on white – and the stated 'claro-
scuros'. Again, abstract shapes dominate; the tension between
shapes and the possibility of another meaning is not resolved, and
the reader is left to slide on the luxurious surface of the poem. It
is noticeable that the poem's title includes 'barroco', rather than
'barroso'. This, I feel, reinforces the abstraction at work, whereas
'barroso', Perlongher's term used to conjure up the Río de la
Plata estuary (1996: 26), would point more towards that socio-
political reality.

Thus Perlongher creates an exaggerated micro-*barroco* from everyday materials that are neither sexual nor literary but with an end product, an abstract shape, that is distinctly literary. Instead of the literary being used as a space for the obscene, here it becomes a space for literary experiment. These short poems then illustrate another movement in Perlongher's trajectory. With the onset of AIDS and the closure of political alternatives by the hardening of neo-liberal policies in Argentina and Brazil, the perversions and anonymous liaisons of the *bocas* no longer offer the same possibilities as before. Thus Perlongher examines the possibility of a pure literary space, and of literary tropes and dynamics that can be used on any base material, not simply observed in the anthropological subject. This movement is reflected in the shift in Perlongher's essay writing around 1987 to 1988 from sexuality towards the *barroco*.

On Kitsch in Perlongher

In an interview Perlongher talked of his desire to mix the poetic with the non-poetic. He called this, perhaps ignoring the more scandalous works of Quevedo (above), 'barroco de trinchera [. . .] una especie de barroco cuerpo a tierra [. . .] Entonces, de ahí puede venir cierto gusto por introducir esas palabras comunes, o vulgares, tal vez, ¿no?' (Friedemberg and Samoilovich, 1992: 31). The material used is not important: 'uno puede, en cierta disposición poética, arrastrar cualquier tipo de referentes' (31). If the materials found 'below', to be dragged along and worked on, are all in Perlongher's eyes potential materials for his *barroco* operation, he also points out another possibility: 'Yo creo que el kitsch puede ser una forma desgradada, desvalorizada o plebeya del barroco' (32). Theodor Adorno defines kitsch as:

> The precipitate of devalued forms and empty ornaments from a formal world that has become remote from its immediate context [. . .] Things that were part of the art of a former time and are undertaken today must be reckoned as kitsch. (2002: 501)

Kitsch, for the critic José Amícola 'pretendido buen gusto' (2000: 99), also related to the German terms 'gemütlich' (acquisitive) and 'Biedermeyer' (from the nouveau riche habit of producing complex and pretentious compound surnames, in this case, from the relatively common names Bieder and Meyer) is related to social processes surrounding the rise of the bourgeois classes in the eighteenth and nineteenth centuries, their attempts at social climbing, and a certain class-disdain held for them by the upper classes and guardians of taste. For Amícola, Perlongher's work is a positive attempt to connect that which the term kitsch initially tried to keep separate:

> En Perlongher, además, lo provocativo de esas categorías genéricas se manifiesta en la contraposición que ofrece la contigüidad de los materiales: los diamantes no sólo no están ausentes de estos textos, sino que se codean con el hule, como el cisne aparece apareado con el *crêpe*, o como el vellocino se presenta junto con la frase despoetizante 'nos caga a piñas en el baño', o 'el ebúrneo guante' aparece junto a 'las agujas [de los tacos de los zapatos exacerbadamente femeninos, pero usados aquí por los travestis] enchastradas de barro', para denunciar en esta mixtura un obsesivo trabajo por la yuxtaposición de lo aristocrático y lo plebeyo, de lo literario y lo presuntamente aliterario, de lo proveniente de la lengua escrita y lo obscenamente oral, de lo paradigmáticamente femenino utilizado como emblema por el travestismo. (2000: 67)

Amícola is right to signal these juxtapositions between the high and the low in Perlongher; however, his use of the term 'despoetizante' is not precise enough. Rather, Perlongher's work creates doubt about what is poetic. There is a double process at work: the poetic becomes less poetic and the non-poetic – that which should be ignored or hidden by literature – becomes more poetic; both are thrown into a zone of indeterminacy in a double process of becoming. This relationship has the effect of reversing the negative charge contained in the term kitsch, which for Perlongher takes on positive values: the kitsch is not something to be excluded as unpoetic but instead that which questions the very term 'poetic'.

This is amply illustrated in the first poem of the *Aguas aéreas* series:

> RECIO EL EMBARQUE, airado aedo
> riza u ondula noctilucas
> iridiscencias enhebrando
> en el etéreo sulfilar:

un trazo
(deleble persistencia)
en el enroque de los magmas
en el cuadriculado del mantel

-mental, la sala
de entrecasas (arte kitsch)
compostelaba medianías
en el corset del voile, leve y violado.
              [. . .]
     (Perlongher, 1997a: 247–8 [1991, Buenos Aires])

The poem was the product of Perlongher's anthropological research into the Santo Daime religion (Perlongher, 1997a: 293 [1991, Buenos Aires]; Friedemberg and Samoilovich, 1992: 32). Not only does Perlongher's poem identify an 'arte kitsch' in the interior of the Santo Daime chapel but it also creates an interior space from kitsch fabrics and clothes: a chequered tablecloth, a net corset. Meanwhile the iridescent lights, reminiscent of the mystical and kitsch painting of the Amazonian artist and mystic Pablo Amaringo (about whose work Perlongher wrote in the long poem 'El Ayahusquero' [1997], subtitled 'Sobre una pintura de Pablo Amaringo'), create a hallucination that equals the fabrics and surfaces of the room in kitschiness. Thus, from Perlongher's anthropological work, both on the sex industry and drug cults, there emerges a re-evaluation of kitsch that deeply informs any supposed *barroco* poetics. Perlongher claimed that the songs and prayers discovered by the adepts of the *ayahuasca* ritual 'configura también una verdadera poética: un barroquismo popular' (1991e: 28 [Buenos Aires]). Perlongher also signalled the effect of living in Brazil as incrusting certain kitsch forms in his poetry: 'el saquito de banlon [a type of nylon jacket, popular in the late 1960s and early 1970s], que sacado de contexto adquiere otra relevancia [. . .] es una imagen de estética kitsch. Estando afuera uno acaba mezclando las lenguas y eso también constituye un elemento estético' (Ulanovsky, 1990: 11).

Thus we can detect in Perlongher's supposed *barroco* poetics a more complex social movement. While *poesía social* may have dealt with kitsch, it is as a deformation of real taste, a failed attempt by the lower classes to associate with the classes above them. Roque Dalton, in *Taberna y otros lugares* (1969), or Ernesto Cardenal in

the poems 'Como latas de cerveza vacías' and 'Detrás del monas-
terio, junto al camino' (1971: 82–3), both criticized the accumu-
lative materialism of the rising classes from a *poesía social*
standpoint. Perlongher, however, identifies kitsch not only as a
genuine trait in the lower-class prostitutes and popular religions
he studied, but also attempts a poetic vindication. This high–low
movement is closer, I feel, to the efforts of the avant-gardes, in
particular in their work on the metaphor, than to the Golden Age
barroco as found in Góngora's work. While Perlongher makes use
of the *barroco* technique of folding, that is not the only *barroco*
trait, and it is not the only technique at work in Perlongher's
complex attempt at aestheticizing and justifying certain popular
cultural forms by giving them literary and social prestige in a
form of poetry that I would call *avant-garde kitsch*.

Last Poems: A Different *Barroco?*

After several years of work focused on Góngora and Lezama Lima,
Perlongher's last poems offer a different and somewhat surprising
literary predecessor, namely Francisco de Quevedo, the figure
somewhat overlooked in Perlongher's earlier work – certainly in
his prose studies – as mentioned above. Similarly, whereas in
many earlier collections Perlongher has lauded in-between and
undecidable states (between genders, countries or epochs, as
described in chapter 2), 'El mal de sí' explores dying as an
unfavourable betweenness. The poem is an address to death, very
much in the tango style.

Detente, muerte:
tu infernal chorreado
escampar hace las estanterías,
la purulenta salvia los baldíos
de cremoso torpor tiñe y derrite,
ausentando los cuerpos en los campos:
los cuerpos carcomidas en los campos barridos por la lepra.

Ya no se puede disertar.

[. . .]

No es lo que falta, es lo que sobra, lo que no duele.
Aquello que excede la austeridad taimada de las cosas

o que desborda desdoblando la mezquindad del alma prisionera.
Mientras estamos dentro de nosotros duele el alma,
duele ese estarse sin palabras suspendido en la higuera
como un noctámbulo extraviado.
(Perlongher, 1997a: 355)

The poem is an impassioned plea for life in the face of death. As
well as defining the nature of death – a clearing out of the body
('su infernal chorreado', 'ausentando los cuerpos'), a destruction
of the faculties ('torpor'), particularly speech ('disertar') – that
follows Deleuze and Guattari's description of the empty or non-
productive Body without Organs,[11] the poem cites Quevedo
(rather than Perlongher's favourite Golden Age poet, Góngora)
in a move that radically changes the tone of Perlongher's appro-
priation of the *barroco*. While many of the quasi-*barroco* tropes I
have mentioned are present, such as the hyperbaton in lines two
and three that draws on Góngora's *culteranismo* (the infinitive
'escampar' and its subject are separated by the verb 'hace', whose
subject is 'muerte' in the opening line), the lines 'Aquello que
excede la austeridad taimada de las cosas / o que desborda
desdoblando la mezquindad del alma prisionera' cite one of the
most discussed lines in Spanish poetry: 'Alma a quién todo un
dios prisión ha sido [. . .]', from Quevedo's 'Amor constante más
allá de la muerte'. Perlongher's association of Quevedo's idea of
love ('dios') trapped inside a soul with pain ('Mientras estamos
dentro de nosotros duele el alma') and dying ('ese estarse sin
palabras suspendido') suggests a need to connect, denied by the
classical constraints of Quevedo's non-sexual unconnected love.
Hence the excess with which Perlongher responds to Quevedo
('lo que sobra', 'Aquello que excede la austeridad') in the poem.
However, without connecting, this excess is fatal, and thus death
comes in the sense of being lost and trapped that ends the poem.

Perlongher's intervention in Quevedo's poetics represents a
criticism of a discourse of order and individual separation. How-
ever, it also represents a radical shift in his poetics and thematics.
Having referred almost exclusively in his *oeuvre* to those poets
charted by Sarduy and Deleuze as part of a nomadic, or *barroco*
tradition (Góngora, Lezama, Mallarmé, Artaud), or the most
excessive poets of *modernismo* (Darío, Casal, González Martínez),
his citing of Quevedo – who attacked Góngora for his neologisms,
his hyperbaton, even his supposed Jewish parentage – shows an

attempt to engage with a different tradition. It also acknowledges the existence of a *barroco* tradition of uniting the high and the low in literature, as in the *barroco* picaresque of *El Buscón*, or Quevedo's satirical, often obscene poems of everyday life.[12] Having worked so hard to establish a pedigree for the *neobarroco* in Argentina as a space for dealing with that written out of official history and literary canons, this new engagement shows Perlongher reconsidering his poetics and engagement with tradition.

Thus it is important not to simplify Perlongher's *oeuvre* by talking about him as a *neobarroco* poet or describing his poetry as *barroco* without qualification or explanation. The *neobarroco* cannot be called a movement, for it often reflects a career path more than a poetics. Perlongher's use of the *barroco* is a complex and mutative formulation, with a difficult relationship to history. This use is also an attempt to create a set of tools for social and literary aestheticization and validation. Oversimplification can mask the many changes, developments and aporia in Perlongher's poetry and poetics and it can also hide the socio-political implications of Perlongher's anthropological relationship to kitsch and the avant-garde kitsch poetics that dominates in Perlongher's use of the *barroco*.

NOTES

[1] A section of this chapter was published in earlier form in the essay, 'Tie Me Up, Tie Me Down: On Masochism, Class and the Barroco in Néstor Perlongher,' *Romance Studies* 22.2 (7/04)

[2] I refer in particular to the critics and poets involved in the publication of *Lúmpenes Peregrinaciones* (Cangi and Siganevich [1996]). In particular see Tamara Kamenszain (1996), Roberto Echavarren (1996) and Susana Cella (1996).

[3] Perlongher's comments on 'Cadáveres' contradict other statements about the genesis of his most famous poem, for example those made in an interview with Friedemberg and Samoilovich: 'Yo me volví a Brasil en ómnibus, y durante el viaje empezó a aparecer ese poema, y después, una vez que llegué a Brasil, en mi casa, vi una especie de inspiración de la que surgió el poema completo. Tengo el original y hay pocos cambios. Entonces, yo diría que me dejé llevar [. . .]' (Friedemberg and Samoilovich, 1992: 31). This seems at odds with Perlongher's suggestion of a complex process at work in the poem. Nevertheless, this second interview was conducted towards the end of Perlongher's life, deep in his mystical phase, when notions of trance

and possession became more important to his poetics, perhaps recolouring other elements.

4 See Jozef in *Hispamérica* 64/65 for a critique of *Caribe Transplatino*, in particular the quality of the proofreading, the omission of certain poets from the selection and the failure of Perlongher to mention the review *XUL* in his introduction.

5 I refer to the edition of this essay in *Medusario* (ed. Echavarren et al.); *Caribe Transplatino* is now rather rare and its entire contents are contained in *Medusario*. The essay by Perlongher is also found in *Prosa plebeya* (1997).

6 Benjamin's work is sometimes entitled *The Origin of German Baroque Drama* as a translation of *Trauerspiel*, literally 'mourning-play'.

7 The not especially notable exception is Luis de Tejeda (1604–80), a near contemporary and follower of Góngora, educated by the Jesuits in Córdoba, Argentina, and skilled in several literary genres, and in particular in the Latinate forms of the *barroco*. Again, Tejeda is a poet not mentioned by Perlongher.

8 Alejo Carpentier is one of the key poles of reference for *neobarroco* theorizing, most often as a contrast to Lezama, Perlongher, Sarduy et al. Perlongher's definition of Carpentier's *barroco* as 'of pure exteriority' sits strangely alongside Carpentier's own pronouncements on the subject: 'el barroco es una suerte de pulsión creadora, que vuelve cíclicamente a través de toda la historia en las manifestaciones del arte, tanto literarias, como plásticas, arquitectónicas, o musicales; [. . .] existe un espíritu barroco' (1987: 106). Carpentier's paper, presented in 1975, considers the idea of a *barroco* spirit. 'El barroco [. . .] se manifiesta donde hay transformación, mutación, innovación' (110); this is, Carpentier suggests, a very American set of traits: 'América, continente de simbiosis, de mutaciones, de vibraciones, de mestizajes, fue barroca desde siempre'. Like Lezama, Carpentier detects the *barroco* in the cathedral of La Habana 'que es una de las más lindas fachadas barrocas que pueden verse en el Nuevo Mundo'. Carpentier talks of Gallegos's novel *Canaima* as *barroco* in that there are descriptions 'en perpetuo devenir' (118), predating the use of the term 'becoming' by Perlongher. The use of Carpentier as a straw man in theories on the *neobarroco* is an area that warrants further and more detailed study.

9 See for example Jean Genet's *The Thief's Diary* (1954 [1949]), where he describes how the discovery of his tube of Vaseline, taken by the police to be evidence of his homosexuality, was for him a source and symbol of pride and identity.

10 Rapisardi and Modarelli also detect *barroco* elements in homosexual subculture. For example, discussing the practice of liaisons in public toilets common under the dictatorship, they talk of 'la vida barroca de estos habitués de las teteras' (2001: 22). Talking of the signs and codes exchanged on street corners and railway platforms, they refer to a '[p]rofusión barroca de códigos particulares, sin duda, donde todo gesto remite a otro' (41). The analogy is with the displacement

at place in the *barroco* metaphor, whereby the use of classical refer-
ences allows the metaphor to become a sliding metonymic chain.

[11] 'A dreary parade of sucked-dry, catatonized, vitrified, sewn-up bodies
[. . .] Empty bodies instead of full ones' (Deleuze and Guattari, 1999:
150); '[. . .] the BwO's [Bodies without Organs] of the plane will
remain separated by genus, marginalized, reduced to means of
bordering, while on the "other plane" the emptied or cancerous
doubles will triumph' (166). The 'empty' or 'cancerous' BwO's, for
example the AIDS patient being cleared out by the hospital tubes,
are those whose attempts to escape stratification (the 'separation')
have failed; rather than connecting with other bodies or the world,
the escape from the body ends in 'baldíos' in Perlongher's poem.

[12] Something of Quevedo's poetics is used in 'Tuyú' (1981), particularly
the fan-like opening up of a molar concept through the repetition of
a noun. The poem was not included in any of Perlongher's collec-
tions or his *Poemas completos*.

Chapter 6

Perlongher's Mysticism[1]

Introduction

The apparent change in Perlongher's work after the publication of his Masters thesis in anthropology (1987) and the emergence of HIV/AIDS in Brazil, whereby he turned his literary and academic attention towards mysticism, in particular the church of Santo Daime in São Paulo and its hallucinogenic drug rituals and, later, the work of the Christian mystics Saint Teresa of Ávila and Saint John of the Cross, has caused consternation amongst Argentine critics. My aim in this chapter is to demonstrate that Perlongher's mystical poetry is more complexly related to his earlier work than previously asserted by these critics. His poetry in the collections *Aguas aéreas* (1991, Buenos Aires) and *El chorreo de las iluminaciones* (1993, Caracas/1997, Buenos Aires)[2] represents neither a complete break from his earlier work, as suggested by Juan José Sebreli (1997) nor another stage in a smooth evolution, as implied by Osvaldo Baigorria (1996) and Flavio Rapisardi and Alejandro Modarelli (2001). Sebreli attacked the last stages of Perlongher's work as being riven with contradictions derived from its sources, 'el surrealismo heterodoxo de Georges Bataille, de Michel Foucault y de Gilles Deleuze. Lamentablemente esta influencia fue la predominante en su última época, llevándolo del demonismo a la mística y aun al esoterismo' (1997: 370).

Osvaldo Baigorria also exhibits some concern in his essay on Perlongher's mysticism:

> Su vinculación con el Santo Daime inaugura la fase final, más controvertida o asombrosa, de ese viaje sobre el filo de la identidad personal. Al contrario de lo que puede pensarse, su enfermedad

no parece haber tenido influencias sobre esta nueva dirección de
sus intereses: Perlongher descubre que es HIV positivo en el 89, en
Francia, bastante después de haber conectado con la iglesia del
Santo Daime. Y su 'devenir bruja' había comenzado aun antes. Por
los años 87/88 – al mismo tiempo en que escribía sus principales
ensayos sobre el neobarroco – comienza a tomar ayahuasca o yagé
[. . .]' (1996: 178).

Unfortunately Baigorria contradicts his own work and that of
others. In the biography of Perlongher's work that he and
Christian Ferrer prepared for *Prosa plebeya,* the authors write:
'1990 [Perlongher] se conecta con la religión de Santo Daime y
comienza a participar en sus rituales' (1997: 257). Rapisardi and
Modarelli suggest that 'en 1987, varios años antes de que se le
anunciase el virus, la Rosa [Perlongher] iba tomando nota de las
prácticas comunitarias del Santo Daime y de los efectos del ritual
de la ayahuasca. [En] 1989 [. . .] se suma al Santo Daime' (2001:
195). Baigorria and, to an extent Rapisardi and Modarelli, are
attempting to deny the link between Perlongher discovering his
illness and his mysticism. However, while Perlongher did not
know he was HIV positive when he became involved with esoteric
religions, he did know that the virus had radically altered the
possibilities for sex as a form of political resistance, as illustrated
in the postscript to the essay 'Avatares de los muchachos de la
noche' and in his long essay *O qué é AIDS* (both 1987, São Paulo).

Instead, an evaluation of the relationship between the poetics,
aesthetics and thematics of poems from these collections and
examples from Perlongher's earlier work reveals a combination of
continuity and change. Perlongher examines some of the prob-
lems and possible solutions within the territorial, literary and
sexual alternatives that his work presents. We can detect therefore
three separate strands to Perlongher's poetry published after
1990. Specifically, these are *mystical masochism,* also fully a part of
his earlier work and related to some of the spatial aesthetics
detailed in chapter 2 and the sexual aesthetics detailed in chapter
4; *mystical withdrawal,* poetically and thematically similar to his
earlier work but aesthetically distinct; and, finally, a *mystical
teleology* or *purpose,* poetically similar to his earlier work but
aesthetically and thematically innovative within his *oeuvre,* in
particular in its complete dependence on the divine.

Mystical Masochism

Perlongher's fifth collection, *Aguas aéreas*, was inspired by the author's experiences attending the rituals of the Santo Daime religion in the late 1980s and early 1990s, in which with the other members of the church he took hallucinogenic drugs and participated in their songs, dances and ceremonies.[3] He also undertook a journey to the religion's headquarters, the Céu de Mapiá colony by the river Purus, in the Brazilian state of Acre. Many of the poems in *Aguas aéreas* describe the religion's rituals and the visions caused by imbibing the drug *yagé*, or *ayahuasca*.[4] Perlongher (1997b: 150 [1991, Buenos Aires]) described this with reference to the work of the German writer and anthropologist Hubert Fichte (1935–86), whose 'ethnopoetry' in works such as *Xango. Die afroamerikanischen Religionen* (1976) and *Petersilie. Die afroamerikanischen Religionen* (1980) aims to renovate the language of anthropology through the adoption of non-scientific language and genres, such as using verse for descriptions of phenomena observed in research.[5] Such is the case with the second poem in Perlongher's series:

TITILAR DE EBONITA, las lilas de la cruz
liman del clavo la turgencia áspera
o paspan el derrame del rosario
por la puntilla del mantel.

Acaireladas convulsiones, si la medusa pincha al pez, tremola
en el remolineo la flotación de un cántico, de un cántaro.

Cantarolan por darle al óleo cenagoso
la consistencia de un velo de noche, por hurtarle
al dios de la floresta la niñez de un escándalo
u otorgarle a la red de iridiscencias pasajeras (tiemblan)
la levedad de un giro en el espacio.

Patrulla el desternillar del álamo veloz la ceremonia
al tiempo que lo desboca con incrustes de strass o lentejuela móvil
que rayan la película devenida traslúcida.
La huida de los cormoranes
y en su lugar las mansas gaviotas del deseo,
el vértigo de los meollos
asombrillando el pajarear

¿Adónde se sale cuando no se está?
¿Adónde se está cuando se sale?

Al lado, o de repente, la musiquilla se aproxima
y avisa que las huellas se hacen barro en la disolución del filafil,
entonces de un tirón se restablece la rigidez de la rodilla (trémula)
y el pico de la flor abre en el témpano la cicatriz de un pámpano

                          rajando

los valles de la misa, los alvéolos
de eso que por ser misa hubo de echarle azogue al ánade,
una mano de espejo a la destreza.
(Perlongher, 1997a: 249–50 [1991, Buenos Aires])

This second poem in the collection allows us to examine the
relationship between Dionysian force and poetic or ceremonial
form that Perlongher highlighted in his writings on the mystical
experience (1997b: 149–54 [1991, Buenos Aires], or 155–73).
Many poems in *Aguas aéreas*, like this one, display formalized
rituals. We can identify this in the poem in the formal elements of
the religious ceremony, its props and rituals, for example 'cruz',
'rosario', 'cántico', and 'cántaro'. The force of the mystical expe-
rience that is held together by these rituals is found in irrational
or pre-rational sensations, involuntary movements and processes
of breaking down, for example the 'deseo', 'convulsiones' and
'disolución' described in the poem. Perlongher, however, struc-
tures the poem so that the form and force elements are both
inseparable and mutually dependent, such as in the link between
music ('musiquilla') and the involuntary movements it inspires
('rigidez de la rodilla (trémula)'). The rituals then are important
for creating a space for experimentation with the dissolution of
the self, connections with others, and non-hierarchical social
organization. For example, the poem details various sensuous
points around a room as part of a synaesthetic recreation of the
space of sensation of the ceremony: the vision of a tablecloth
('mantel') implying the central altar of the Daime church; the
cross and rosary mentioned above; the musical sounds ('musiq-
uilla'); and the bright lights and points of reflection that may be
kitsch decoration but could equally be the flashing lights that
begin the *ayahuasca* vision ('strass', 'lentejuela móvil'). Within this
space the self becomes problematic as it journeys outside the body
and the implied space or point of view it normally occupies
('*¿Adónde se sale cuando no se está?*'). I would argue that this
autonomous space, whereby the division between self and other

and the organization of social interaction on the basis of individualism are overcome, is very close to the TAZ space created in Perlongher's early poems, as outlined in chapter 2. The division Perlongher seems to be implying in this poem is the same one he draws in essays such as 'Poesía y écstasis' (1997b: 149–54 [1991, Buenos Aires]) between the disorganized and descendent 'salir de sí' of illegal drugs and sex, as portrayed in his earlier poems, and the organized and ascendent 'salir de sí' of the mystical experience.

The structure in Perlongher's poem by which this occurs, whereby force and form are mutually dependent, is closely related to Perlongher's writings on the possibility of mystical poetry. In 'Poesía y écstasis' Perlongher quoted this very poem and observed:

> Lo puro dionisíaco es un veneno, imposible de ser vivido, pues acarrea el aniquilamiento de la vida. Para mantener la lucidez en medio del torbellino, hace falta una forma. Sabemos que esa forma es poética. Intuimos que puede ser divina. (Perlongher, 1997b: 153)

Perlongher suggests that pure Dionysian force is fatal; elsewhere in the same essay he compares this to the nearly terminal experiences of Antonin Artaud with *peyote* in Mexico. The form required to hold the ecstatic experience together, Perlongher suggests, can be found in Santo Daime:

> En el que las expediciones visionarias por las infractuosidades transpersonales [...] son puntuadas y orientadas por himnos musicales, recibidos por inspiración divina por los correligionarios, que obran como faro y guía en el asombroso arrobamiento de la fuerza, devolviendo así lo divino a la forma del éxtasis que es la poética. (153)

Perlongher is comparing religious ecstasy, where formal elements guide the experience so that it does not become too dangerous, with other forms of ecstasy, for example sex or secular drug use, which do not have a formal element. He draws heavily on the work of Friedrich Nietzsche (1844–1900), who in *The Birth of Tragedy* (1872) suggested that the Dionysian and the Apolline are intrinsically linked and, while different, function together. The Dionysian is a force that breaks down barriers: 'all the rigid and hostile boundaries that distress, despotism or "impudent fashion"

have erected between man and man break down' (1993: 17).
However, there is a key divide in the Dionysian, on which
Perlongher does not dwell, between the *Dionysiac Greeks*, who had
the form offered by Apollo as control, and the *Dionysiac Barbarians*,
whose sexual excesses showed the 'savage beasts of nature [. . .]
unleashed' (18). One might offer as a parallel in Perlongher's work
the Dionysian *Barbarian* experiences of gay men looking for prosti-
tutes on the streets of São Paulo, or hippies experimenting with
hallucinogens, and the organized, ritualized experiences of Daime.
Nietzsche stresses the potential danger of the pure Dionysian but
demonstrates how in Greek tragedy (as in Perlongher's work)
ceremonial art allows the deadly Dionysian forces to be experi-
enced safely: 'art [. . .] alone can turn these thoughts of repulsion
at the horror and absurdity of existence into ideas compatible with
life [. . .]' (40).

There are a number of anomalies in the comparison that
Perlongher suggests, following Nietzsche, between prostitution
and drugs as a way of dissolving the individual and organized
esoteric religions. Firstly, the formal elements of his poems do not
alter radically with the attempts to write poetry about Daime.
There is no greater evidence of rhyme, metre or formal concerns
in the *Aguas aéreas* series than elsewhere in his *oeuvre*. As with
Perlongher's earlier poems, the same tropes are at work as in
Góngora's verses. The opening stanza of poem II employs quasi-
hyperbaton, the suppression of connectives, Latinate gerundives
and classical references but, whereas in Perlongher's poem they
are not held together by a sense of formal unity, in Góngora
syntax and form work as a unified whole. One might say that
Góngora's work contains a proliferating set of points within the
framework of the poem as a whole, whereas Perlongher's poem
uses the same tropes to create a proliferating set of points that are
related through tension that cannot be resolved, even briefly, into
a whole. This difference further reveals the connections between
Perlongher's chronologically and thematically distanced works,
for example those analysed in chapter 5.

Secondly, if we examine his work on the sex trade in São Paulo,
we will notice that Perlongher *does* highlight formal elements:

> Es preciso, sin embargo, ver cómo, en el dispositivo de la
> prostitución viril, los flujos nómades pueden ser recapturados y
> reconvertidos. [. . .] Doble tensión ésta, que retoma las díadas

deseo/interés, acaso/cálculo: pasión por el riesgo, pasión por el código [. . .]: *las sobrecodificaciones del socius* serían, en sí mismas, deseadas. (1997b: 55 [1987, São Paulo] my italics)

While Perlongher was keen to highlight the nomadic potential of male prostitution, he also outlines formal elements, for example the minutely detailed system of naming sexual roles, and the subtleties that denote price and desirability.[6] Furthermore, in *Aguas aéreas* II, Perlongher draws on elements from his overtly sexual poetry. The 'cántico' recalls the central and titular element in his unanthologized poem 'Cántiga' (1981), where the song and dance offers a provocative challenge to clear divides between the sexes. The ceremony in *Aguas aéreas* II is filled with unholy dirt, for example the 'óleo cenagoso' – muddy or slimy oil – on which the dance takes place. Similarly, 'deseo' is as much a factor in this poem as in any of his earlier works, even those of *Parque Lezama*, such as 'Leyland' (1997a: 194–5 [1990, Buenos Aires]), which portray contracts and sex between the *michê* and the client.

The attitude to the individual in Perlongher's mystical poem is also similar to his earlier works. If we recall how the becoming-woman in 'Ethel' (1981) or 'Daisy' (1983) was traced in parts and poses of the body, or how the prostitutes in 'Leyland' (1990) or 'Vahos' (1988) existed as parts of bodies – skin, thighs and penises in particular – and masculine clichés such as strength, erectility and hardness, then the fragmented bodies in *Aguas aéreas* II – 'rodilla', 'cicatriz', 'mano' – as well as reflecting the fragmented, many-centred form of the poem, also stress Perlongher's contin- ued reliance on his earlier themes. While he may be describing a mystical experience, at this stage the ceremony he describes is as physical and dirty as in his earlier poems, and there is no radical change from his earlier work.

Furthermore, the poem also exhibits a key element from Perlongher's earlier poetry in keeping with its Nietzschean approach, what Bersani (1995: 94) calls 'self-shattering jouis- sance', an impulse of self dissolution particularly found in the practice of sadomasochism (S/M) and identified by practitioners of S/M as a form of 'cosmic ecstasy' (93).[7] This is the phenom- enon in Perlongher's poem whereby the ceremony presents a means, perhaps temporarily, of destroying the individual or, more specifically, the fixed relationship between a body and a self. This is found in a number of areas of the poem. Firstly, *Aguas aéreas* II

focuses on movements of flight, such as the 'huida de cormo-
ranes', that reflect the flight of the self. Secondly, alongside the
fragmented portrayal of the body, the poem also conflates sepa-
rate forms of perception, for example in the confusion of time
and space described by the phrase 'Al lado, o de repente',
whereby physical proximity is taken also to be temporal proximity.
Furthermore, as something of a summary of these elements, the
poem suggests an emptying of the self in the lines '*¿Adónde se sale
cuando no se está? / ¿Adónde se está cuando se sale?*' The question is,
of course, unanswerable, for the masochistic, self-shattering jouis-
sance of the mystical ceremony as described by Perlongher, his
'salir de sí', denies the very existence of the self of the 'se'. As Leo
Bersani and Ulysse Dutoit suggest, in art that questions the
principium individuationis, like Perlongher's, the Dionysian dom-
inates and the self is radically challenged. They add, 'sexuality is
perhaps as close as we come (short of death) to the beneficial
destruction of the empirical individual, a destruction that is
identical to the body's most intense concentration on its own
capacity for sensations' (1993: 142). For Perlongher, however,
now that with the emergence of HIV/AIDS sexuality does not
seem to stop short of death, the religious ceremony and its
portrayal in poetry offer a formally controlled method of dissolv-
ing the individual.

Perlongher's final collection of poetry, *El chorreo de las ilumina-
ciones*, explores a very similar aesthetic. Prior to Perlongher's
death, he had broken with the Santo Daime religion and,
although he still used *ayahuasca* privately, according to Baigorria
(1996: 179–80), he felt that the religion could not offer the
medical help that his severe condition required. Perlongher had
been awarded a Guggenheim scholarship for a project uncom-
pleted at the time of his death, an *auto sacramental* or mystery play,
which Sara Torres (Rapisardi and Modarelli, 2001: 200) claims
was heavily influenced by the Christian mystics. The first poem in
the collection, 'Tema del cisne (I)', draws on *modernista* tech-
niques and classical mythology:

> Undoso el que avanzara por los rizos
> del espejo laqueado, su pezcuello
> dócil al mando del cendal declina
> rayado el rutilar de su plumaje.
>
> Quien por interrogar las inestables

corrientes donde anega su pellejo
arruga de nerviosas denticiones
la quilla que traslúcida corría

por parques de reflejos azulados,
impávido el azor, la crista altiva,
arriesga el hundimiento en ese anclaje.

Porque, por más que mírese a los hados,
no se retarda la fatal carrera
si tempestuoso pie pisa la pluma.
(Perlongher, 1997a: 297)

Perlongher's poem, his most 'correct' sonnet, portrays the immi-
nence of the poet's death using Golden Age form and *modernista*
symbolism. The swan, the *modernista* bird par excellence, whose
curved neck represents the unanswerable question for the poet
who cannot but question, as in Ruben Darío's 'Yo persigo una
forma' (Jiménez, 1994: 204 [1901]), is drawn from the symbolist
poetry of Stéphane Mallarmé (1842–98) and the Classical myth of
Leda, raped by Zeus in the shape of a swan. Perlongher here
offers an image of the questioning that he has carried out in his
poetry and anthropology: the swan, cipher for the poet, is adrift
like the earlier anthropological 'Kayak' (Perlongher, 1997a: 234
[1988, Buenos Aires]). Perlongher reframes his earlier projects
with a mystical intent ('mírese a los hados') and also with a
morbid sense of inevitability ('no se retarda la fatal carrera').
Difficulty is seen in terms of darkness and waters, an experiment
of going into the powerful unknown. This unknown may well
destroy the poet in painful and unexpected ways, as suggested by
the final line, where an alliterative sequence inextricably links the
poetic project embodied in the plume ('pluma') to violent
destruction, being squashed by the 'tempestuoso pie'. Hence the
use of the sonnet, clearer syntax, the swan and a logical method
similar to his essays in a poem that reflects on a poetic project that
has met its fatal end. Hence also Perlongher's adherence to a
form that is not entirely strict, given that the forces in operation
are strong enough to annihilate the poetic project; eight of the
fourteen lines stress on syllables two, six and ten but others do
not; the rhyme scheme is uneven and finishes on 'pluma', a word
that does not rhyme. One could suggest then that this seemingly
unequal struggle between deathly force and poetic form illus-
trates a characteristic of many poems in the final collection, for

example 'Gemido', 'Decepción', 'El mal de sí' and 'Roma', written after Perlongher's break from Santo Daime and the onset of full-blown AIDS whereby death is accepted as inevitable and the real physical effects of illness are drawn harshly into focus.

The ideas of the Golden Age mystic Saint Teresa of Ávila on the mystical experience are of help here, particularly with regards to the relationship between spiritual pleasure and physical pain:

> Era tan grande el dolor [of the mystical experience] que me hacía dar aquellos quejidos y tan excesiva la suavidad que me pone este grandísimo dolor [. . .] No es dolor corporal sino espiritual, aunque no deja de participar el cuerpo algo, y aun harto [. . .] Pues tornando este apresurado arrebatar el espíritu es de tal manera que verdaderamente parece salir del cuerpo y por otra parte claro está que no queda esta persona muerta, al menos ella no puede decir sí está en el cuerpo o si no, por algunos instantes. (Martí, 1981: 395 [1565])

Saint Teresa's insistence on the inseparability of pleasure and pain and the intimate relationship between the physical and the spiritual in the mystical experience allows us to draw the connection to the masochistic mysticism in Perlongher's earlier poems, whereby suffering, be it from the Daime ceremony or AIDS, despite its potentially lethal effects, becomes potentially divine.

An examination of the poem, 'Herida pierna', from *Austria-Hungría*, can help trace connections to his earlier work and also allow us to consider further whether this strand of Perlongher's mystical poetry presents as dramatic a change as commentators (above) might lead us to suspect.

> Coser los bordes de la herida? debo? puedo? es debido?
> he podido? suturarla doliente ya, doliéndome
>   rastreramente husmeando como un perro
>   oh señor a sus pies oh señor con esa pierna
>   atada amputada anestesiada doblada pierna
> [. . .]
> O estoy? ando? metiendo los estiletes en el muslo
>   para que arda para que mane
>   haciéndole volcar lechoso polvo en la enramada
>   ampliándola estirándola
> [. . .]
> No me hagas caso, Morenito, no la hagas
> así, tan prominente y espantosa la herida lo que hiende
>   la penetración del verdugo durante el acto del suplicio

durante la hora del dolor del calor
de la sofocación de los gemidos
impotente como potente bajo esa masa de tejidos
arbitrarios como bandidos asaetados por los chirridos
[. . .]
Debo chupar? mamar? de ese otro seno herido
desangrado con la pierna cortada con la daga
en la nalga ah caminar así, rauda cual ráfaga
montañas de basura mágicas y luminosas
ser lúcida? ahora, hoy?
tumbada cual yegua borracha cual chancha echada
cual vaca animal animal
No me hagas caso, Morenito: vé y dile la verdad a tus padres
(Perlongher, 1997a: 47–8 [1980, Buenos Aires])

As intimated briefly in chapter 3, the poem creates a relationship
of guilt and humiliation between the narrator-voice and other
subjects, for example the 'verdugo', a torturer or executioner,
and family members ('padres', 'madre'). The former is repeatedly
placed in subordinate positions, as various animals ('yegua',
'chancha') and a naughty child, and is the object of violence,
being cut ('cortado'), bled ('desangrado') and suffocated ('sofo-
cación'). This relationship is highlighted as one of impotence to
potency ('impotente como potente') but one in which impotence
becomes a form of potency. Alongside this we encounter surpris-
ingly esoteric vocabulary, for example the 'montañas de basuras
mágicas y luminosas'. This magical, luminous material stands in
keen contrast to the dirty subservience that dominates the poem.
The flashes of light within the scenes of abjection and humiliation
are a glimpse of an unspecified divine. Thus there is a suggestion
of martyrdom, the sacrifice of one's self for a greater end, and
illumination, as in the process of spiritual enlightenment. The
poem, like Perlongher's later mystical work, seems to suggest that
the adoption of a physically degraded position whereby one
voluntarily accepts violence and humiliation, can be not only
empowering but, also, like the sufferings of martyrdom, can be a
form of *ascesis*[8] to the divine. This aesthetic is also found in the
work of Jean Genet (1910–86), an author Perlongher spoke of as
being important to his early poems (1997b: 15 [1988, Buenos
Aires]). In many of his works Genet proposes a form of mystical
humiliation, generally related to homosexuality and transvestism.
In the novel *Notre-Dame des Fleurs* (1944), Genet writes:

> [Darling] walked down the Rue Dancourt, drunk with the hidden splendour (as of a treasure) of his abjection [...] (1988: 70)
> His life is an underground heaven thronged with barmen, pimps, queers, ladies of the night, and Queens of Spades, his life is a heaven. (73)
> Slowly but surely I want to strip [Divine] of every vestige of happiness so as to make a saint of her. (82)

Genet's characters in *Notre-Dame des Fleurs* are portrayed as marginal martyrs. Through them, Genet raises perversion, hunger, theft, betrayal and abjection to the level of virtues and, like perverse extensions of Saint John of the Cross they become, through their spectacular self-denial and suffering, saintly. Genet's technique, like Perlongher's, is to ally the low, dirty and humiliated with the mystical, so that the underworld becomes *ascesis* to the divine.

However, the poems by Perlongher we have examined and Genet's novel, while remarkable in their courting of the marginal and abused, do not necessarily offer a radical challenge to the structures of domination – be they sexual or economic – that frame such positions. While Perlongher reveals the sordid attraction of humiliation, there is a strong suggestion that his writing accepts the structures whereby such humiliation is imposed rather than sought. In the wider context, while members of the gay rights movement's adoption in the 1980s and 90s of terms such as 'queer' and 'dyke' as affirmative has the powerful effect of rendering harmless a term of abuse, it does not challenge the dominant social order's capacity to invent and impose such stigmatizing language. As Bersani suggests, 'resignification cannot destroy' (1995: 51). In his lauding of the social position of the scapegoat and the concomitant lauding of mystical, martyrological suffering in *Aguas aéreas* and *El chorreo de las iluminaciones*, Perlongher does not suggest a practical way out other than to celebrate what in effect is the only option available for many. This masochistic mysticism is fundamentally linked to the imminence of death, or one might say, to use Bersani's terms, that it is 'death complicit'. Bersani offers a critique of the aesthetic of mystical humiliation through S/M found in authors such as Genet: 'masochistic jouissance is hardly a political corrective to the sadistic use of power' (1995: 99). Problematically, Perlongher's mystical masochism does not challenge structures of violence and power but, in fact, willingly subscribes to and replicates them for the purposes of desiring pleasure, be it spiritual or sexual. This movement, while subversive at a surface level, suffers the key problem of being ultimately complicit with death.

On the evidence of these intertextual references I would argue that Perlongher's 'mystical turn' is not as sudden as many commentators attempt to suggest and, furthermore, that the physical intensity of Perlongher's earlier work, although abounding in references to the sordid and painful, contains an aesthetic whereby humiliation and suffering are, perhaps problematically, perceived as having divine qualities. Perlongher's project is still dependent on kitsch and sexual elements, for example the academic relationship between the middle-class poet and researcher and working class anthropological or poetic subjects, or the destruction of the self through sexual, violent or chemical means. Perlongher's poems of mystical masochism thus have key thematic, aesthetic and poetic links to his earlier work.

Mystical Withdrawal

Another set of poems in Perlongher's last two collections creates different thematic and aesthetic alternatives, specifically in the movement of *mystical withdrawal*. After poem XIX of the *Aguas aéreas* series, where the Santo Daime ceremonies and visions reach their conclusion with the vision of a god ('el sereno entregarse de un dios . . . ' Perlongher 1997a: 273 [Buenos Aires, 1991], ellipsis in original), poem XX marks a change by tracing a journey inland and into the Amazon rainforest:

> Zambullen la ondulación chispas de espumas suave, verde
> claro, en reflejos de magma vegetal que a la madera de la proa as-
> tillan, al hacer restallar en el derretimiento de la luz. Ruido
> de espumas y olor de aguas mareosas en el deslizamiento (todo se
> vuelve lento) por el Purus y las madejas en remolinos entroncadas
> que hacen de galería a la hirsuta piragua.
> [. . .]
> No más que un instante íg-
> neo en la numinosa constelación de lejanías (porque nos alejamos
> de la costa interior para internarnos por túneles de ramajes, severa
> incrustación del palo en la madera) [. . .]
> (Perlongher, 1997a: 274 [1991, Buenos Aires])

The poem marks a change in aesthetic in that it traces a movement away from the city. The ceremony and related details are no longer present. Instead, the poem describes a journey through the Amazon rainforest, 'por el Purus', the river by whose banks the *Daimeros* have their colony. Despite the absence of drug-related details – cups or purges, for example – thematically there still operates in this poem the same process of breaking up monads – the self, the body – that occurs in the ceremony poems. Sensations, for example lights and watery reflections dominate the poem, while non-reflecting surfaces begin to reflect ('incrustación del palo') through the play of light on water and light takes on the quality of water ('derretimiento de la luz'). The poem reveals the sensitivity of the *Daimero* to synaesthesia, even when not necessarily using *ayahuasca*. Furthermore, in its focus on such sensations, it seems to suggest a non-rational, perhaps pre-linguistic contact with the world, in keeping with the *ayahuasca*-induced dissolution of the self.

Whereas the work carried out in *O negócio do michê* might be described as a drift – around São Paulo – and a descent – in terms of income, class, legal position, and physically onto the street, down into nightclubs or public toilets – into the city, Perlongher's movement here is also a drift, in the kayak on the river's current, but one that is characterized as up, towards the light and the divine ('numinosa constelación'), back to the source of the river, away from the city ('por el Purus'), and towards a geographical periphery, in terms less of class or social position than of the physical isolation of the religion's headquarters, away from the coast and the southern cities that dominate Brazil politically and economically. Another vital change here is that in the journey upstream on a river, Perlongher is drifting along a path that *already exists*, unlike those traced in his earlier anthropology.

Poem XXI continues this journey and follows Guattari's thinking within the framework of the Amazonian journey:

EL JUEGO DEL CLAROSCURO en la echada hojarasca, como un calco, estampaba de ramilletes puntillistas la oscilación de los andariveles. Había el peligro de la gran serpiente fluvial, la amenaza sombría de la raya, la sonrisa desconfiada de los yacarés y la raída sombra de una tortuga al sumergirse entre las estelas alborotadas. Todo tan leve y al mismo tiempo tan caliente, tan exhausto. Nos doblega con su inmensidad el cielo como un tapado celeste inspirado

en Femirama. Una sutil femineidad cincela con delicadeza los cuer-
pos trabajados (a tachas) de los que reman y sus gestos ágiles como
panteras en el marihuanal. No es fácil abstraerse en lo celeste cuan-
do estas superficies bronceadas nos deslumbran con su acento de
canto. Sin embargo, se tiende a lo sublime, sublime resplandor.
(Perlongher, 1997a: 275 [1991, Buenos Aires])

Perlongher's poem demonstrates two areas of his mystical with-
drawal. Firstly, he displays his continued reliance on French
post-structuralist theory. The many animals in the poem go
beyond Amazonian naturalist realism and also seem to represent
the mystical possibilities of the shamanic becoming-animal, while
the forest goddess 'Femirama' reveals the mystical experience
as the becoming-woman of the forest ('rama', branch, is
feminized, 'femi'). Thus Perlongher's mystical escape is still
couched in terms drawn from Félix Guattari's *Molecular Revolution*
(1977). The bodies of the rowers are engaged in becoming-
woman – 'una sutil femineidad cincela con delicadeza los cuer-
pos' – that recalls Perlongher's suggestions about the becoming-
woman of the *michê* (1997b: 50 [1987, São Paulo]). Furthermore,
in the suggestion of a feline air to the rowers' movements ('gestos
ágiles como panteras'), Perlongher moves from this becoming-
woman to a becoming-animal. Meanwhile, there is a play between
the hardness of the bodies and the subtlety, as softness and
attention to the blurring of differences, of becoming-woman or
animal. For Perlongher, despite other changes in his poetry that
may have occurred with his involvement in Santo Daime, Guatta-
ri's suggestion that the becoming-woman is the first step in
escaping phallocentrism and, with it, the stratification of norma-
tive capitalism and heterosexuality, still provides a guiding trope
for his assessment of the revolutionary possibilities that he detects
in the religion. As Guattari (1984: 228 [1977]) observed, and
Perlongher seems to concur here, only by breaking away from the
'phallic rat race inherent in all power formations' can man
engage in becoming-woman and, from there, go on 'to become
animal, cosmos, words, colour, music'. Thus Perlongher's with-
drawal shares its theoretical basis with his earlier work.

Secondly, and vitally, this poem shows Perlongher trying to *avoid*
sex. Despite the sexual abstinence of members of Santo Daime
(Perlongher, 1991e: 29 [Buenos Aires]), the poem describes
strong sexual attraction towards co-religionaries, described as
'superficies bronceadas'. The same connections of desire between

parts of bodies exist as in earlier poems. The sexually charged description of the becoming-woman/-animal of the rowers echoes the depiction of the *michê* in *Parque Lezama* and *O negócio do michê*, particularly in the racial and linguistic exoticism of the 'superficies bronceadas' with their 'acento a canto'. However, two phrases ('abstraerse en lo celeste', 'se tiende a lo sublime') reveal that Perlongher is seeking the intensity of desire but, at the same time, trying to refrain from sexual contact. I would suggest that in this poem Perlongher approaches what Bersani calls 'non-relational pederasty', a type of non-sexual, non-relational sexual relation (1995: 123). Unlike the death-complicit shattering of the ego in S/M, which we observed in Perlongher's work, above, or the sedentary couple, easily recoverable by the state, this non-relational relation is neither easily stratified nor potentially fatal. Prostitution and the nomadic wandering and anonymous sexual liaisons that accompanied it, and the withdrawal from the city of the Santo Daime religion, offer the same possibilities for escaping the individual through desiring-connections. However, while the former are dangerous, through AIDS and frequent outbreaks of violence (Perlongher, 1997a 35–40 [Buenos Aires, 1988]), yet increasingly accepted within the neo-liberal marketplace and so thus tamed of the possibilities for unleashing becomings that challenge the dominant social order (Perlongher, 1991c [Buenos Aires]), the latter, organized through the structure of a religion, represents a more feasible alternative, distanced from the market, yet relatively safe. Through his journey away from the city to the community of Céu de Mapiá and his mystical withdrawal away from sex, Perlongher appears to be seeking the concrete existence of the type of alternative communities he traced in his earlier poems, as described in chapter 2. However, as we saw with the analysis of the spaces found in early poems and in the description of the Santo Daime ceremony – a ceremony whose participants, we must remember, then return to their own homes and jobs the next day – these spaces exist as *Temporary* Autonomous Zones. In the community of Céu de Mapiá, legally recognized by the Brazilian state, there exists an organized Autonomous Zone. This would suggest a key thematic change in the mystical withdrawal of Perlongher in that the new form of social organization is one that is in many ways concrete. However, Perlongher's poems do not dwell on the details of the colony, instead focusing on journeys and visions. Thus the aesthetic change, withdrawing and moving away from sex, instead of the theme of community, is key.

Despite Perlongher's break with Santo Daime, *El chorreo de las iluminaciones* continues to trace a similar aesthetic of mystical withdrawal. There is a strong aesthetic of distance, often in relation to illness. Rather than the intense contact that dominated earlier poems – with *michês*, or in the religious ceremony – the final collection proposes more non-relational relations that, as I shall examine, offer new and intriguing socio-political alternatives to his earlier work.

The title of 'Albañiles Desnudos (I)' is drawn from a late nineteenth and early twentieth-century theme in painting used as a means for portraying the male nude.

Con temple atisbo desde la ilusión de los tules bíceps lardos
lerdez de movimientos en el aire desnudo tachonado
de cuerpos que se tasan a la luz espléndida del cuelgue
de las cuerdas tonsado el hálito frío de la brisa
vespertina agitando calzones desde lo alto de sí, donde
se arroja.
    Cata la turmalina rociada trepidez
de polvos que se echan al vacío desde arriba
de un mueble:
      cuece andamios la costa
inefable su jalde borroneo,
en balde la cosquilla de la roca en la nube.
Vecina a las inspiraciones abre los brazos socorriendo
la distracción de la pupila en las hamacas paraguayas.

Tizne del morenillo y el resbalar oleoso de los huevos.
Los huecos en la cima, el portland los rellena con su balde
irguiendo toscamente las arenas del sueño en el serrallo.
Hay una confusión de abedules erectos, la contorsión, la
          distorsión arquean
arqueros apostados en las almenas liminares
cuyo salto doblega al malandrín en el torneo deseante.

Y húmeda flecha moja la entretela sudada.
(Perlongher, 1997a: 301 [1992, Buenos Aires])

Again we see Perlongher exoticizing working-class and darker-skinned men, as in the description of 'bíceps' and the reference to 'morenillo', and of course in the choice of central subject matter, Brazilian builders. An interesting artistic analogy is drawn.

Prior to the focus on the builder as a source of artistic subject matter, one of the most common life subjects was the female dancer. In the paintings of Toulouse-Lautrec (1864–1901) and others, the showgirls and can-can dancers of Montmartre are often, by implication, prostitutes, part of an exploration of metropolitan bohemian decadence. Thus Perlongher's portrayal of the artistic subject matter of the nude builder seems to suggest that once again he is dealing with male, or in his terms 'masculine', prostitutes, aestheticizing them through poetic presentation.

Perlongher's poem inhabits a similar territory to his earlier sexual poems, in particular in its relationship between poet-observer and working-class men, yet with a new distance and withdrawal. The poem's language juxtaposes two quite distinct fields: the mercantile body at work ('albañiles', 'bíceps', 'calzones', 'polvos', 'mueble', 'portland', 'arenas') and the classical in register and theme ('temple', 'ilusión', 'tonsado', 'vespertina', 'serrallo', 'arquero', 'almenas', 'malandrín', 'torneo', 'flecha'). The mercantile elements are dealt with in Perlongher's thesis, for example 'cuerpos que se tasan a la luz espléndida del cuelgue' recalls 'la conversión de las intensidades libidinales en signos monetarios' (1993a: 108). There is a 'sintaxis de la piel' (1997a: 108) and a 'gramática de los cuerpos' (108) that connect the body to exchange value. Again we find Perlongher validating the sexual-charged relationship of poet to macho proletarian men through analogy to the classical and academically respected.

The poem exhibits a play between metaphor (i.e. 'a poem that describes sexual relationships with proletarian men using classical references') and a drift away from metaphor; the effect is achieved through long comma-less enumerations (lines one to five), an accumulation of nouns ('la turmalina rociada trepidez / de polvos') and the inflation of clauses through conjunctions and prepositions ('abre los brazos socorriendo / la distracción de la pupila en las hamacas paraguayas'), all of which are closely related to the poetics of the (non-)metaphor we examined in chapter 5. It has elements that can be read as sexual metaphors for builders or as a *barroco* castle scene ('arqueros apostados en las almenas liminares'). The last line thus offers several possible readings; intriguingly, its two parts offer literal readings, each of which calls for a metaphorical reading of the other. For example:

húmeda flecha (arrow) moja la entretela (i.e. bloodies the guts)
or
húmeda flecha (i.e. ejaculation) moja la entretela (wets the lining,
where 'entretela' is a synonym of 'forro', and therefore condom)

An irresolvable tension is thereby created between two possible readings (among many). As in the mystical experience a close and dynamic relationship is created between pleasure and pain. A chiasmus effect distances the reader, through uncertainty and literariness, from the presentation of sex. This is further reinforced by the constant references to visions and observation, for example 'ilusión', 'sueño', 'atisbo', and 'pupila'. It is this physical distance from the sexual act itself that distinguishes the poem. Perlongher described the anthropological immersion of his research and the poems in *Parque Lezama* that dealt with prostitution as a form of 'participative observation' (Ekhard and Bernini, 1991: 85). Here we have physical distance and near nostalgia in the consideration of potential sexual partners.

This distance – the male gaze that implies status as a prostitute, as in Toulouse-Lautrec's paintings or Perlongher's poem, the latter framed by his own isolation through sickness – is commented upon by Bersani (1995). He argues that writers such as Marcel Proust (1871–1922), André Gide (1869–1951) and Genet, although by no means gay-affirmative, can offer a radical challenge to homophobia and the society in which it predominates through their attacks on conventional relations between persons, in particular through their desexualization of the erotic or, in other words, through their ability to complicate received social classifications and expand the possibilities of pleasure beyond genital sexual contact. In the case of Gide's novel *L'immoraliste* (1902), Bersani detects what he calls '*a nonsuicidal disappearance of the subject*' (99, italics in original). To explain this, one might call on Perlongher's earlier poems and anthropology. If the behaviour of the client seeking the dissolution of his ego in the exchange with the *miché* is masochistic, it is also potentially suicidal with inherent risks of violence. With the appearance of AIDS, sex becomes very visibly unsafe. Bersani (1995: 21) argues that, 'the heightened visibility conferred on gay men by AIDS is the visibility of imminent death, of promised invisibility.' Similarly, the Daime ceremony dissolves the self through extreme physical sensation but, after Perlongher became increasingly affected by AIDS-related illness, it became excessively dangerous for his health. So in comparison to the development of the mystical masochism we detected in Perlongher's poems that interacted with the work of Genet, these late, distanced poems offer a different aesthetics. As Bersani suggests, the strange relationship that Gide's protagonist undertakes in observing beautiful Arab boys without ever engaging in sexual intercourse, or that of Perlongher's poet-observer, is a form of 'nonrelational pederasty' (123). For Bersani, this circumventing of the couple or the interpersonal relationship offers a new possibility, that of 'declining to participate in any sociality at all' (168). Despite the seemingly nihilistic connotations, this turning away from the relational relation, the community and the intimately conjoined couple has a radical potential: bodies project 'out of themselves, out of any absorption in each other' (165). What is important for our reading of Perlongher's work here is that the combination of a sexually distanced sexuality and the overriding mystical background allows Perlongher to formulate in these last poems possibilities for anti-social socialization that move beyond his sexual aesthetics in purpose and dynamic, out into the cosmos, while maintaining the sexual vocabulary and tone, and which interact with the theoretical and practical problems of alternative politics and sexuality after HIV/AIDS.

Mystical Teleology

Where Perlongher's last two collections differ most radically from their earlier counterparts is in those poems that seem to suggest a mystical teleology, whereby the poems turn aesthetically and thematically towards the divine and suggest a divine purpose underlying human activity and the organization of the world. After a series of poems in verse that describe the Daime ceremony and visions, the sixth poem in the collection reverts to the prose form used in many of the poems of *Parque Lezama*:

ACRÍLICO (ACRE LÍRICO) * más que esplendor volumen tornaluz
luz fría acuática su raye (intersección de élitros, choque o ba-
llet de *vagalumes*, niágara) de guante calza el espesor glaseando el
manatí de una cutícula de nubes, cutis níveo, glostora de nivea, en
la ampulosidad del ademán glorioso disponíase el zarpe de la raya,

cuadriculado en vértigo, craquelé, sin dejar de ser ruina, pegoteado
de babas, la rebaba de nácar estirada en el borde de su vaina de
vals, ríspido enroque que trastoca los estremecimientos en connu-
bios, leves, alados, casi voiles, manatíes sirena, bosques río, pues el
milagro de su sobresalto, al cascar, en granadas, los aretes de espar-
to, les despertaba napas de titilante ánade, vacío, vagabundo, su ter-
sura de plumas en el cauce azaroso, no nada sino que se deja llevar,
ser arrastrado, en el remolineo de las hélices por el torrente panta-
noso, escándalo de espumas la ola orín, agua de porcelana en el
chorro de joyas, un portland numinoso al recubrir da vuelta al pul-
po como un guante, perla que se revela en goma o nace caucho, do-
lido por el acre o el acíbar, en lenguas marejadas de un-ungüento
encantado.

*Caetano Veloso (Perlongher, 1997a: 256 [1991, Buenos Aires])

The poem is evidence of Perlongher's application of poetic
techniques from his earlier work, in this case the drifting (non-)
metaphors discussed in chapter 5, but with a new mystical pur-
pose. For example, the poem displays a play between ceremonial
and sexual language. The first details the purge and the visions in
the Daime ceremony; hence '*ACRE LÍRICO*' offers bitterness
('acre'), suggesting the vomiting that takes place, and the lyrical
ordering of a hymn ('lírico'). We also have 'acíbar', aloes, a bitter
herb with purgative effects, together with lights and illuminations
('tornaluz', 'luz', 'vagalume', Portuguese for glow-worm), recall-
ing the hallucinogenic phase of abstract visions in an *ayahuasca*
trip. The second is distinctly sexual, particularly those elements
that imply sheathing and ejaculation: 'glaseando el manatí' recalls
the crude metaphors for sexual activities we saw in chapter 5; 'la
rebaba de nácar estirada en el borde de su vaina' uses high
register terms ('vaina', 'nácar') that suggest sexual activity; 'da
vuelta al pulpo como un guante' is reminiscent of many of the
metaphors and slang terms for condoms found in *Hule* (1989),
including the title itself; while 'perla que se revela en goma o nace
caucho' combines a shining white noun with two terms for rubber
in equally suggestive fashion. It is strange then that within
Perlongher's ceremony poems he seems to have found space for a
portrayal of sexual intercourse. This is given a focus by the central
cultismo 'connubios', a marriage couple. However, one must be
careful not to imply that Perlongher is writing here *about* penises,
condoms and ejaculation, for a number of reasons. While
'manatí' and 'guante' may be very close to the type of slang used

to describe sexual practices in earlier poems, here they are not simply metaphors for the initiated. Perlongher problematizes the ghettoization of slang metaphors through the employment of the (non)metaphor; 'ánade' – which might be interpreted as 'ano' – is juxtaposed to 'su tersura de plumas en el cauce azaroso'. There is greater weight and space given to the description of the 'ánade' than of an 'ano', and so thus the poem turns away from the portrayal of a sexual scene.

Nevertheless, if Perlongher were just removing the street context and language that can overdetermine such elements sexually, then there would be no difference to his abstract literary *barroco*, as outlined above in chapter 5. However, while words such as 'ánade', previously sexually suggestive, as in 'Ánade, caracoles' (1997a: 97–9 [1987, Buenos Aires]), appear in these poems, they are not only desexualized but, furthermore, are orientated in a different direction. This new direction is indicated by a central set of terms in the poem, specifically related to the perception of flight and light: 'élitros', 'vagalumes', 'vértigo', 'leves', and 'alados'. While the poetics of this poem is not radically different to that seen before, the key aesthetic difference is that instead of the movement within this territory being traced down, into the darkness, toward the genitals, or in the mud, or 'away', as in the poems of mystical withdrawal, now, while the dirt and lowness may still be present, the poem is tracing a journey upwards. At the same time, the poet is facing in the opposite direction to before, towards God, thematically exhibiting a faithful belief in the divine as a central reference point. Perlongher's desire is now closer to its Latin root, 'sidus', stars.

The penultimate poem of the collection, 'Paso de la serpiente', offers a further insight into the reworking of Perlongher's thematics and aesthetics that takes place in the collection:

1.
DE LA SERPIENTE EL PASO traslúcido
babea en el instante el eco que se abomba
o tapiza de jades, como un pespunte verde
alza coloraciones en el giro del espacio increado,
trasnatural, su giba en roce desleyente
borra casi olvidando las leyendas del jabón
mas del halo al halarlo resurgen contraseñas
o anulares que enseñan la lucidez del paso.

2.
SERPENTINA DE COBRAS en el ballet mohave
mojándose a la sombra de espiraladas araucarias
por marcar en la hiedra la levedad de un paso
que es en verdad el paso de la hierba por el aire
mojado de los círculos de ojos hueros en salitrosos
vidrios fintas de macramé escandiendo la cítara
pupilar, su enamorado colibrí la córnea
cornea simulando en la alfombra del musgo
en lo aguado del aire ese rocío del humo en su
dehiscencia.
(1997a: 289 [1991, Buenos Aires])

Perlongher's poem sees him turning elements from his sexual
poetry towards the divine. In particular he traces shapes and
patterns suggestive of the drift and tactile sensation in his poems
detailing the activities of the *bocas* of São Paulo, for example
'serpiente', 'paso', 'roce', 'serpentina', 'espiraladas', 'círculos',
and 'finta'. However, Perlongher's poem is also close in content to
those detailing mystical visions, with its synaesthesia ('el eco que
se abomba', 'roce desleyente'), and anthropomorphic creatures
('serpiente', 'enamorado colibrí'). Thus there is a clear overlap
between the mystical experience and the poetic presentation of
prostitution. Furthermore, the piece demonstrates the presence
of a poem by José Lezama Lima (1910–76), 'Rapsodia para el
mulo', a poem that offers an *ars poética* for the Cuban's *neobarroco*
poetry. Lezama's *neobarroco* was, as we observed in chapter 5, very
important to Perlongher's interaction with the *barroco*:

[. . .]
Su don ya no es estéril: su creación
la segura marcha en el abismo.
Amigo del desfiladero, la profunda
hinchazón del plomo dilata sus carillos.
Sus ojos soportan cajas de agua
y el jugo de los ojos
– sus sucias lágrimas –
son en la redención ofrenda altiva
[. . .]
(Jiménez, 2000: 476 [1949])

Lezama's poem sees poetic production ('creación') as a play
between force ('abismo') and form ('la segura marcha'). How-
ever, as in the work of Nietzsche's Dionysian Greeks, these

elements are not in opposition but are conjoined and indivisible in the poetic project; the mule is thus an 'amigo del desfiladero', hence the poet must negotiate with the danger of the Dionysian. There is in this dirty and emotional project ('sus sucias lágrimas') the possibility of divine 'redención'. Thus Perlongher's poem, through the intertextual reference to Lezama, reinforces the mystical experience as a source of poetic creation or, more precisely, as the force that finds form in poetics, as in the other mystical poems we observed above.

However, Perlongher's work also interacts with another work by Lezama, as underlined for different reasons by Alberto Moreiras (2002). The 'serpiente' is a key element in chapter 9 of Lezama Lima's *Paradiso* (1966), where it is used in the Dionysian phallic procession: 'Cada una de las cuatro lanzas están empuñados por doncellas y garzones desnudos, que en cada uno de los descansos acarician la espiral de la serpiente fálica' (1988b: 270). The serpent, a Dionysian phallus, is the apogee of the explicit homosexuality in the chapter. However, in Perlongher's reworking, rather than being an erotic symbol, the serpent is one of the ascetic, asexual, ascendant visions of his mystical experience. Thus while Perlongher's literary and philosophical influences are not radically altered in the collection *Aguas aéreas*, the orientation of the work does change, not only geometrically in the movement up but also in relation to the body, whereby the erotic is turned to the divine.

Turning to *El chorreo de las iluminaciones*, 'Luz oscura' similarly exhibits Perlongher turning towards divine teleology. The title is an oxymoron drawn from mysticism and its epigraph is from the work of Saint Teresa of Ávila ('recio martirio sabroso').[9] It displays a now familiar play between physical pain and spiritual pleasure.

> Si atrevesada por la zarza el pecho
> arder a lo que ya encendido ardía
> hace, el dolor en goce transfigura,
> fría la carne mas el alma ardida,
>
> en el blanco del ojo el ojo frío
> cual nieve en valle tórrido: el deseo
> divino se echa sobre lanzas ígneas
> y muerde el ojo en blanco el labio henchido.
>
> Funambulesca beatitud la suya,
> de claroscuros, que al soltar el pliegue

de luz inunda el esplendor febeo.

"No es resplandor que nos deslumbra, sino
una blancura suave y el resplendor difuso
que alto deleite da a la vista y no
la cansa, ni la claridad que se ve para ver
esta hermosura tan divina".
(Perlongher, 1997b: 304, italics in original)

Perlongher's poem again displays the relationship between mys-
tical force and poetic form. The first eleven lines of 'Luz oscura'
follow the sonnet form. The poem is dense in *barroco* tropes: the
faithful use of hendecasyllables (before the italicized section),
very rare in his work; the quasi-hyperbaton of the first six lines;
fully functioning hyperbaton in the third stanza; the chiasmus
stretched over four lines in the second verse ('el blanco del ojo
[. . .] el ojo en blanco'); and *conceptista* comparison of opposites
('dolor en goce transfigura'). Furthermore, there is direct refer-
ence to *barroco* characteristics, as described in chapter 5: 'claro-
scuro'[10] and 'pliegue'.[11] The poetic form, as we saw in 'Tema del
cisne I' demonstrates a more faithful application of Golden Age
formulas. However, Perlongher's poem highlights the strength of
force at play by allowing the first two stanzas to drift semantically,
by including only limited rhyme and also by varying the metre
between three, four and five stresses per line with varied feet. This
is reinforced by the final stanza, a quote from Saint Teresa that
exceeds the confines of the sonnet form in rhyme, line length and
metre.

   This is still in keeping with Perlongher's mysticism in that it
insists on both force and form or, as Nietzsche (1993: 14; 1999:
120) would have it, the inseparability of the 'Dionysiac' and the
'Apolline'. If Perlongher maintained, as discussed above, that the
dissolution of the self in the orgy or in secular drug use fell too
much on the side of the Dionysian (more accurately the Diony-
sian *Barbarian*) and therefore led to a 'descending', or suicidal
'salir de sí', the rituals of Daime proposed an ecstasy which takes
its form from the religious expression, the dances, hymns and
rituals, what Perlongher called the 'poetics' of Daime (1991e: 28).
The break with Daime is accompanied in Perlongher's work by an
intense focus on mystical pain, often indistinguishable from
pleasure. However, without the formalized rituals of the religion,
this pain – the pain that dominates *El chorreo de las iluminaciones* –

as observed by Sara Torres in her discussion of Perlongher's illness, accompanied as it was by virulent lung infections and sudden weight loss (Rapisardi and Modarelli, 2001: 199–200), could not be controlled. However, Perlongher finds in the mystical pain-pleasure of Saint Teresa a religious form, the directing of pain upwards to God, which can offer some control to the experience of painful death. Perlongher's extension of the cosmic ecstasy of S/M is to remove the sexual pleasure found in poems such as 'Herida pierna' (above) and inscribe pain totally within the framework of religious teleology.

The opening stanza therefore creates a dynamic set of binary relationships: 'zarza' / 'pecho'; 'dolor' / 'goce'; 'carne' / 'alma'. This relationship suggests the spiritual possibilities of physical pain. Alongside the final quote, this recalls a rapture recounted by Saint Teresa:

> Veíale [Jesus] en las manos un dardo de oro largo, y al fin del hierro me parecía tener un poco de fuego; éste me parecía meter en el corazón algunas veces y que me llegaba a las entrañas; al sacarle, me parecía que las llevaba consigo y me dejaba toda abrasada en amor grande de Dios. (Martí, 1981: 393)

The image is of opening oneself up to pain so as to achieve divine ends. That which is physically damaging to the body is in some way morally beneficial to the soul. Perlongher and Saint Teresa are both lending corporeal sensations a purpose other than the search for intensity, instead turning them towards the divine. Curiously, Perlongher's reworking of Teresa's cosmology again demonstrates the presence of Jean Genet. As the Frenchman wrote in *Notre-Dame des Fleurs*, 'I was his at once, as if (who said that) he had discharged through my mouth straight to my heart' (1988: 53). The masochism of Perlongher's mystical pain and Genet's sexual submissiveness recalls the cosmic ecstasy that Bersani discussed in relation to S/M (1995). We have discussed the problems that Bersani attributes to the supposedly death-complicit nature of these writings. The masochism in Perlongher's poem is no longer sexual and is informed by a new purpose. Unlike the other mystical poems of masochism or distanced relations, this poem and others in *El chorreo de las iluminaciones*, including the final poem 'Roma' (1997a: 361 [1993, New York]), exhibit a different teleological aesthetic.

Saint Teresa's quote deals with the overwhelming physical force of the mystical experience. Teresa Bielecki (1994:48), a Carmelite follower of Saint Teresa, observes:

> Sex is disguised mysticism [. . .] Eroticism, a preoccupation with genitality, is a deflection of real energy and the end of any mystical possibility [. . .] Sex is a need, Eros is a desire [. . .] Eros is the longing to enjoy such deep and wide-ranged dimensions of relatedness – all originating from a critical center and tending towards an ultimate end.

This approach to desire offers a radical alternative to Perlongher's earlier view of it as flow, connection and flight, as drawn from Deleuze and Guattari; the Teresan mystical desire is also a movement out of the body but it is logocentric and teleological ('critical center', 'ultimate end'). Nevertheless, Bielecki characterizes this experience as a radical attack on binary systems:

> In Hebrew there are no separate words for 'body' or 'soul' [. . .] Only in the mystical experience is the dilemma of duality resolved. For to the mystic is given the unifying vision of the One in the All and the All in the One [. . .] Saint Teresa, the grand wild woman of Avila, teaches us to live life in its total polarity: agony and ecstasy, warring and wedding, madness and reason, masculine and feminine, action and contemplation, discipline and wildness, fast and feast [. . .] Life is not either-or but both-and. (1994: 99, 115)

However, rather than replace the binary with the multiple or the rhizomatic, the new term is Oneness. Two aspects of Perlongher's poem suggest this change in perspective from the rhizomatic, anti-hierarchical thinking of Deleuze and Guattari to the Christian mystics: the overwhelming light in the poem ('luz', 'esplendor') and a qualifier for desire, emphasized by enjambment: 'deseo / divino'. Perlongher, like Saint Teresa, subscribes desire and physical pain fully within a religious telos. Perlongher speaks in 'Luz oscura' of a '[f]unambulesca beatitud'; the root of the first word is tightrope-walking (from the Latin, 'funis', rope and 'ambulare', to walk). This image brings together danger, the abyss – like that of Lezama's mule – but also a purpose to the line of flight. Bielecki again offers a clue to Perlongher's work: 'Jesus Himself on the cross, the greatest balancing act of all, a miracle of tension, that becomes a miracle of balance' (1994: 116). This difficult movement is summed up by another student of Saint Teresa, Elizabeth Teresa Howe: 'Progress to mystical union is a

paradoxical exercise on the part of the soul [...] it abandons
created things as well as its own passions, desires, and will, it
approaches the transcendent reality of mystical unions with the
creator' (1988: 323–4). The 'salir de sí' is still vital to Perlongher's
poem; now, though, it is not just that. Perlongher's mysticism here
contains the same play between force and form, the same over-
flowing excess, the same intensity of physical sensations, but now
informed aesthetically and thematically by a sense of purpose
specifically related to the divine in Christianity.

In a similar fashion, 'Alabanza y exaltación del Padre Mario'
takes the form of a long prayer with refrains and imprecations for
the priestly figure of the title. Much of the poem stands in radical
contrast to Perlongher's earlier poetics, particularly with regard to
light and darkness. Perlongher can also be seen dealing with the
contradictions and paradoxes thrown up by a meeting between
experimental poetics and teleological religious systems. This
occurs in particular with Perlongher's treatment of the up/down
binary. Whereas in previous poems Perlongher has moved down
(to the anus, the genitals, the petticoats, or the sewer), in the fifth
stanza Perlongher negatively valorizes such a movement:

> Oh Padre
> Cúrenos
> la salud y las escoriaciones del alma y los pozos del trauma y las he-
> ridas que hilan en el fondo de sí de cada cual las babas de la sierpe
> y nos enriedan la cabeza enrulada hasta hacernos perder toda ra-
> zón y arrastrarnos enloquecidamente con el absurdo sueño de salir
> por abajo bajando descendiendo sin ver que la iluminación viene de
> arriba como un sol que fijo sobre los ventanales de voile atravesán-
> dolos de luz divina luz de la que irradian sus ojos claros ojos abrien-
> do una vereda de fulgor en la tiniebla floreciéndola (332)

In chapter 2 I discussed the valorization of ascesis proposed by
this poem, a reversal of his earlier aesthetic. There is, however,
another key difference in the section. Perlongher suggests a new
element for his thematics, the notion of curing, as revealed in the
imprecation 'cúrenos / la salud'. We have seen in *Aguas aéreas*
that Perlongher cultivated extreme physical sensations, while
most of the poems in *El chorreo de las iluminaciones* can be divided
between those that suggest an anti-social sociability and those that
suggest a form of mystical masochism that seems to see death as
inevitable. This poem differs in that it seeks a cure. One can relate

this to Perlongher's late fascination with popular faith healing, an interest not revealed in his writing outside this poem. However, as Sara Torres points out, after his participation in Santo Daime ended for health reasons, 'vino su fascinación con el Padre Mario, un cura sanador [. . .] de González Catán [a suburb of Buenos Aires], donde iba en peregrinación cuando ya habían comenzado los síntomas de la enfermedad' (Rapisardi and Modarelli, 2001: 198). Again, however, despite the change in subject matter and the new aesthetic of curing, the same academic relationship to working-class practices exists as in his anthropology and poetry.

The aesthetic of curing offers a contrast to Perlongher's early reaction to AIDS. The essay 'Disciplinar os poros e as paixões' (1983) and his book *O qué é AIDS* (1987) attacked medical and judicial discourses that promoted safe sex as a means of preventing the spread of HIV; however, in later interviews, Perlongher seemed to recant his early, combative stance:

> La expansión de la enfermedad fue mucho más grave de lo que 7 u 8 años atrás uno se podía imaginar. Ahora es un momento para auxiliar a los enfermos y en el que la cuestión de la muerte nos obliga a repensar el tema del hedonismo individual occidental. En un primer momento mi reacción fue decir: 'resistamos'. Ahora me doy cuenta de que en muchos aspectos me equivoqué. Y en relación con la enfermedad, le tengo temor y respeto, la tengo en cuenta. (Ulanovsky, 1991: 11)

The change that Perlongher highlights is that AIDS moved from being a distant menace to a real threat and, with it, death became a far more immediate threat. Bersani (1995: 97) criticizes the 'death-complicit' aesthetic of many gay theorists. However, the question Perlongher's work raises is how one avoids being death-complicit when death is brought into the closest possible focus by terminal illness. Perlongher's last poems approach the near impossibility of answering this question without recourse to metaphysics or mysticism.

In Perlongher's final collections we can detect three key aesthetics: firstly, the masochistic aesthetic of mystical suffering; secondly, the non-relational relation that questions conventional notions of sociability; and, thirdly, the notion of an all-encompassing mystical purpose or teleology. His mystical poems are related to the perceived end of possibilities presented by political activism, sex and prostitution but still show the strong influence of the sexual aesthetics that he developed in his earlier poems and of the avant-garde kitsch/quasi-*barroco* poetics examined in chapter 5. Indeed many of these last poems draw directly from Perlongher's earlier activism and writings. His poetry still highlights the Dionysian and attacks the individual. However, the mystical elements in the last two collections offer alternatives that are perceived as in some way safer and more formal than before.

NOTES

1   A section of this chapter was published in the *Modern Language Review*, 99, 1 as 'Perlongher's Mysticism: Towards a Reappraisal'. I am grateful to the MLR and MHIZA for permission to reuse material.
2   The collection was published in two separate versions, firstly as a short collection of four poems in Caracas (1993), and secondly as the final section of thirty-one poems in *Poemas completos* (1997).
3   See Perlongher (1997a: 293 [1991, Buenos Aires]), where he thanks the 'Centro Ecléctico de Fluyente Luz Universal, "Flor de las aguas"' for the privilege of having been allowed to take the sacred liquid.
4   See Schultes and Hofman (1980) and *www.ayahuasca.com* for a description of *ayahuasca*, its use and effects. *Ayahuasca*, also known as *caapi, natema, pindé,* or *yajé,* means 'vine of the ancestors' or 'vine of the souls' in Quechua. It is drawn from the bark of *banisteriopsis caapi* and mixed with extracts from other plants such as *peganum harmala* (Syrian rue) or *psychotria viridis* to form a powerful brew that contains hallucinogenic alkaloids including harmaline, harmine, d-tetrahydroharmine and N,N-dimethyltryptamine. The latter, alongside the Monoamine Oxidase Inhibitors found in the brew, cause strong psychotomimetic and purgative effects.
5   Perlongher commented on the collection *Aguas aéreas* in an interview from 1992: 'yo escribía después de la ceremonia, generalmente, o al otro día. [...] [E]l cambio principal es que se trata de un libro unitario, a diferencia de todos mis otros libros' (Friedemberg and Samoilovich 1992: 31).
6   This approach is close to the theories of Michel Maffesoli, with whom Perlongher studied in Paris in 1990 (Rapisardi and Modarelli, 2001: 199) and who highlighted 'orgiasm', the dissolution of the self or the *principium individuationis*, as one of the essential factors of modern social life (Maffesoli, 1993: xv). Problematically, there is a difference between Perlongher's *demand* that his readers leave themselves in the 'salir de sí', and Maffesoli's suggestion, expounded in *The Shadow of Dionysus*, that orgiasm is the defining characteristic of contemporary socialization. Whereas Perlongher's writing has the tone of a call to revolution, Maffesoli reveals this as significantly less revolutionary than Perlongher might like.

7   I am aware of the objections raised by, for example, Deleuze to the terms 'sadomasochism' and 'S/M', based on his reading of Sacher-Masoch's *Venus in Furs*, as outlined in *Coldness and Cruelty* (1989). However, I follow Bersani in using the term to describe a very specific set of largely homosexual practices such as bondage, beatings and humiliation between explicitly or implicitly consenting adults, as opposed to the largely heterosexual contracts, suspensions and beatings in Sacher-Masoch's work.

8   I use the word *ascesis* to translate Perlongher's term 'ascesis', normally translated as 'asceticism'. Perlongher's term, from the Greek *asketikos*, from *askein*, to exercise, implies not only the self-denial of asceticism but also a spiritual ascent to the divine.

9   The title also suggests Saint John of the Cross's 'En una noche escura' (1980: 77–8 [circa 1578]), a poem which uses the allegory of sexual union between lovers to describe the mystical communion with the divine, and follows Saint John's doctrine of suffering and being despised.

10   See Carilla (1972: 18), and also Perlongher's poems 'Superficies paganas' (1997a: 128) and 'Formas barrocas' (129), both from *Hule* (1989).

11   See Deleuze (1993: 3) and Perlongher's introduction to *Caribe Transplatino* (1996: 19–30).

Conclusion

'It was always the becoming he dreamed of, never the being.'

(F. Scott Fitzgerald, 1987: 27)

'Keep away from the boats, but keep near them.'

(Herman Melville, *Moby Dick*)

'A good book, like a good girl, spells out the implications at the end, so that there is nothing to do but close the book and buy another.'

(Kappeler, 1986: 220)

What then are the constants in Perlongher's work, the recurring tropes in the avatars of his *oeuvre*? Perlongher's written engagement with marginal groups, be they *rockeros*, anarchists, *travesti* prostitutes, Brazilian *michês*, *Daimeros* and faith healers, takes working-class and lumpenproletariat subjects and aestheticizes them through poetic, academic and critical means. In this aestheticization, there are four constants. Firstly, Perlongher interacts with avant-garde writings, be it the historical Latin American vanguard – Girondo, Molina, and others – or his contemporary pseudovanguard in the *neobarroco*. Secondly, Perlongher employs modern European thinking, in particular the work of Deleuze and Guattari, in his prose and his poetry. Thirdly, Perlongher traces and explores spaces for desire and the ways in which it questions the unity of the individual. Finally, Perlongher focuses incessantly on the body; here I concur with Nicolás Rosa (1997) in seeing Perlongher's poetry as an attempt to reinstate in language the body that Lacanian psychoanalysis claims is denied. The pure physicality of Perlongher's poetry – the nonsense, sound games and liquid sequences – is an attempt to write the body in poetry and also to write on the body of the reader. His poetry offers tools for reading other difficult, neo-avant-garde, visceral or esoteric poetry, in particular through its demonstration of the need to allow a poem to perform poetically through close and formal readings while letting the poem detonate through its interactions with other works and the world.

Thus what I call Perlongher's 'poetic search for an Argentine marginal voice' can be regarded as an artistic trajectory through various alternative positions that responds to some of the most pressing political and sexual developments in Argentina and Brazil in recent years, whereby the use of the body, as inscribed in poetry, becomes a radical experiment in attacking the dominant social discourses and orders in those countries. Vital to this is Perlongher's engagement with foreign theorists, many of whose works Perlongher was active in importing into the political, literary and academic fields of Brazil and Argentina, and who are becoming increasingly important to recent interpretations of socio-political reality. This is particularly the case in Argentina in the wake of the economic collapse of December 2001 and the subsequent political upheaval, especially the discrediting of organized political parties that led to the emergence of new people's assemblies, or in Brazil with the increased importance of grass-roots socialist groups, as in the city of Porto Alegre with its socialist local government, or in recent indigenous resistance and political movements in Mexico and Bolivia. Perlongher's trajectory has a strong avant-garde tendency, in that his aesthetics and thematics develop ahead of most of the other alternative artists and political thinkers of the time. It is also class-based, dominated as it is by an intense and physical relationship with lumpenproletariat sectors. At the same time, seeking publication in various media – the political pamphlet, the feminist review, the academic thesis, the literary interview, poetry collections, the anthology, the review, or the introduction – allowed him to engage provocatively with the broadest audiences available for his work.

I conclude then by offering the suggestion, perhaps anathema to many readers and critics of Perlongher's work, that there is much greater similarity between Perlongher's work and the Argentine canon than perhaps has previously been admitted and that Perlongher has the right to a position alongside the writers of founding texts such as *El matadero* (1839), *Civilización y barbarie* (1845) or *Don Segundo Sombra* (1926). Like Echeverría's tale, dirt, the body and unwholesome sexuality are central; alongside Sarmiento, Perlongher engages in an aestheticizing of the lumpenproletariat and the working class through imported and inherited intellectual models; as in Güiraldes's novel, Perlongher matches the avant-garde to the popular. However, Echeverría was scathing about the occupants of the slaughterhouse; Sarmiento's admiration for the skills of the gaucho *baqueanos* and *rastreadores* was admitted begrudgingly; and Güiraldes's resolution is firmly on the side of the ruling classes. Perlongher's fascination with the *travestis*, prostitutes and shaman engaged in dangerous journeys at the edge of individual identity, is an honest and visceral one. Throughout his career he is politically revolutionary. Vitally, Perlongher's critical background comes from a rigidly anti-Platonic, anti-humanist background, a very different continental tradition to the one sought out by Sarmiento, specifically the anti-rational, anti-Platonic philosophy of Deleuze and Guattari, Nietzsche, and Bataille. Perlongher can thus be identified as a self-questioning, post-structuralist heir to earlier national allegories.

Works Cited

Please note, for ease of reference, I include in the text the place and date of first publication of major works to which I make reference.

Primary Sources: Works by Perlongher and Interviews Given

Ekhard, M. and E. Bernini. 1991. 'Néstor Perlongher: El negocio del deseo', *ESPACIOS de Crítica y producción*, 10: 82–6

Friedemberg, D. and D. Samoilovich. 1992. 'Perlongher: El barroco cuerpo a tierra', *Diario de Poesía*, 22: 31–2

Molina, D. 1988. 'Paseando por los mil sexos', *Fin de Siglo*, 8: 16–17

Perlongher, N. 2001. *'Evita Vive' e Outras Prosas*, ed. J. Schwartz, tr. J. Vianna Baptista (São Paulo: Iluminuras)

— 1999a. *El negocio del deseo. La prostitución masculina en San Pablo*, trans. by M. Irigoyen (Buenos Aires: Editorial Paidós)

— 1999b. 'Nueve meses en París', *Hispamérica*, 84: 53–7

— 1997a. *Poemas completos 1980–1992* (Barcelona: Seix Barral)

— 1997b. *Prosa plebeya* (Buenos Aires: Ediciones Colihue)

— 1997c. 'Tuyú', 'degradée' and 'Mme. Schocklender', in *The XUL Reader*, ed. E. L. Grossman (New York: Roof Books), pp. 24–31

— 1996. 'Prólogo', in *Medusario*, ed. R. Echavarren and others, pp. 19–30

— 1994. *Lamê*, ed. R. Echavarren, tr. J. Vianna Baptista (Campinas: Universidade Estadual de Campinas)

— 1993. *La prostitución masculina* (Buenos Aires: Ediciones de la Urraca)

— 1992. 'Argentina's Secret Poetry Boom', tr. M. Smallman, *Traves(s)ia: Journal of Latin American Cultural Studies*, 1.1: 178–184

— 1991a. *Aguas áereas*: II, III, IV, V, VI, *Hispamérica*, 58: 59–63

— 1991b. 'Cavidad de la luna', *Cuadernos Hispanoamericanos*, 495: 79–82

— 1991c. 'La desaparición de la homosexualidad', *El Porteño*, 119: 12–15

— 1991d. 'La loca de los ocho', *Página 12*, section *Cultura*, 1 September 1991, p. 8

— 1991e. 'La religión de la ayahuasca. Éxtasis sin cilicios', *El Porteño*, 116: 26–9

— 1990. *Parque Lezama* (Buenos Aires: Editorial Sudamericana)

— 1989. *Alambres*, 2nd ed. (Buenos Aires: Ediciones Último Reino)

— 1988a. *El fantasma del SIDA*, tr. O. Pedrozo (Buenos Aires: Puntosur Editores)
— 1988b. 'Formas neobarrocas', *Nicolau*, 19: 16–17
— 1988c. 'Kayak' and 'Urol', *Fin de Siglo*, 8: 18–19
— 1987a. *Hule* (Buenos Aires: Ediciones Último Reino)
— 1987b. *O negócio do michê: Prostituição viril em São Paulo* (São Paulo: Brasiliense)
— 1987c. 'Para lá de toda culpa', *Leia Livros*, 109: 38
— 1987d. 'Polifonia necessária', *Leia Livros*, 106: 37
— 1986. 'Molina y Valentín: El sexo de la araña', *Tiempo Argentina*, section *Cultura*, 29 June 1986, pp. 34
— 1985. 'Disciplinar os poros e as paixões', *Lua Nova*, 2.3: 35–7
— 1984. 'El sexo de las chicas', *XUL*, 6: 25–8
— 1983a. 'Evita Lives', in *My Deep Dark Pain is Love*, ed. W. Leyland, tr. E. A. Lacey (San Francisco: Gay Sunshine Press), pp. 98–104
— 1983b. 'Um "Nuevo Verso" Argentino', *Leia Livros*, 63: 6
— 1983c. 'As viagens da vanguarda', *Leia Livros*, 62: 21
— 1981a. 'Prostitución homosexual: El negocio del deseo', *Revista de Psicología de Tucumán*, 3/4: 69–81
— 1981b. 'Rivera', 'Tuyú', 'El circo' and 'Cántiga', *XUL*, 2: 25–7
— and A. Nigro. 1980. 'El boom de la poesía argentina subterránea', *Mutantia*, 3: 64–74
— S. Pérez Álvarez and R. S. Llarguez. 1980. *La familia abandónica y sus consecuencias* (Buenos Aires: EUDEBA-CEA)
Saavedra, G. 1991. 'Privilegio las situaciones del deseo', *Clarín*, section *Cultura y nación*, 26 December 1991, pp. 2–3
Ulanovsky, C. 1990. 'El SIDA pusó en crisis la identidad homosexual', *Página 12*, 19 September 1990, p. 11

Secondary Sources: Critical and Biographical Work on Perlongher

Amícola, J. 2000. *Camp y posvanguardia. Manifestaciones de un siglo fenecido* (Buenos Aires: Editorial Paidós)
Baigorria, O. 1996. 'La Rosa Mística de Luxemburgo', in *Lúmpenes Peregrinaciones: Ensayos sobre Néstor Perlongher*, ed. A. Cangi and P. Siganevich, pp. 175–80
Bueno, W. 2003. 'Néstor Perlongher e suas autonomias textuais', *http://www.estado.estadao.com.br/editorias/2001/03/31/cad923.html* [accessed 22 January 2003]
Canaparo, C. 2001. *El perlonghear. Postulado de un pensamiento posracionalista* (Buenos Aires: Zibaldone Universidad)
— 1998. *El perlonghear* (Buenos Aires: La Protesta Ediciones)
Cangi, A. and P. Siganevich (eds). 1996. *Lúmpenes Peregrinaciones: Ensayos sobre Néstor Perlongher* (Rosario de Santa de Fe: Beatriz Viterbo)
Cella, S. 1996. 'Figuras y nombres', in *Lúmpenes Peregrinaciones*, ed. A. Cangi and P. Siganevich, pp. 148–74

Chauvié, O. 1998. 'El neobarroco en cuestión', in *Las operaciones de la crítica*, ed. A. Giordano and M. C. Vázquez (Rosario de Santa Fe: Beatriz Viterbo), pp. 109–20

Echavarren, R. 1999. 'Prólogo', in *El negocio del deseo. La prostitución masculina en San Pablo*, by N. Perlongher, pp. 1–10

— 1997. 'Prólogo', in *Poemas completos*, by N. Perlongher, pp. 7–16

— 1996. 'Prólogo', in *Medusario*, ed. R. Echavarren and others, pp. 11–17

— 1991. 'La revolución neobarroca', *http://www.henciclopedia.org.ur/echavarren/neobarroco.html* [accessed 25 April 2002]

— J. Kozer and J. Sefamí (eds). 1996. *Medusario. Muestra de poesía latinoamericana* (Mexico: Fondo de Cultura Económica)

Ferrer, C. 1996a. 'Bibliografía establecida', in *Lúmpenes Peregrinaciones*, ed. A. Cangi and P. Siganevich, pp. 205–18

— 1996b. 'Escamas de un ensayista', in *Lúmpenes Peregrinaciones*, ed. A. Cangi and P. Siganevich, pp. 181–93

— and O. Baigorria. 1997. 'Obra de Néstor Perlongher' and 'Itinerario biográfico', in *Prosa plebeya*, by N. Perlongher, pp. 249–57

Fogwill, R. E. 1994. Letter to the Editor, Diario de Poesía, 29: 40

— 1993. 'Yo creía en el gusto', Diario de Poesía, 27: 3–4

González, H. 1996. 'Introito', in *Lúmpenes Peregrinaciones*, ed. A. Cangi and P. Siganevich, pp. 9–16

Jozef, B. 1992. Review of Caribe Transplatino by N. Perlongher, *Hispamérica*, 64/65: 204–6

Kamenszain, T. 1997. 'El canto del cisne', in Poemas completos, by N. Perlongher, pp. 367–70

— 1996. 'De noche, Góngora', in *Lúmpenes Peregrinaciones*, ed. A. Cangi and P. Siganevich, pp. 101–4

Kuhnheim, J. 1999. 'La promiscuidad del significado: Néstor Perlongher', *Revista Iberoamericana*, 187: 281–92

Moreno, M. 1996. 'Personal', in *Lúmpenes Peregrinaciones*, ed. A. Cangi and P. Siganevich, pp. 194–7

Panessi, J. 1996. 'Detritus', in *Lúmpenes Peregrinaciones*, ed. A. Cangi and P. Siganevich, pp. 44–62

Patiño, R. 2003. 'Intelectuales en transición. Las revistas culturales argentinas (1981–1987)' *http://www.fflch.usp.br.dlm/posgraduacao/espanol* [accessed 5 March 03]

Rapisardi, F. and A. Modarelli. 2001. *Fiestas, baños y exilios. Los gays porteños en la última dictadura* (Buenos Aires: Editorial Sudamericana)

Rosa, N. 1997. *Tratados sobre Néstor Perlongher* (Buenos Aires: Ars)

— 1987. *Los fulgores del simulacro* (Rosario de Santa Fe: Universidad Nacional del Litoral)

Schettini, A. 1997. 'El escritor insaciable', *La Nación*, 15 March 1997, p. 14

Other Works Cited

Adorno, T. 2002. 'Kitsch', in *Essays on Music*, ed. R. Leppert, tr. S. H. Gillespie (London: University of California Press), pp. 501–5

Acevedo, Z. 1985. *Homosexualidad: Hacia la destrucción de los mitos* (Buenos Aires: Ediciones del ser)

Alonso, A. M. and M. T. Koreck. 1993. 'Silences: "Hispanics", AIDS, and Sexual Practices', in *The Lesbian and Gay Studies Reader*, ed. H. Abelove, M. A. Barala, and H. Donghi (London: Routledge), pp. 110–19

Alpert, M. 1969. 'Introduction', in *Two Spanish Picaresque Novels*, ed. M. Alpert (Harmondsworth, Middlesex: Penguin), pp. 15–34

Altamirano, C. 1986. 'El intelectual en la represión y en la dictadura', *Punto de vista* 28: 115–18

— (ed.). 1971. *Poesía social del siglo XX: España e Hispanoamérica* (Buenos Aires: Centro Editor de América Latina)

Álvarez, A. G. 2000. 'The City Cross-dressed: Sexual Rights and Roll-backs in De la Rúa's Buenos Aires', *Journal of Latin American Cultural Studies*, 9.2: 137–55

Ángel, R. 1992. *Rebeldes y domesticados: Los intelectuales frente al poder* (Buenos Aires: Ediciones El cielo por asalto)

Anguita, E. and M. Caparrós. 1997. *Voluntad. Una historia de la militancia revolucionaria en la Argentina 1966–1973* (Buenos Aires: Ediciones Norma)

Artaud, A. 1988. *Selected Writings*, ed. S. Sontag (Berkeley: University of California Press)

Avelar, I. 1999. *The Untimely Present. Postdictatorial Latin American Fiction and the Task of Mourning* (Durham, NC: Duke University Press)

Baciu, S. (ed.) 1974. *Antología de la poesía surrealista latinoamericana* (Mexico D.F.: Joaquín Mortiz)

Bataille, G. 1987. *Eroticism* (London: Marion Boyars)

Benedetti, M. 1981. *Los poetas comunicantes* (Montevideo: Marcha Editores)

Benjamin, W. 1977. *The Origins of German Tragic Drama*, tr. J. Osborne (London: NLB)

Bersani, L. 1995. *Homos* (Harvard: Harvard University Press)

— and U. Dutoit. 1993. *Arts of Impoverishment: Beckett, Rothko, Resnais* (Harvard: Harvard University Press)

Bey, H. 2002. 'TAZ. The Temporary Autonomous Zone', in *Cultural Resistance Reader*, ed. S. Duncombe, pp. 113–18

— 1991. *T. A. Z. The Temporary Autonomous Zone, Ontological Anarchy, Poetic Terrorism* (New York: Autonomedia)

Bielecki, T. 1994. *Holy Daring. An Outrageous Gift to Modern Spirituality from Saint Teresa the Grand Wild Woman of Avila* (Shaftesbury: Element)

Borges, J. L. 1970. *Labyrinths* (Harmondsworth, Middlesex: Penguin)

— 1957. *Ficciones* (Buenos Aires: Emecé)

Bourdieu, P. 1993. *The Field of Cultural Production* (Cambridge: Polity Press)

Braidotti, R. 2000. *Sujetos nómades*, tr. A. Bixio (Buenos Aires: Editorial Paidós)

Breton, A. 1974. *Manifestoes of Surrealism*, tr. R. Seaver and H. R. Lane (Ann Arbor: University of Michigan Press)

Brittain, F. (ed.) 1962. *The Penguin Book of Latin Verse* (Harmondsworth, Middlesex: Penguin)

Bronfen, E. 1992. *Over Her Dead Body: Death, Femininity and the Aesthetic* (Manchester: Manchester University Press)

Bürger, P. 1984. *Theory of the Avant-Garde*, tr. M. Shaw (Manchester: Manchester University Press)

Butler, J. 1999. *Gender Trouble. Feminism and the Subversion of Identity* (London: Routledge)

Calvera, L. 1990. *Mujeres y femenismo en la Argentina* (Buenos Aires: Grupo Editor Latinoamericano)

Cardenal, E. 1971. *Poemas* (Barcelona: Seix Barral)

Carilla, E. 1983. *Manierismo y barroco en las literaturas hispánicas* (Madrid: Editorial Gredos)

— 1972. *La literatura barroca en Hispanoamérica* (New York/Madrid: Anaya)

— 1946. *El gongorismo en América* (Buenos Aires: Instituto de Cultura Latino-Americana)

Carpentier, A. 1987. *Tientos, diferencias y otros ensayos* (Barcelona: Plaza y Janés)

Carrera, A. 1972. *Escrito con un nictógrafo* (Buenos Aires: Editorial Suda-mericana)

Cerro, E. 1989. *Las mirtilas* (Buenos Aires: Ediciones Último Reino)

Cixous, H. and C. Clément. 1993. *The Newly Born Woman* (Minneapolis: University of Minnesota Press)

Collins Concise Dictionary Fourth Edition 1999 (Glasgow: Collins)

Cowley, M. 2002. 'Exile's Return', in *Cultural Resistance Reader*, ed. S. Duncombe, pp. 312–16

Dalton, R. 1969. *Taberna y otros lugares* (Vedado, Cuba: Casa de las Américas)

Deleuze, G. 2001. *Pure Immanence. Essays on a Life*, tr. A. Boyman (New York: Zone Books)

— 1994a. *Difference and Repetition*, tr. P. Patton (London: The Athlone Press)

— 1994b. 'He Stuttered', in *Gilles Deleuze and the Theater of Philosophy*, ed. C. V. Boundas and D. Olkowski (London: Routledge), pp. 23–9

— 1993. *The Fold: Leibniz and the Baroque* (London: The Athlone Press)

— 1990. *The Logic of Sense* (London: The Athlone Press)

— 1988. *Bergsonism*, tr. H. Tomlinson and B. Habberjam (New York: Zone Books)

— and F. Guattari. 2000a. *Anti-Oedipus: Capitalism and Schizophrenia*, tr. R. Hurley, M. Seem and H. R. Lane (Minneapolis: University of Minnesota Press)

— 2000b. *Kafka. Toward a Minor Literature*, tr. D. Polan (Minneapolis: University of Minnesota Press)

— 1999. *A Thousand Plateaus: Capitalism and Schizophrenia*, tr. B. Massumi (London: The Athlone Press)
— 1994. *What is Philosophy?* (London: Verso)
— and L. von Sacher-Masoch. 1989. *Masochism: Coldness and Cruelty. Venus in Furs* (New York: Zone Books)
Derrida, J. 1994. *Spectres of Marx* (London: Routledge)
Duncombe, S. (ed.). 2002. *Cultural Resistance Reader* (London: Verso)
Dutrénit Bielous, S. 2002. 'Se cruzan los relatos: memoria personal y reconstrucción histórica' [unpublished paper, Instituto Mora]
Echavarren, R. 1994. *Ave roc* (Montevideo: Baja la luna nueva)
— 1980. *La planicie mojada* (Caracas: Monte Ávila Editores)
Egurbide, P. 1982. 'La voz sindical', *Cambio 16*, 26 April 1982, p. 82
Ekins, R. and D. King. 1996. *Blending Genders. Social Aspects of Cross-dressing and Sex-changing* (London: Routledge)
Escudero Chauvel, L. 1996. *Malvinas: El gran relato* (Barcelona: Editorial Gedisa)
Fichte, H. 1992. *Detlev's Imitations*, tr. M. Chalmers (London: Serpent's Tail)
Fitzgerald, F. Scott. 1987. *This Side of Paradise* (Oxford: Bodley Head)
Fogwill, R. E. 1992. 'Muchacha punk', in *Buenos Aires*, ed. J. Forn (Barcelona: Anagrama), pp. 45–73
Foster, D. W. and V. Ramos Foster. 1973. *Luis de Góngora* (New York: Twayne Publishers)
Foucault, M. 2000. 'Preface', in G. Deleuze and F. Guattari *Anti-Oedipus: Capitalism and Schizophrenia*, pp. xi–xiv
— 1991. *Discipline and Punish*, tr. A. Sheridan (London: Penguin)
— 1984. *The Foucault Reader*, ed. P. Rabinow (Harmondsworth, Middlesex: Penguin)
— 1976. *The History of Sexuality. Volume I: The Will to Knowledge*, tr. R. Hurley (London: Penguin)
Frank, T. 2002. 'Why Johnny Can't Dissent', in *Cultural Resistance Reader*, ed. S. Duncombe, pp. 316–27
Galeano, E. 1981. *Días y noches de amor y de guerra* (Barcelona: Editorial LAIA)
Gelman, J. 1980. *Hechos y Relaciones* (Barcelona: Editorial Lumen)
— 1968. *Poemas* (Vedado, Cuba: Casa de las Américas)
Genet, J. 1988. *Our Lady of the Flowers*, tr. B. Frechtman (London: Paladin)
— 1954. *The Thief's Journal*, tr. B. Frechtman (Paris: The Olympia Press)
Girondo, O. 1998. *Persuasión de los días. En la masmédula* (Buenos Aires: Editorial Losada)
— 1996. *Veinte poemas para ser leídos en el tranvía. Calcomanías* (Buenos Aires: Editorial Losada)
Gobello, J. 1998. *Nuevo Diccionario Lunfardo* (Buenos Aires: Ediciones Corregidor)
— and L. Payet. 1959. *Breve diccionario lunfardo* (Buenos Aires: A. Peña Lillo)
Góngora y Argote, L. de. 1997. *Soledades* (Bristol: Classical Press)
— 1991. *Poesía selecta*, ed. A. Pérez Lasheras and J. M. Micó (Madrid: Clásicos Taurus)

González Tuñón, R. 1977. *Poesías* (Vedado, Cuba: Casa de las Américas)

Gordon, L. 1995. *Aspects of Gender. A Study of Crossdressing Behaviour* (Waltham MA: IFGE Publications)

Guattari, F. 1990. 'Restauração da cidade subjectiva', *Jornal do Brasil,* section *Idéias/ENSÁIO,* 29 September 1990, pp. 4–6

— 1984. *Molecular Revolution,* tr. R. Sheed (Harmondsworth, Middlesex: Penguin)

Habermas, Jürgen. 1996. *The Structural Transformation of the Public Sphere. An Inquiry into a Category of Bourgeois Society,* tr. T. Burger and F. Lawrence (Cambridge MA: MIT Press)

Harvey, D. 2000. *Spaces of Hope* (Edinburgh: Edinburgh University Press)

Hayward, J. (ed.) 1973. *The Penguin Book of English Verse* (Harmondsworth, Middlesex: Penguin)

Hebdige, D. 1979. *Subculture: The Meaning of Style* (London: Routledge)

Heidegger, M. 1999. *Contributions to Philosophy (From Enowning),* tr. P. Ermad and K. Maly (Bloomington and Indianapolis: Indiana University Press)

— 1993. *Basic Writings,* ed. D. Farrell Krell (London: Routledge)

Hobsbawm, E. 1998. *Behind the Times. The Decline and Fall of the Twentieth-Century Avant-Gardes* (London: Thames & Hudson)

Howe, E. T. 1988. *Mystical Imagery. Santa Teresa de Jesús and San Juan de la Cruz* (New York: Peter Lang)

Jiménez, J. O. (ed.) 2000. *Antología de la poesía hispanoamericana contemporánea 1914–1987* (Madrid: Alianza Editorial)

— 1994. *Antología crítica de la poesía modernista hispanoamericana* (Madrid: Hiperión)

St. John of the Cross. 1990. *Obra poética* (Barcelona: Acervo)

Kappeler, S. 1986. *The Pornography of Representation* (Minneapolis: University of Minnesota Press)

Kaufman, A. 1997. 'Notas sobre los desaparecidos', *Confines,* 4 July 1997, pp. 29–34

Kosofsky Sedgewick, E. 1985. *Between Men. English Literature and Male Homosocial Desire* (New York: Columbia University Press)

Kuhnheim, J. 1996. *Gender, Politics, and Poetry in Twentieth-Century Argentina* (Gainesville: University Press of Florida)

Lamborghini, O. 1973. *Sebregondi retrocede* (Buenos Aires: Ediciones Noé)

— 1967. *El fiord http://www.literatura.org/OLamborghini/Fiord.html* [accessed 17 October 2001]

Lemebel, P. 2000. *Loco afán. Crónicas de un sidario* (Barcelona: Editorial Anagrama)

Lezama Lima, J. 1988a. *Muerte de Narciso. Antología poética,* ed. D. Huerta (Mexico D.F.: Ediciones Era)

— 1988b. *Paradiso* (Madrid: Archivos)

Lucy, N. 1997. *Postmodern Literary Theory: An Introduction* (Oxford: Blackwell)

Luxemburg, R. 1989. *Reform or Revolution,* tr. 'Integer' (London: Bookmarks)

— 1986. *The Mass Strike* (London: Bookmarks)

— 1976. *The National Question. Selected Writings*, ed. H. B. Davies (London: Monthly Review Books)

— 1973. *Leninism or Marxism*, tr. K. Eaton (Leeds: I. L. P. Square One Publications)

Maffesoli, M. 1993. *The Shadow of Dionysus. A Contribution to the Sociology of the Orgy*, tr. C. Linse and M. K. Palmquist (Albany NY: State University of New York Press)

Marcuse, H. 1991. *One-Dimensional Man* (London: Routledge)

— 1987. *Eros and Civilization: A Philosophical Inquiry into Freud* (London: Ark)

Martí, J. 1981. *Diccionario del pensamiento de Santa Teresa de Jesús* (Valencia: Edicep)

Masiello, F. 1992. *Between Civilization and Barbarism: Woman, Nation and Literary Culture in Modern Argentina* (Lincoln, Nebraska: University of Nebraska Press)

— 1987. 'La Argentina durante el proceso: Las múltiples resistencias de la cultura', in *Ficción y política: La narrativa argentina durante el proceso military*, ed. D. Balderstone and others (Buenos Aires: Alianza Editorial), pp. 11–30

Massumi, B. 1999. *A Users Guide to "Capitalism and Schizophrenia". Deviations from Deleuze and Guattari* (Cambridge MA: MIT Press)

Molina, E. 1984. *Obra completa. Tomo 1. Prosa. "Una sombra donde sueña Camila O'Gorman" y otros textos* (Buenos Aires: Ediciones Corregidor)

— 1978. *Obra poética* (Caracas: Monte Ávila Editores)

Moreiras, A. 2002. 'Mules and Snakes: On the Neo-baroque Principle of De-Localization' [paper presented at the *Journal of Latin American Cultural Studies* / Birkbeck College Summer Conference, 19 June 2002]

Moreno, M. 2002a. 'Interview with Horacio González', *Journal of Latin American Cultural Studies*, 11.2: 14–50

— 2002b. 'Interview with Alejandro Kaufman', *Journal of Latin American Cultural Studies*, 11.2: 137–42

— 2002c. 'Interview with Eduardo Grüner', *Journal of Latin American Cultural Studies*, 11.2: 157–62

Müller, A (ed.). 1999. *Nuestros poetas y las Malvinas* (Buenos Aires: Ediciones Corregidor)

Nietzsche, F. 2002. *Beyond Good and Evil*, tr. J. Norman (Cambridge: Cambridge University Press, 2002)

— 1999. 'The Dionysiac World View', in *The Birth of Tragedy and Other Writings* (Cambridge: Cambridge University Press), pp. 117–38

— 1996. *On the Genealogy of Morals*, tr. D. Smith (Oxford: Oxford University Press)

— 1993. *The Birth of Tragedy*, tr. S. Whiteside (London: Penguin)

Ortíz, R. 1982. 'Más allá de sus diferencias, la CGT y la CNT-20 adhieron a la reivindicación de soberanía', *Convicción*, 3 April 1982, p. 8

Piglia, R. 1994a. *Artificial Respiration*, tr. D. Balderstone (Durham NC: Duke University Press)

— 1994b. 'Masoquismo de Fogwill', *Diario de Poesía*, 28: 5

— 1992. *Cuentos con dos rostros* (Mexico: UNAM)

— 1990. *Crítica y ficción* (Buenos Aires: Siglo Veinte Editorial)

Pound, E. 1954. *Literary Essays* (London: Faber & Faber)

— 1951. *ABC of Reading* (London: Faber & Faber)

Preminger, A. and T. V. F. Brogan (eds) 1993. *The New Princeton Encyclopedia of Poetry and Poetics* (Princeton, NJ: Princeton University Press)

Puente, E. de la and D. Quintana. 1988. *Rock! Antología de la poesía rock argentina desde 1965* (Buenos Aires: El juglar editorial)

Quevedo, F. de. 1984. *Antología poética* (México D.F.: Origen/OMGSA)

— 1977. *La vida del buscón llamado Don Pablos* (Oxford: Pergamon)

Quilis, A. 1969. *Métrica Española* (Madrid: Ediciones Alcalá)

Reynolds, S. 2002. 'Generation Ecstasy', in *Cultural Resistance Reader*, ed. S. Duncombe, pp. 119–31

Rowe, W. 2000. *Contemporary Poets of Latin America: History and the Inner Life* (Oxford: Oxford University Press)

— 1996. *Hacia una poética radical. Ensayos de hermenéutica cultural* (Rosario de Santa Fe/Lima: Beatriz Viterbo/ Mosca Azul Editores)

Saldías, A. 1958a. *Historia de la Confederación Argentina. Vol 4: Los aliados contra Rozas* (Buenos Aires: Ediciones Cenit)

— 1958b. *Historia de la Confederación Argentina. Vol 5: Rozas y Lavalle* (Buenos Aires: O.C.E.S.A.)

Salvador, N. 1962. *Revistas Argentinas de Vanguardia (1920–1930)* (Buenos Aires: Universidad de Buenos Aires)

Sarduy, S. 1974a. *Barroco* (Buenos Aires: Editorial Sudamericana)

— 1974b. *Big Bang* (Barcelona: Tusquets Editor)

Sarlo, B. 1988. 'El campo intelectual: Un espacio doblemente fracturado', in *Represión y reconstrucción de una cultura: El caso argentino*, ed. by S. Sosnowski (Buenos Aires: Editorial Universitaria de Buenos Aires), pp. 95–106

— 1987. 'Los militares y la historia: Contra los perros del olvido', *Punto de vista*, 30: 119–22

Schultes, R. E. and A. Hofman. 1980. *Plants of the Gods* (London: Hutchinson)

Sebreli, J. J. 1997. 'La historia secreta de los homosexuales en Buenos Aires', in *Escritos sobre escritos, ciudades bajo ciudades* (Buenos Aires: Editorial Sudamericana), pp. 275–370

Sifuentes-Jáuregui, B. 2002. *Transvestism, Masculinity and Latin American Literature* (New York: Palgrave)

Sola, G. de. 1967. *Proyecciones del surrealismo en la literatura argentina* (Buenos Aires: Ediciones Culturales Argentinas)

Sontag, S. 1967. *'Against Interpretation' and other essays* (London: Eyre & Spottiswode)

Tarsis, J. de, Segundo Conde de Villamediana. 1990. *Poesía impresa completa*, ed. J. F. Ruiz Casanova (Madrid: Cátedra)

Taylor, D. 1997. *Disappearing Acts* (Durham NC: Duke University Press)

Terán, O. 1993. *Nuestros años sesentas. La formación de la nueva izquierda intelectual argentina 1956–1966* (Buenos Aires: Ediciones El cielo por asalto)

Todorov, T. 1988. *Literature and Its Theorists*, tr. C. Porter (London: Routledge & Keegan Paul)

— 1982. 'A Complication of the Text: the *Illuminations*', in *French Literary Theory Today* (Cambridge: Cambridge University Press), pp. 223–37

Torre, J. C. and L. de Riz. 1993. 'Argentina since 1946', in *Argentina since Independence*, ed. L. Bethell (Cambridge: Cambridge University Press), pp. 243–364

Trotsky, L. 1975. *'Culture and Socialism' and a Manifesto 'Towards a Free Revolutionary Art'* (London: New Park Press Publications)

— 1971. *Literature and Revolution* (Ann Arbor: University of Michigan Press)

— 1962. *'The Permanent Revolution' and 'Results and Prospects'*, tr. J. G. Wright and B. Pearce (London: New Park Publications)

— 1957. *Radio, Science, Technique and Society* (London: New Park Publications)

Tzara, T. 1981. *Seven Dada Manifestos and Lampisteries*, tr. B. Wright (London/New York: John Calder/Riverrun Press)

— 1975. *Selected Poems*, tr. L. Harwood (London: Trigram)

Unruh, V. 1994. *Latin American Vanguards: The Art of Contentious Encounters* (Berkeley: University of California Press)

Vallejo, C. 1998a. *Los heraldos negros* (Madrid: Cátedra)

— 1998b. *Trilce* (Madrid: Cátedra)

— 1988. *Obra poética. Edición crítica*, ed. A. Ferrari (Madrid: Colección Archivos)

Verani, H. J. 1996. 'The *Vanguardia* and its Implications', in *The Cambridge History of Latin American Literature vol. II*, ed. R. González Echevarría and E. Pupo-Walker (Cambridge: Cambridge University Press), pp. 69–113

Vezzetti, H. 2002. 'Scenes from the Crisis', *Journal of Latin American Cultural Studies*, 11.2: 163–71

Vich, C. 2000. *Indigenismo de vanguardia en el Perú* (Lima: Fondo Editorial de La Pontificia, Universidad Católica)

Virilio, P. 1998. *The Virilio Reader*, ed. J. Der Derian (Oxford: Blackwell)

Newspapers, Journals and Reviews

The Buenos Aires Herald
Cambio 16
Clarín
Diario de Poesía
Folha de São Paulo
Página 12
El Porteño
Punto de vista
XUL

Websites and Electronic Resources

http://www.ayahuasca.org

Cerati, G., Z. Bosi and C. Alberti. *Comfort y música para volar. Soda Stereo Unplugged*. Soda Stereo. 1996. 74321 41491–2

Encyclopaedia Britannica Deluxe Edition CD ROM 2001. BJDLX01/01

http://www.henciclopedia.org

http://www.literatura.org

http://www.poesia.com

Index

Please note: for references to Perlongher, his works, and aspects of his writings, readers are advised to consult the table of contents.